ENNISCORTHY
The
Forgotten Republic

Pat Doran

Enniscorthy The Forgotten Republic © 2021 by Pat Doran. All Rights Reserved.

All rights reserved. No part of this book may be reproduced in any form or by any electronic or mechanical means including information storage and retrieval systems, without permission in writing from the author. The only exception is by a reviewer, who may quote short excerpts in a review.

Cover designed by Cover Designer
Cover Photograph Pat Doran

ISBN-13-979-8-4854-4558-4

To Lauraine and Sam,
Thanks again for your patience.

This book is dedicated to the memory
of Joe Doyle

Introduction

The seed for this book was sown one Friday night in 2016. I was watching the Late Late Show which featured an interview with one of the most prominent broadcasters on R.T.E.. He was discussing his new book about the 1916 Rising. It was just a passing comment he made that struck me deeply, he said quite flippantly, that apart from Ashbourne in County Meath, the Rising was confined to Dublin. This was news to me, coming from Enniscorthy, where in 1916 the Volunteers held the town for a period of four days and were the very last to surrender. The fact that the host of the show did not question this statement was no surprise, for if it didn't happen in Dublin it didn't happen.

Not that this was a new phenomenon. It is worth noting of the 260 plus local men and women who submitted State Pension claims for their military service during the Rising, only seventy had their claims accepted. As Deputy Richard Corish stated in a debate in Dáil Éireann on the 2nd of July 1942.

"The Departments of Finance and Defence insist the Enniscorthy men had no contact with the enemy. (However) These Enniscorthy men came out to establish the Republic and were prepared to die for the Republic if necessary. They came out under the order of Pearse, and they never thought the struggle was going to end so quickly."

On the 1st of July 1936 a delegation from Enniscorthy were in front of the Referee and Advisory Panel for Military Pensions. The Referee compared the Enniscorthy claimants to those from Cork who had marched to Macroom during Easter Week. One of the delegation, T.D. Sinnott replied.

"I certainly cannot see how you can put people marching out to Macroom on the same level. They made no attempt to establish a military control of the area. There was no military control assumed anywhere except Enniscorthy except Dublin and Galway…..The position in Enniscorthy must have been considered of some

importance. Here was a party of unarmed and undisciplined and whatever reports the man in charge of the British troops had about these men, he came to the conclusion it would be a wise thing to allow two of their men-officers-accredited by him in Dublin to get a written order from Pearse for the men in Enniscorthy to surrender."

Over the following years I started to peruse the online military archives and began reading the evidence and statements of those involved. To my personal surprise I came across two of my Great Grandfather's files. I had never realised they had played a part in 1916. With further exploration I found files belonging to a Great Aunt and Uncle. I began to wonder how many people like myself had no knowledge or only the vaguest indication that their relatives were involved. The thought then occurred to me, what if I could put their stories together, to give them a voice if you like. For the majority of people the names of the leaders are familiar, while the rank and file are known only in some instances from stories passed down through the generations. Reading the names of those involved over a hundred years ago you cannot be but surprised with the familiarity of them. These are names which are still relevant in the town today.

It was not until early 2021 that I decided to go ahead with this book. The catalyst for it was the sudden death of my cousin Joe Doyle of The Duffry. Joe had informed my wife of his plan to write a book about the Civil War in Enniscorthy and had great plans for it and its launch! After his death I found myself returning to the research I had already done, it was like Joe had given me a shove to get on with it.

This book is based on the accounts, statements and references by and for the men and women who applied for a Military Service Pension, many were refused while some were successful many years after their first application. It was an arduous journey, the Republic they fought for was guilty of turning its back on many of its sons and daughters.

Throughout the book you will see the names "Antwerp" and "The Dump" referenced. Antwerp was the name given to the Volunteer headquarters at the bottom of Mary Street which itself is at the bottom of Slaney Street. The Dump refers to the munitions factory and cavern which was dug out at the back of the Keegan home at number 10 Irish Street.

After all my research I came up with 596 individuals, men and women, who either played a part in the Easter Rising in Enniscorthy or were arrested and interned in the aftermath. For 268 of these people I try to tell their story in a concise and factual way, although many have stories which would be worth a book of their own. The rest I name and where they lived or where they came from. Included in the 596 are 17 Wexford people who served in Dublin or Galway during that momentous time.

Finally, I do not claim that the list of people mentioned as participating in the 1916 Rising in Enniscorthy is definitive, however, I have done my best to include everyone I could find and if I have omitted anyone I am truly sorry.

Pat Doran. October 2021.

The Volunteers and the Rising

The Irish Volunteers were formed in November 1913 in response to the formation of the Ulster Volunteers. By Christmas over one hundred Enniscorthy men had joined. The purpose of the organisation was to protect the proposed implementation of Home Rule the following year. When World War One broke out in August 1914, Home Rule was on the statute books but was then postponed due to the war. On September 20th, John Redmond the leader of the Irish Parliamentary Party made a speech at Woodenbridge County Wicklow, calling for the Volunteers to enlist in the British army and fight in the war. The militant nationalist members of the Volunteer Executive bitterly opposed this and rid the executive of all Redmondites. However, most rank-and-file Volunteers followed Redmond and a new movement the National Volunteers was established. This became known as the split.

The Witness Statement of James Cullen on the 25th of January 1956.

"The split occurred in the Volunteer movement directly as a result of John Redmond's appeal to the Volunteers to join the British Army. "

In Enniscorthy, unlike other towns in Wexford, the leaders of the Volunteers were I.R.B. (Irish Republican Brotherhood) members and they kept the pro Redmondites and supporters of the Irish Parliamentary Party from any position of power in the organisation. There was over one hundred members of the I.R.B. enlisted in the town's Volunteers. However, in the rest of the county the majority of rank-and-file members joined the National Volunteers.

Enniscorthy was made up of three Volunteer Companies, A, B, and C. A was the town Company, B was the area of St. John's Street while C was The Shannon Company. After the split A and B merged together as A Company while C Company remained neutral before throwing their lot in with the Irish Volunteers.

In his Witness Statement dated the 20th of September 1955, John Carroll described Volunteer activities.

"Parades were held twice weekly. The training included foot drill, arms drill, musketry and scouting. Occasionally on Sundays we would have route marches, field exercises and manoeuvres. The Company took over the club rooms in Mary Street as headquarters which later became known as "Antwerp".

And.

"Each Volunteer paid a weekly subscription to Company funds and in addition, anyone who could afford to do so subscribed weekly for the purchase of his rifle and uniform. In the case of the poorer members who could not afford to buy their rifles and uniform, the Company Captain Seamus Rafter, bought them for them out of his own pocket."

Over the following months and with mounting casualties in the Irish Divisions, Redmond and his party's popularity were dealt a terminal blow. In contrast, the Irish Volunteers increased their membership modestly from 1914-16. They were much better organised and trained than their National compatriots.

The 1916 Easter Rising began on Monday the 24th of April in Dublin when approximately twelve hundred men and women from the Irish Volunteers, Irish Citizen Army and Cumann na mBan seized some strategic sites in Dublin including the G.P.O. The number of Volunteers was smaller than anticipated due to their leader Eoin McNeill learning of their plans and issuing orders for its cancellation the previous day.

Outside of Dublin, Enniscorthy would be the only other location where the Volunteers would raise the Tricolour.

James Cullen again.

"About a week before Easter 1916 a man named Sullivan, he was not Gearóid O'Sullivan, came to Seamus Rafter's house. He told us, Seamus Rafter, myself and a few other I.R.B. men, that a general rising throughout the country had

been decided upon and that we were to rise at 6 p.m. Easter Sunday. We did not give this information to the rank and file."

On Easter Sunday the full Company gathered outside "Antwerp" on Mary Street and set off on a route march around Vinegar Hill and the town. On their return they were ordered to stand down but to be on alert for any emergency. Late on Easter Monday night and early Tuesday morning, Peter Galligan one of the Enniscorthy leaders met with James Connally, Pádraig Pearse and Joseph Plunkett in the G.P.O.. He received orders to hold Enniscorthy and its railway station. Connolly had realised the strategic position the town held with the rail lines from the ports of Rosslare and Waterford going through it. He believed the British would use these ports to mobilise troops and supplies for Dublin. Connolly also ordered that they should not attempt to try and seize the local R.I.C. barracks for it would waste too much of the meagre ammunition which the Volunteers had.

At sunrise on Tuesday morning Galligan set off by bicycle for Enniscorthy. He would not arrive until the Wednesday evening after a journey of over 150 miles and many detours to avoid the British. When he reached the outskirts, he met a local Volunteer delivering bread and told him to contact all the leaders and instruct them to report to "Antwerp". At this meeting Galligan informed them of their orders from Dublin.

Over the years writers have differed on the number of Volunteers who marched from Irish Street to the Athenaeum that fateful Thursday morning, some have said a hundred while others three hundred and five hundred. I feel the number was one hundred or less owing to the Witness Statements of the following.

Captain Peter Paul Galligan on the 17th of December 1948.

"The Battalion was mobilised about 2 a.m. on the following (Thursday) morning and was about 100 strong when mobilisation was completed."

Lieutenant Thomas Doyle on the 30th of November 1954.

"… When we got there, I saw only about 80 other Volunteers standing in the street. Rifles and shotguns were being handed out to them. Keegan's house in Irish Street was the first headquarters for the Irish Republic. With about 90 men we marched to the Athenaeum…"

And James Cullen.

"Early on Thursday morning, 27th of April, about one hundred men answered the call."

Cullen goes on to describe what happened next.

The Athenaeum was taken over as headquarters and the Tricolour hoisted over it and volleys fired in salute. Armed outposts were placed at all approaches to the town. Bedding and foodstuffs were commandeered. Members of Cumann na mBan established a food kitchen and cooked for the Volunteers. All shops were ordered to close, and food tickets were issued to the people to get food. No one was allowed to leave the town without a permit. A police force was established to preserve order and to ensure that all instructions were carried out. About two hundred men came in from the country during the week to take part in the Rising.

Lt. Thomas Doyle.

"When the people of the town woke up in the morning and saw the Volunteers all armed, they did not know what was after happening. At 8 o'clock that morning when the people were on their way to work, the Volunteers told them that there would be no work that day as the Republic was proclaimed. That morning some of the banks were taken over by Captain Etchingham. We placed guards in them and told the managers to lock up everything and if anything went wrong they were to report to us.

Orders were given to go to all the hardware shops in town and bring back all the guns and shotgun cartridges that were in them. John N. Greene's, Lar Codd's, Donohoe's Ltd. were visited. They were told that they would be paid for them later on.

…there was a notice posted around the town asking all the people who had firearms to hand them in before 12 o'clock. Some of them did not do so, and reports came in that certain people had guns but did not hand them up. I got orders to raid their houses. I first went to Kerr's the jewellers in Slaney Street. I told him a report had been handed in that he had some arms in the house. He said he only had two revolvers and he kept them for his own protection. I told him to hand them up and we would give him all the protection he wanted. He said to me "When you go up, tell Commandant Rafter I would like to have one of them." I saw Commandant Rafter and told him what Mr. Kerr said. He then sent back one of the revolvers to him. At that time, if anyone had something against you, they would send in a report that you had arms in your house and get you raided- and send us on a fool's errand. It was not a nice job, we had to do it when reports were sent in."

Peter Paul Galligan.

"After we mobilised on Thursday morning Father Murphy and Father Coady came to our headquarters. This was early in the morning. Father Murphy was anxious to join us. He asked what our prospects of success were. I told him that the arms ship had been sunk and that we were only carrying out our orders and I believed there was no hope of success. I asked him to give us his blessing which he did. He then left us. There was a branch of Cumann na mBan in the town and nothing, but admiration and appreciation is due to those girls together with some local girls who joined them."

Galligan also spoke of the attempt to rouse the Volunteers in New Ross.

"A mobilisation order to mobilise his Company was sent to Seán Kennedy at New Ross. He failed to do this, and a second order was sent to him. Kennedy's father met the man who carried the orders and told him that if he did not leave the town he would shoot him. New Ross never officially mobilised, but as far as I remember a number of men reported to Enniscorthy."

Seamus Doyle stated in his Witness Statement on the 12th of October 1949.

The R.I.C. were confined to their barracks and all gas and water cut off from them. All motor cars and cycles in shops were seized."

The above statements were given years after the Rising but at least one participant recorded the events in real time through his diary. That was Seán Etchingham.

"We have had at least one day of blissful freedom. We have had Enniscorthy under the laws of the Irish Republic for at least one day and it pleases me to learn that the citizens are appreciably surprised. We closed the public houses. We established a force of Irish Republican police, comprising some of Enniscorthy's most respectable citizens, and a more orderly town could not be imagined. Some may attribute this to the dread of our arms. Yet, strange to state it is not true. True, we commandeered much needed goods from citizens who were not in the past very friendly to our extreme views. The wonder to me is how quickly a shock changes the minds of people...."

Etchingham goes on to write about the Volunteers intentions.

"How Enniscorthy mobilised on this morning makes me feel optimistic. We never intended to attack the police barracks or post office of Enniscorthy, or elsewhere. The action of Constable Grace in firing the first shot resulted in a desultory fire. It brought about a casualty to a little girl and a wound to himself. We hold all the town and approaches. We have cut the wires, blown up the Boro Bridge and so assured that the men of Dublin will not have added to their foes further reinforcements through Rosslare."

The shooting of Constable Grace is mentioned in the Witness Statement of John (Seán) Whelan on the 21st of November 1955.

"We allowed a doctor to go into the barrack to treat his wound, but he did not succeed in saving the constable's leg as it was amputated after the surrender."

Whelan also dispelled some myths.

"Some writers say that we occupied historic Vinegar Hill and that we made no real effort to rouse the country or to maintain the initiative. Those statements are not true."

Etchingham's diary again.

"The police are in a bad way in this isolated barrack by the Quay. We have some difficulty in keeping the fighting heroes of our little army from capturing the building. We refuse to allow this, though we know the besieged would welcome an attack of rotten egg-throwers to give them an excuse of surrendering. Indeed this is confirmed by the result of an interview arranged by us between the besieged and the members of the Enniscorthy Urban Council. The District Inspector Hegarty assured the deputation that he regretted he could not accede to their terms to lay down arms and don the ordinary clothes of citizens of the Irish Republic. We will not waste ammunition on this little force which will come out to satisfy the searching demand of the stomach.

The town is very quiet and orderly. We are commandeering all we require, and we have set up different departments. The people of the town are great. Our order to close up the public houses shows to what extent these buildings are in disorder. We are all discussing the bright prospect and even our most bitter enemies give to us unstinted praise. The manhood of Enniscorthy is worth its manhood. They are working for us like the brave hearts they are. God bless you all brave people of this historic old town.

On Thursday night Volunteers from the Ferns Company arrived in Enniscorthy. Patrick Ronan from his Witness Statement on the 14th of October 1949.

"That night with about twenty men marched into Enniscorthy. This number was increased to about fifty later on."

Of the next day James Cullen stated.

"On Friday Bob Brennan arranged for a party of about 50 Volunteers to parade through the town so as to impress the people. Comdt Galligan, who was in charge

of field operations, organised a column to proceed to Ferns, where they would attack and capture the R.I.C. barracks and continue on to Dublin. Late on Saturday Comdt Galligan with between forty to fifty men marched to Ferns."

John (Seán) Whelan.

"On Friday we extended our line to Ferns and had almost reached Gorey when Dame Rumour came to Enniscorthy on Saturday and told us that the Volunteers had surrendered in Dublin and that British troops had landed in Wexford and were marching on Enniscorthy."

On Saturday evening a "Peace Committee" consisting of the Parish Administrator Rev. Fitzhenry and some prominent local businessmen arranged to speak to the leaders and ask them to surrender.

Etchingham wrote.

"We discuss things and ultimately agree to recognise an armistice. We discuss terms of peace conditionally on the English Military Authorities issuing a proclamation in the four towns of Wexford of this action and that we will not compromise in one comma our principles. We are not averse if almost a bloodless blow wins Independence.

Seamus Doyle stated.

"On Saturday night the Administrator of the Catholic Parish of Enniscorthy sent for me and talked about the hopelessness of our cause and tried to convince me to give up our effort. He made no impression on me. Later, a deputation headed by him and consisting of the businessmen in the town interviewed us with the same object, but without result. This deputation asked permission to go to Wexford to see the Commander of the British troops there. They were allowed to go. They returned to Enniscorthy with the news of the surrender in Dublin…

We did not believe about the surrender in Dublin when the information was brought to us by the deputation. It was decided the best thing to do was one of us to surrender to Colonel French in Wexford and with his permission travel to Dublin to seek confirmation. This proposition was conveyed to Colonel French who agreed and suggested that two officers should travel to Dublin. Etchingham and I travelled to Wexford on a pass supplied by Colonel French."

On Sunday morning Doyle and Etchingham were brought by a military car to Arbour Hill where they spoke to Pádraig Pearse who officially ordered them to surrender. While they were making their way to Dublin a car carrying a white flag arrived in Ferns. It contained the Parish priest of Camolin and an R.I.C. District Inspector with a surrender letter from Pearse. They were escorted to Enniscorthy and delivered it to the Athenaeum.

Seamus Doyle again.

"We returned to Wexford where we saw Colonel French. He asked us did we get what we wanted. We said we did. We got in our own car and returned to Enniscorthy. Colonel French did not discuss surrender with us. On arrival in Enniscorthy a conference of officers was called. The order was received with mixed opinions but finally it was decided to obey the order. The decision arrived at was that the officers would surrender if the men were allowed to go free. The civilian deputation went to Wexford to Colonel French with this offer and returned and gave us the impression that Colonel French agreed to this and that he would take our surrender at 2 p.m. the following day."

Thomas Francis Meagher later stated in his Witness Statement on the 12th of April 1955.

"On Sunday we were instructed to return to Enniscorthy. Some went by car; the others marched back. When we arrived at the Athenaeum, we learnt that the late Seán Etchingham and Seamus Doyle had gone to Dublin to get verification from Pearse of the order to surrender and that they had an interview with P.H. Pearse the first President of the Republic, in his prison cell and that he had ordered our officers to comply with the order to surrender…We were addressed by Seán Etchingham, Seamus Doyle, Commandant Seamus Rafter and Captain Robert Brennan. They explained to us that our comrades in Dublin had surrendered and that we must comply with the order received from Pearse to surrender. Father

Pat Murphy then attached to the Mission House, also told us to mind our arms that Ireland would need them again."

Colonel French took the surrender at 4 p.m. the following afternoon and handed the leaders over to the R.I.C. in Wexford.

A member of Cumann na mBan Maria Fitzpatrick stated in her Witness Statement on the 25th of January 1956.

"Things moved pretty fast then. The rats all came out of their holes to welcome the British soldiers. It was sad to see our brave leaders accepting death to save the rank and file."

In the aftermath there was over 260 arrests with over half of them interned in Frongach Camp in North Wales. The final word goes to Seán Etchingham.

""Well we have had a few days Republic in Enniscorthy."

1917-1923

In March 1917 the Volunteers were re-organised in the town. Over the following years members who had served in the Rising participated in the general activities of their Company's. This included digging trenches and felling trees to block roads, raiding for arms and materials and the seizure of minute books and rate books. In March 1918 a party of fifty local Volunteers were sent to Waterford to protect Sinn Féin Election officials and supporters from intimidation in the city's Bye- Election following the death of the Irish Parliamentary Party leader John Redmond. After the General Election held in December of the same year, Volunteers guarded the ballot boxes which were stored in the courthouse over the Christmas Holidays.

During the War of Independence their activities increased. Operations carried out by the Volunteers included the attack on the R.I.C. barracks in Clonroche, a raid for petrol at the railway station in which over 800 gallons was seized, a raid on Davis's foundry in St. John's for materials used in the manufacture of munitions. Some Enniscorthy Volunteers were also involved in the killing of R.I.C. District Inspector Percival Lea Wilson in Gorey in June 1920. This killing was carried out on the orders of Michael Collins who had witnessed Wilson mistreat Thomas Clarke after his arrest in 1916.

Other notable killings in this period included that of spies James Doyle of Ballycarney in September 1920, Fredrick Newsome in Slaney Place in February 1921, the Skelton Brothers near Ballindaggin in March the same year and James Morrisey near Marshalstown a couple of months later. A member of an R.I.C. bicycle patrol was killed in an ambush near Inch in May 1921, an attack which left another policemen seriously wounded. In December the same year, an R.I.C. Constable named William Jones, who was stationed in Newtownbarry (Bunclody) was shot and killed in a licensed premises in the village. All these killings involved at least one or more Volunteer who participated in the Rising in Enniscorthy.

At the outbreak of the Civil war at the end of June 1922, many former comrades found themselves on opposing sides. On the 2nd of July, open warfare broke out between the Free State soldiers and the I.R.A. in the town. This became known as the "Battle of Enniscorthy". The fighting lasted for four days before the Free State troops in the Castle and the old R.I.C. barracks on the Abbey Square surrendered. They were relieved of their weapons and then given safe passage from the town. The cost of the battle was two dead I.R.A. men and several wounded on both sides. The town itself was badly damaged. A few days later the Free State Army returned to the town in larger numbers and retook it, but not before the I.R.A. set fire to the courthouse. They then went on the run to the country and established small flying columns who returned to the town occasionally to engage the Free State troops.

One of the most brutal incidents occurred on the night of October the 10th, when two Free State Army officers were assassinated on Main Street after attending Mass. In the confusion that followed, four women were wounded in the crossfire by Free State soldiers who believed they were under attack. The two officers that were killed both came from the local area, one from Marshalstown and the other from Ballindaggin. Both men were Volunteers and members of Active Service Units during the War of Independence, and both men died from bullets fired by former comrades.

The Men and Women of Sixteen

Edward Balfe (The Shannon) C Company. Balfe joined the Volunteers in 1913. He was one of five brothers who took part in the Rising. According to his Witness Statement for the Bureau of Military History dated the 12th of March 1956, on the first morning he was awoken by loud banging on his door and the cry.

"Come on! Come on! The boys are out."

Balfe and his brothers leapt out of their beds and made their way downtown. The first thing he noticed was all the telegraph lines had been cut on the street. After reporting to the Athenaeum where a H.Q. had been established, Balfe was ordered to the Turret Rocks, which overlooked the R.I.C. barracks in the Abbey Square, to take up a sniping position. Volleys of shots were fired, and fire was returned. Later that morning an ambulance pulled up outside the front door of the barracks and a Constable named Grace was carried out on a stretcher by four other officers and placed in it. The Volunteers held their fire while this happened. Balfe was sent to Ferns on the Friday evening and remained there until the surrender on Sunday night. He evaded arrest.

Balfe re-joined in 1917 when the Volunteers were reorganised. For the next few years he took part in the general activities of his Company. In early 1920 he was promoted to the rank of acting Brigade Commandant. In April, he helped organise an attack on the R.I.C. barracks in Clonroche, this attack involved Company's from around the district as well as Wexford and New Ross. The attack lasted for a couple of hours. Towards the end of the summer, he relayed orders from G.H.Q. in Dublin, to burn all unoccupied R.I.C. barracks in the area.

In October 1920 Balfe and four others were arrested in a house on Irish Street. They were lined up and marched to the R.I.C. barracks, along the way he was prodded forcefully several times in the side with a bayonet. After giving their names and addresses they were then marched to the courthouse, which was the headquarters of the Devonshire Regiment. The men were placed in cells and then assaulted. Balfe had a revolver shoved in his mouth on three separate occasions. For three mornings running they were brought outside naked to be washed. They were individually made stand on a concrete slab while buckets of ice-cold water was thrown on them with such force, it made it impossible for them to keep their balance. They were then scrubbed with a hard yard brush. Once finished they were told to run back to the cells while trying to avoid the kicks and punches of the soldiers. Back in their cell all they had to dry themselves with was their own clothes. They received no rations and what food they had was brought by their families. Four days after their detention they were taken by lorry to Rosslare, where they boarded a British destroyer the H.M.S Valorous and sailed to Cobh. They disembarked and were brought to the Bridewell Barracks in Cork. After spending two nights there they were transferred by lorry to a military detention camp. After a couple of weeks Balfe was brought to trial, found guilty and sent to Cork jail. He spent several months there before he was transferred by train to Kilkenny.

In November 1921 Balfe was one of twenty plus prisoners who tunnelled out of the prison. He made it as far as Ballymurphy where he met some friends from Enniscorthy who were attending a coursing meeting. They brought him to Enniscorthy where he spent the night in another friend's house. The following morning Balfe went to a Volunteer camp near Kyle where he spent a week before he was assigned to take charge of a foundry on the Blackstairs Mountains which was making munitions. Edward Balfe died in his 83rd year in 1972.

James Balfe (The Shannon) C Company. James was one of Edward Balfe's older brothers. Like his brothers, he mobilised on the first morning of the Rising. After reporting to the Athenaeum he held post at three different locations that day, first at the bridge, then on the Railway Corner in Templeshannon before finally at Brownswood Cross. On Friday he was a member of a detail sent out of town to raid certain houses in the district for arms and supplies. On Saturday morning Balfe took up a sniping position on the Turret Rocks. He later stated before the Military

Service Pensions Board on the 9th of February 1940, that he fired a few rounds at the R.I.C. barracks. That night he was placed on outpost duty at Blackstoops Cross. On Sunday he was on patrol around the town. After the surrender, Balfe handed in his gun at the Athenaeum and was instructed to go to the Wexford Road to remove any roadblocks. He then went on the run and avoided arrest.

Balfe re-joined the Volunteers in 1917 and took part in their general activities. He guarded ballot boxes in the courthouse over the Christmas Holidays after the 1918 General Election. In the period 1920-1921 he took part in actions such as a raid on the Enniscorthy Asylum (St. Senan's) for minute/rate books. He carried bombs to a safe house in Killagoley which were used in the attack on the R.I.C. barracks in Clonroche in April 1920. Balfe was also involved in the raid to steal a large quantity of petrol from the railway station the following month, this raid yielded the Volunteers over 800 gallons of petrol. He stored rifles and ammunition where he worked, these weapons were later delivered to a column in Kiltealy. He did not participate in the Civil War.

After applying for the Military Service Pension, Balfe received word that he was deemed ineligible in June 1941, but that he could appeal the decision. He appealed with supporting evidence from several of his commanding officers but was still rejected. As a provision of the 1934 Act stated that the appeals referee's decision was final, his application was closed. On the 29th of June 1945, Balfe wrote a letter to the Minister of the department responsible which closed with the following lines,

"I would be grateful to you if you would give me a fair break. I consider it degrading to myself and my children not to be recognised for my past during the Insurrection."

He was met with the standard reply that the referee's judgement was final. It would not be until 1949 and the passing of the Military Service Pensions Amendment Act that Balfe's case and hundreds like it could be reopened. It was June 1951 before he was finally awarded his pension. James Balfe died in St. John's Hospital at the age of 70 in 1955.

John Balfe (The Shannon) C Company. Like his brothers, Balfe was mobilised on the Thursday morning of the Rising. He was a member of the squad of men who were sent to the Turret Rocks to snipe on the R.I.C. barracks. After this he was sent to Salville Cross to prevent people entering the town. Over the following days he was posted to Templeshannon, Clonhaston, Drumgoold, Davis's Mill and Lambert's Sawmill. After the surrender Balfe evaded arrest. He re-joined in 1917 and took part in several Volunteer operations including the raid for petrol at the railway station. At times he held ammunition and arms in his house. John Balfe died in St. John's Hospital in 1964 at the age of 82.

Michael Barnes (Ferns) Ferns Company. Barnes joined the Volunteers in 1915 and served with the Ferns Company. During the Rising he was engaged as a dispatch rider between Ferns and Enniscorthy. Following the surrender Barnes was arrested and deported shortly afterwards. He was interned in Wandsworth Jail in London and then sent to Frongach Camp in North Wales.

Upon his release he re-joined his Company and was appointed an officer. In 1920 Barnes moved to Enniscorthy and joined the local Company with whom he served until The Truce. There are no records of him taking part in the Civil War. In later years he moved to Dublin and obtained employment with Dublin County Council. During World War Two (The Emergency) he joined the Defence Forces. Barnes applied for the Military Service Pension in 1934 but was denied it. He did not appeal the decision at the time. After the passing of the Amendment Act in 1949 he applied again and in 1956 was awarded his pension. Michael Barnes died in Dublin in 1968 aged 69.

Thomas Barnes (Ferns) Ferns Company. The older brother of Michael Barnes, Thomas Barnes joined the Volunteers in 1914. Before the

Rising he was employed in the Kynoch munitions factory in Arklow. As part of his Volunteer duty he reported back to his Company Commander about troop strength and movements in the Arklow area. Once the Rising had begun he left Arklow and joined his Company in Enniscorthy. He returned to Ferns on the Friday and spent the remaining days up until the surrender on outpost and sentry duty around the village. After the surrender he was part of a small convoy of cars that set off for Enniscorthy. On the way the car in front which contained Peter Galligan crashed leaving four of the passengers injured. Barnes and another Volunteer drove to Newtownbarry (Bunclody) and brought a doctor back to the scene. He then proceeded to Enniscorthy and assisted with the disposal of weapons and munitions.

Barnes was arrested the next day and deported shortly after. He was interned in Wandsworth Prison and Frongach Camp before he was released three months later. In 1917 Barnes moved to Cork where he joined a Volunteer Company. From this time up until approximately four months before The Truce he was principally involved in the production of munitions. However, on one occasion he was involved in the capture of a spy named Nolan. After Nolan was tried and found guilty, Barnes was a member of the firing squad who executed him. In July 1921 Barnes was diagnosed with Tuberculosis and sent to a sanatorium in Doneraile. He played no further part in any activities. In later life he worked as a Customs Officer in Schull and Skibbereen. Thomas Barnes died on New Year's Eve 1963 at the age of 69.

James Bernie (Ferns) Ferns Company. James Bernie joined the Ferns Company of the Volunteers in 1914. When the Rising began he marched with members of his Company to Enniscorthy and carried out sentry duty in the town. The following day he was ordered to return to Ferns, where he served until Sunday night. After the surrender Bernie evaded capture and over the course of the next week took an active part in recovering arms and ammunition that had been hidden by captured Volunteers. In late 1916 due to unemployment, Bernie left for England only to return shortly after when conscription of Irishmen living there was introduced. Once home he re-joined his old comrades. However, due to dire circumstances he had to leave for England once more in search of employment. Bernie eventually settled in Lancashire and married an English Woman. In 1952 he applied for the Military Service Pension but was turned down. In response he wrote a letter dated the 21st of November 1952, part of which read.

"One must wonder what grounds six years' service during this period could be deemed insufficient."

By 1955 he was awarded his pension and issued with his certificate of service. He returned the certificate immediately stating it was not a true and accurate record of his service. His concluding remarks read.

"This miserable document is a mockery and I have no place for it."

Bernie was not arguing about his pension amount but saw his record as a matter of principle. In a letter dated the 11th of July 1967 he wrote.

"I here again renew my appeal against the brutal document which is supposed to be my service certificate. This I will do until I go to my grave. Kindly give us credit for knowing what we were doing in 1916."

He continued writing for several years. A note on the bottom of a department memo dated the 26th of August 1975 gave an inclination of how some of the Pensioners were thought of.

This man is a bit irrational.

James Bernie died in 1976 over 60 years after the Easter Rising, he was 79 years old.

Thomas Bishop (The Shannon) C Company. Thomas Bishop was 16 years old when he joined the Volunteers on the 1st of April 1916. He served for the duration of the Rising carrying out such duties as digging trenches, felling trees and carrying dispatches. He was not arrested after the surrender. In 1917 Bishop re-joined the organisation and served until The Truce. In March 1922 Bishop joined the National Army and fought throughout the "Battle of Enniscorthy" in July. After the Civil War Bishop worked as a labourer and then as a part-time postman before he emigrated to Cardiff in 1929 to seek full-time employment. He returned to Enniscorthy before the start of the Second World War. Thomas Bishop died in 1985 at the age of 85.

Edward Black (Hospital Lane) A Company. Edward Black enlisted in the 18th Foot Royal Irish Battalion of the British Army at the age of 18 in 1904. When he returned home to Enniscorthy he joined the I.R.B. and then the Irish Volunteers at their inception. He mobilised on Easter Sunday and spent every night bar Tuesday in "Antwerp" on standby. On the Thursday morning he arrived at the Athenaeum armed with a rifle. In his interview with the board for his Military Service Pension on the 8th of December 1937, Black stated he took a position at the top of Castle Hill and fired 10 to 12 rounds at policemen standing outside the R.I.C. barracks. He spent the rest of Thursday on outpost duties. On Friday morning Black stated he went to the Turret Rocks and again fired on the barracks. He spent the remainder of his time before the surrender commandeering supplies and on patrol. Black was arrested on the following Wednesday and deported shortly afterwards. He was interned in Stafford Jail and Frongach Camp in North Wales before he was released at the end of August. He had no further involvement with the Volunteers.

Before the Rising, Black had been employed in Davis's Flour Mill but on his return his employment was terminated. He remained unemployed for the next five years until he was reinstated in Davis's in 1921.Edward Black died in the Wexford County Hospital in 1947 aged 71.

Patrick Boland (Ferns) Ferns Company. Patrick Boland joined the Volunteers in early 1914. During the Rising he served both in Ferns and Enniscorthy. He delivered dispatches between the two locations and assisted in the occupation of the R.I.C. barracks in Ferns. After the surrender he was arrested and deported. Boland was interned first in Perth Jail in Scotland and then Frongach Camp in North Wales. He was released on the 23rd of December 1916. In 1917 Boland joined the Bree Company and served with them until he moved to Dublin, there he joined the 4th Battalion of the Dublin Brigade in 1918. In January 1919 he went to England and did not return until April 1920. Once back he joined E Company 2nd Battalion North Wexford Brigade.

Boland joined the National Army on the 4th of March 1922. During the Civil War he served as Corporal of the Guard at Kilkenny Prison, where one night he suffered serious injuries after falling from a wall while investigating strange noises. He spent three months in the Infirmary before going home on sick leave. While at home his house was raided by Anti-Treaty Irregulars who warned him he had three hours to leave, or he would be shot. He returned to light duty at the Kilkenny Barracks until he was discharged as being medically unfit to serve. In 1925 Boland moved to England where he married an English woman and settled in Barrow on Furness, Lancashire. Patrick Boland died in 1938 at Chorley Hospital at the age of 47. On the 9th of October, a few months after his death, his wife Margaret wrote a letter to Eamon De Valera in desperation for help in the support of herself and two young boys, a part of her letter read.

"In the search for employment my status as the widow of an Irish soldier is a distinct handicap."

John Boyne (The Shannon) C Company. John Boyne joined the Volunteers in 1914. He spent the night before the Rising at "Antwerp". Early the next morning he marched with the main body of Volunteers from Irish Street to the Athenaeum. After a H.Q. had been established there he was sent to Clonhaston Cross to erect roadblocks. Later Boyne was sent to the Turret Rocks with a rifle to fire on the R.I.C. barracks. Sleeping at night in the Athenaeum, he spent four days in total on the

Rocks. Once the surrender was announced, he handed in his rifle and ammunition and evaded arrest. He was "on the run" for several weeks. Boyne re-joined in 1917 and served until 1921 during which time he carried out the routine duties of a Volunteer. He took no part in the Civil War. John Boyne died at the age of 69 in 1949.

Patrick Boyne Jr. (The Shannon) C Company. Patrick Boyne Jr. joined Na Fianna Éireann in 1914 and by the time of the Rising was nearly 16. On the Thursday morning he was mobilised at 4 a.m.. After a H.Q. had been established in the Athenaeum, he was given a shotgun and sent with a party of Volunteers to the Turret Rocks. There he was ordered to guard the positions of the men who were sniping at the R.I.C. barracks below. After he was relieved a few hours later, Boyne took it upon himself to fire several shots at the barracks, (Boyne's statement before the Military Service Pensions Board on the 29th of November 1938) which was well out of his weapons range. For this action he was reprimanded. He was then placed on sentry duty at the corner of Old Church Street and Castle Hill. He slept in the Athenaeum that night. On Friday, Boyne was sent with a dispatch to Ferns and on his return took up outpost duty at Salville Cross. Boyne participated in the recruiting parade around the town on Saturday afternoon, after which he was placed on sentry duty outside the Athenaeum. On Sunday evening, Boyne who was armed with a pike, helped hold back the crowd that had gathered on the Market Square upon hearing the rumours of the surrender. Once it was official, he helped load arms and munitions which were then taken away and hidden. He then went home and successfully evaded arrest..

Boyne re-joined in 1917 and up until The Truce participated in several Volunteer operations, including the attack on the R.I.C. barracks, the stealing of Rate Books from the Enniscorthy Asylum, the raid on the County Sherriff's residence for arms, the raid on the railway station for fuel and the raid on Davis's foundry, where he was employed, for equipment to manufacture munitions. After the latter raid Boyne was dismissed from his job, having been identified as one of the raiders. With the spoils of the raid on Davis's, Boyne was sent to Corrageen near Mount Leinster to help establish a forge. He would spend four months there manufacturing grenade casings. On his return to Enniscorthy, Boyne joined the newly formed Republican police force and was soon appointed Sergeant. After The Truce he was a member of the first group of men who went to Beggars Bush to join the National Army in early 1922. He spent a month there before he was posted to the barracks in Kilkenny.

A couple of months later, after the split in the army over The Treaty, Boyne was among the 35 men who deserted with their rifles and equipment. He headed straight for Enniscorthy and joined the I.R.A. garrison in the courthouse. During the "Battle of Enniscorthy" Boyne fought at Bennett's Hotel and Yates's wool store on the Quay. He spent the next few months on the run before leaving for England when his health began to fail. He returned after the ceasefire. In later years Patrick Boyne Jr. lived in Ballymun Dublin. He passed away at the James Connolly Memorial hospital in 1988 at the age of 88.

Patrick Boyne Snr. (The Shannon) C Company. Patrick Boyne Snr. was the father of Patrick Jr; he joined the Volunteers in 1914. On the morning of the Insurrection he was handed a rifle and took a position on Castle Hill where he covered the R.I.C. barracks. He did not fire any shots. For the remainder of the week Boyne was on street patrol around the town and sleeping in the Athenaeum. After the surrender he went home but after the military started arresting men he went on the run for three weeks, sleeping in sheds and fields. Boyne re-joined in 1917 but had little involvement up to The Truce save for carrying dispatches to Wexford on several occasions. He took the Anti-Treaty side in the Civil War. Patrick Boyne Snr died in 1953 at the age of 78.

William Boyne (Irish Street) A Company. William Boyne joined the Volunteers in early 1914. Not long after joining he also became a member of the I.R.B.. Boyne played an active role in the preceding years to the Rising. He was involved in the procurement of arms and materials and helped make munitions in the "The Dump", which was the name given to the shed and cavern at the rear of the Keegan house on Irish Street. On the night before the Rising information was received that a British troop train was to pass through Enniscorthy with reinforcements for Dublin. Four men including Boyne were detailed to lift rails off the track at the Boro Bridge three miles outside the town. They made their way in pairs so as not to raise suspicion. As they started to loosen the rails, they were observed by a patrol of R.I.C. men in a nearby wooded area who immediately opened fire. The Volunteers returned fire, (Boyne would later state he fired four rounds from his revolver) and made to escape. One of them who was not familiar with the area, jumped down the wrong side of the tracks and was captured. Another was injured as he escaped. Boyne helped this Volunteer back to the local hospital attached to the County Home.

When he returned to H.Q. in "Antwerp" he was ordered to mobilise the Shannon Company, after which he caught a few hours' sleep in Antwerp. He then helped distribute rifles to the men before being tasked with the job of securing the railway station. Boyne spent the remainder of Thursday at the station and slept in the Athenaeum that night. On Friday morning he participated in raids for arms and motor vehicles outside the town. On his return he was sent to the "The Dump" to manufacture munitions. He spent Friday night in the Athenaeum. On Saturday morning Boyne was back in "The Dump", later he was placed on sentry duty at the top of Castle Hill. On Sunday, Boyne spent most of the day hiding arms and munitions. He was back in the Athenaeum in time to listen to the address of Fr. Fitzhenry asking the Volunteers to lay down their arms. He had already hidden his. His last involvement would be the clearing of blockades on the Dublin Road. He returned to his home at 11 o'clock Monday morning.

Boyne was arrested by the military the following Wednesday on the bridge and deported not long afterwards. He was incarcerated in Stafford Jail for seven weeks before he was released. He returned home to find he had lost his job as a carpenter. In 1917 Boyne briefly re-joined the Volunteers before leaving Enniscorthy to find work. He first went to Cork and then to Liverpool and Swansea. He returned in 1919 and for a few months prior to The Truce in 1921, helped his old comrades with the manufacturing of munitions. Boyne played no part in the Civil War. In the 1934 local elections Boyne was elected to the Town Council as a representative of Fianna Fáil. By 1944 he was suffering from severe heart problems and was no longer able to work so he applied for a Special Allowance under Section 7 of the 1943 Army Pension Act which stated.

That such a person is incapable of self-payment by reason of age or permanent infirmary of body or mind.

The Department requested he attend a hospital in Dublin for a full medical examination in May. Boyne's doctor refused to let him travel due to his health. He said he believed that Boyne could die on the journey. However, the Department insisted, and that August, Boyne made the journey and attended the hospital. The medical examiners declared that they believed Boyne at his age could recover so they advised against him receiving the Special Allowance. William Boyne died in April 1945 aged 49, eight months after this diagnosis. His death and treatment prior to it caused consternation to his old comrades, one of whom was Thomas Brennan a T.D. for Wicklow and who was a Commandant in the North Wexford Brigade during the War of Independence. He wrote a stinging letter to the Department a few weeks after Boyne's death, which included the lines.

"…sometime later he was notified that he was not entitled to the allowance and when I inquired I was told that his illness was not that of a permanent nature, neither was it, for it killed him a few weeks ago."

John Brady (Irish Street) A Company. John Brady joined the Volunteers at their inception in 1913 at the age of 16. On the first morning of the Rising he marched with the main body of Volunteers from Irish Street to the Athenaeum. After a H.Q. had been established there, Brady was sent with a party of Volunteers to the Turret Rocks. He later stated in his interview before the Military Service Pensions Board on the 8th of December 1937 that he personally fired up to 20 shots at the R.I.C. barracks. On Friday, Brady was on sentry duty at Brewery Hill while on Saturday he was on outpost duty at Clonhaston Cross. On Sunday he was involved in the collection and hiding of arms and munitions, Brady hid rifles at the sewage works by the Slaney. After the surrender he evaded capture.

Brady re-joined the newly reformed organisation in 1917 and for the next two years was involved in the manufacturing of munitions. In 1919 he participated in three raids for arms and a raid on the railway station for petrol. He also followed and spied on policemen patrolling the town at night. In the months preceding The Truce Brady stored weapons belonging to other Volunteers, whose homes were raided on a regular basis. He took no part in the Civil War but was known to hold sympathies for the Anti-Treaty side. John Brady died on the 14th of April 1966, just two weeks shy of the 50th Anniversary of his involvement in the Insurrection, he was 68 years old.

John Breen (Templeshannon) A Company. John Breen was a member of the I.R.B. before he joined the Volunteers in 1913. He worked as a coachbuilder in the Rock Factory at the base of the Turret Rocks. After been called early on the morning of the Rising Breen went directly to "Antwerp" armed with his Mauser rifle. He was met by a Volunteer who informed him that the H.Q. had been moved to the Keegan's house on Irish Street. When Breen got there he was ordered to cut the communication lines to the railway station which were located at the mouth of the tunnel on the west side of the railway bridge. Once he returned to Irish Street he swapped his heavy Mauser for a lighter Martin-Henry rifle. Breen then marched to the Athenaeum with the main body of men. After a headquarters was established at the Athenaeum, Breen was assigned a sniping position at the top of Castle Hill, from where he fired at the front door of the R.I.C. barracks. (testimony before the

Military Service Pensions Board on the 29th of November 1938) After been there for approximately an hour and a half, he was recalled to the front of the Athenaeum, where as a member of the designated firing party, he fired three shots in salute after the Tricolour was raised. Shortly after this an officer emerged from the Athenaeum to ask for any Volunteers who had experience with explosives. Breen raised his hand. He was sent with four other men to blow up the Boro railway bridge outside the town. However, armed with only blasting paper and a fuse they only succeeded in damaging one of the bridge's parapets.

On his return, Breen was ordered to the roof of the Castle. He would remain there overnight and was not relieved until Friday evening. Throughout his time on the roof Breen did not fire a shot. He spent the remaining days of the Rising in the vicinity of the Athenaeum. After the surrender, he helped load lorries with arms and ammunition. He hid his own rifle in the Rock Factory. On Monday morning Breen went on the run and did not return home for three months. For the next few years he made casings and shells in his factory that were then brought to the "The Dump" and "Antwerp" to be filled with gunpowder and explosives. John Breen lived in Templeshannon and died in 1975 aged 83

Joseph Breen (Ferns) Ferns Company. Joseph Breen joined the Volunteers in 1914. During the Rising he brought fuel from Enniscorthy to Ferns and stood post there until the surrender. Breen was arrested on the 3rd of May and deported shortly afterwards. He was interned in Wandsworth Jail and in Frongach Camp until he was released on the 1st of August. Breen re-joined in 1917 and took part in the general activities of his Company. In March 1920 he was obliged to go on the run and joined up with the North Wexford Flying Column until The Truce. During the Civil War he was a member of the Free State Army garrison in Ferns at the time it was attacked by Anti-Treaty Irregulars. Joseph Breen died in 1955 at the age of 60.

Mary Breen (Slaney Street) Cumann na mBan. Mary Breen (nee Cullen) joined Cumann na mBan in 1914. On the morning of the Rising she reported to the Athenaeum for duty. She was assigned to the dressing table in the first aid section. Since there was not a lot of call for first aid she helped out with the cooking and prepared basins of hot water for tired Volunteers to soak their feet in. Breen spent the entirety of the Rising in the Athenaeum. Over the following months she helped to collect money for the families of the Volunteers interned. She also sent food parcels to the prisoners. After the death of Seamus Rafter, Breen marched with her Cumann branch at his funeral. On several occasions her home was used as a safe house for on the run Volunteers. She ceased her activities in 1919. Mary Breen died in 1970 at the age of 83.

Myles Breen (Ferns) Ferns Company. Myles Breen was Joseph Breen's older brother; he joined the Volunteers in 1914. During the Rising he served in Enniscorthy and Ferns. His various roles included patrolling, commandeering of arms and supplies and sentry duty. He was arrested on the Wednesday following the surrender and deported shortly afterwards. Breen was interned in Wandsworth Jail and Frongach Camp until his release in the first week of August.

During the War of Independence Breen served as a Lieutenant, a Captain and as Battalion Commandant. He was involved in several operations including the seizure of Excise Books in Gorey and the attack on the R.I.C. barracks in Clonroche. In June 1920, Breen acted as a scout for the I.R.A. party who shot dead R.I.C. District Inspector Lea-Wilson in Gorey. In March the following year he went on the run and became O/C for the North Wexford No. 2 Column. This column was responsible for the ambush near Inch of a six-man R.I.C. cycle patrol in May 1921 which left one policeman dead and another badly wounded. After The Truce Breen trained men in camps to be ready for action should it be broken. Breen was automatically appointed Commandant in the National Army on its formation and remained in situ until the end of the Civil War. Myles Breen died at the age of 87 in 1981.

Robert Brennan (Wexford) Brigade Q/M Wexford Brigade. Robert Brennan became a member of the I.R.B. in 1907 and joined the Volunteers at their inception in 1913. He was also an organiser of branches of the Gaelic League. Brennan worked for The Echo Newspaper as a journalist and was the Wexford correspondent for The Irish Times for a period. During the Rising, Brennan was one of the leaders based in the Athenaeum. After the Surrender he was sentenced to death, but the sentence was commuted to 5 years penal servitude. He served his time in Dartmoor, Lewes and Pentonville Jails before he was released in June 1917. From 1918 Brennan ran the publicity wing of Sinn Féin. He also served on the intelligence staff of the Volunteers under Michael Collins. In the Civil War he sided with the Anti-Treaty forces and worked as a propagandist for them. Brennan served as a diplomat in Washington for several years around the time of the outbreak of World War Two. He was also one of the founders of The Irish Press. Robert Brennan died in Dublin in 1964 at the age of 83.

Una Brennan (Oylgate) Cumann na mBan. Una Brennan (nee Anastatia Bolger) was the wife of Robert Brennan; she joined the Wexford branch of Cumann na mBan in 1915. In March 1916, when she found out the Rising was imminent, she bought iodine and material to make bandages. Brennan brought a quantity of bandages and other medical supplies to Enniscorthy shortly before Easter Week. The night before the Insurrection she travelled to Enniscorthy and reported for duty at the Athenaeum early the following morning. Throughout the rest of the week Brennan remained there helping to set up beds and organising meals for the Volunteers, as well as other tasks. She remained with her husband until he was arrested on the Monday afternoon. Brennan was inactive until the summer of 1919, at which time she was residing in Dublin. She carried dispatches and hosted meetings in her house on numerous occasions. In November 1920 the Brennans had to go on the run, they stayed in various houses around the city using aliases. From 1921 until the Civil War she worked out of the newly established Office of Foreign Affairs and after choosing the Anti-Treaty side assisted her husband in running propaganda. When Seamus Doyle appeared before the Military Pensions Advisory Board on the 8th of March 1946 he was asked about Brennan. He said the following about her.

"…she was a very forceful personality; you can take that from me."

Una Brennan died in Dublin in her 70th year in 1958.

Fintan Burke (Georges Street) A Company. Fintan Burke joined the Volunteers at their inception in 1913 and the I.R.B. a short time after. Before the Rising he was involved in raids for arms and munitions. Burke was a member of a small group of Volunteers who hid munitions in an abandoned house two miles out of town in Kilcannon. This house was known to the men as *"The Haunted House"*. On Good Friday and Holy Saturday, Burke helped transport these munitions to "The Dump", where they were made ready for use by Easter Sunday evening when the Rising was originally to begin.. After Eoin McNeill's counter orders the Volunteers were in a state of limbo. Burke remained on guard duty at Keegan's until the Wednesday evening.

When Peter Galligan returned from Dublin with the orders from Pearse and Connolly, Robert Brennan despatched Burke and another Volunteer to Wexford with a message for his wife. The message was for her and whatever men who were ready to immediately come to Enniscorthy. However, as Burke approached her house he was set upon by R.I.C. men and Special Constables who had been lying in wait. They searched and threatened to shoot him but all they found was a revolver on him., the message he had to deliver was a verbal one. The next morning, he was brought before British Army officers who remanded him to Waterford Jail. From there he was sent to Richmond Barracks in Dublin where he shared a cell with four other men, one of whom was future Taoiseach

Seán Lemass. Burke was deported, and later interned in Wakefield Prison and Frongach Camp from where he was released in August 1916.

Burke re-joined the Volunteers in 1917 and served with them up to his departure for the United States in May 1920. He settled in New York and in the following year assisted Patrick Keegan with the procurement of arms which were shipped back to Ireland. Burke lived in New York for the rest of his life working as a carpenter. During World War Two he served in the United States Coast Guard and was based at Coney Island. Fintan Burke died In Flushing, Queens in 1966, a few months after returning from Enniscorthy where he attended the 50th Anniversary celebrations of the Rising. He was 73 years old.

George Butler (Ferns) Ferns Company. George Butler joined the Volunteers in 1914. As a member of the Ferns Company, he marched to Ballinahallin Wood on the outskirts of Enniscorthy and set up camp on the Tuesday of Easter Week. The following day he was sent on his own into Enniscorthy to receive instructions. He was told to return to Ferns and raise more men. For the remainder of the Rising Butler was on armed duty in Enniscorthy, Ferns and Camolin. After the surrender he evaded capture and was on the run for six weeks. In 1917 he helped reorganise the Ferns Company and was appointed as 2nd Lieutenant. Up until The Truce he took part in Volunteer activities including the torching of R.I.C. Barracks' and several ambushes. After The Truce was declared on the 11th of July 1921, Butler served as a policeman in Ferns until the 8th of February the following year. As a member of the National Army, he fought in Enniscorthy and Ferns when they were attacked in July of 1922 by Anti-Treaty forces. George Butler died in 1973 at the age of 80.

Anastasia Byrne (Old Church) Cumann na mBan. Anastasia Byrne (nee Walsh) joined Cumann na mBan in 1914. On the morning of the Rising, while making her way to the Athenaeum from her home she came under fire from the R.I.C. barracks as she crossed the bridge. Once at the Athenaeum Byrne was sent to Kelly's Chemist in Slaney Place for medical supplies. For the remainder of the week she helped in dressing beds, cooking and general duties. She also delivered dispatches on several occasions.

After the surrender her father, Volunteer Patrick Walsh was arrested and interned. Byrne minimised her activities in order to help her mother and after marrying the following year ceased altogether. However she did attend the funeral of Seamus Rafter in September 1918 as a member of Cumann na mBan. In a summary of her application for a Military Service Pension, the Referee wrote on the 11th of January 1939.

Applicants Easter Week service appears to be satisfactory, but I am of opinion she dropped out after that. Her domestic duties claimed her full-time then.

Anastasia Byrne died in 1945, she was 50 years old.

Edward Byrne (The Duffry) A Company. Edward Byrne joined the Volunteers in 1914 and took part in all their activities. During the Rising he was tasked with sentry duty, road blocking and the procurement of supplies. He was arrested and interned for a period after the surrender. In 1917, Byrne re-joined the Volunteers and served until The Truce. In this period, he was involved in several raids for arms and the attack on the R.I.C. barracks in Clonroche. Byrne was also involved in the large raid for petrol at the railway station in May 1920. From July 1921 until the following June, Byrne served as a Republican police officer and claimed to have tied numerous offenders to the Cathedral's railings. During the Civil War he fought on the Anti-Treaty side and took part in the "Battle of Enniscorthy". Edward Byrne died from Tuberculosis at the age of 45 in 1936.

John Joseph Byrne St. Patrick's Place) Unaffiliated. John J. Byrne worked as a solicitor's assistant in the practice of P.J. O'Flaherty & Sons at the time of the Rising. On the first evening of the Rising he volunteered for duty at the old R.I.C. barracks on Court Street. He was made a member of the Irish Republican Police and given a red armband with the initials I.R.P. on it. He patrolled the streets until midnight alongside Volunteer Edward Byrne. He then returned to his home in St. Patricks' Place.

Early the next morning Byrne was summoned to the Athenaeum by Commandant Seamus Rafter and was put to work typing proclamations and military orders. He spent all day Friday and Saturday in this endeavour. After the surrender Byrne was not arrested, however, he was dismissed from his position in O'Flaherty's' for his role in the Insurrection. John Joseph Byrne died in 1961 at the age of 63.

Patrick Joseph Byrne (The Duffry) A Company P.J. Byrne joined Na Fianna Éireann in 1914 and by the time of the Rising was a member of the Volunteers. Having stood prepared throughout the first three days of Easter Week, Byrne reported to Irish Street early on Thursday morning and marched with the main body of men to the Athenaeum. Once a H.Q. had been established there, Byrne was selected for the firing party who fired the salute after the Tricolour was raised above the building. From there he was sent on outpost duty to Summerhill.

Later in the morning Byrne was recalled to H.Q. and went with the party of Volunteers sent to commandeer coal from O'Neill's coal yard on the Mill Park Road. Byrne was standing guard at The Echo Newspaper office on the opposite side of the road from the coal yard when shots were fired by the R.I.C. men in the Bank of Ireland, according to his statement before the Military service Pensions Board on the 8th Of February 1940, he stood out into the street and fired twice with his shotgun at the source of the shots. The R.I.C. ceased firing and the volunteers continued with their raid. That evening Byrne was placed on guard duty at the Gas Yard and remained there until the following morning. On Friday he was assigned to the transport section and given the responsibility of recording the comings and goings of vehicles to the Athenaeum. Byrne carried out this assignment until the surrender on Sunday night. He was arrested the following Tuesday and sent to Wellington Barracks in Dublin, from where he was released three weeks later due to his age.

Byrne re-joined in 1917 and participated in the routine activities of his Company. In the aftermath of the attack on the Clonroche R.I.C. barracks in April 1920, Byrne was badly injured when a bomb went off accidently near where he was standing. He was brought to a house in Ballindaggin where he was treated for his wounds before he was transferred to Jervis Street Hospital in Dublin for an operation. After he was discharged he was brought to a safe house in Carlow to recuperate. Once well enough, Byrne returned to Enniscorthy only to find out he was a wanted man. He returned to Carlow and joined the Brigade there. Byrne was involved in several operations in the Carlow area including the torching of the R.I.C. barracks in Borris and the sniping on barracks' in Bagenalstown, Goresbridge and Gowran.

Byrne was also involved in the killing of two alleged spies in Borris on March the 15th 1921, a local pharmacist named William Kennedy who was believed to be colluding with the R.I.C. and Michael Dempsey his solicitor from Enniscorthy. In 1924 the family of Dempsey were awarded £2,500 in compensation from the Free State government in recognition that he was an innocent man and not a spy. After The Truce Byrne returned to Enniscorthy and at the outbreak of the Civil War chose the Republican side. During the "Battle of Enniscorthy" he carried dispatches to Gorey and Blessington. After the evacuation of the town by the Republican forces he was instructed to try and reorganise the Republican faction left in the town, but due to disagreements between them he decided to end his service. In later years he opened a shop on The Duffry. Patrick Joseph Byrne died at his residence on The Duffry in 1967, he was 69 years old.

Patrick Byrne (Ross Road) A Company. A member of both the Volunteers and the I.R.B., Patrick Byrne worked as a carter for The Mill Park Brewing Company. During the Rising he was involved in the blocking of roads. After the surrender he evaded arrest. Byrne re-joined in 1917 and used his position to help move arms and munitions on several occasions. He also helped in the manufacture of said munitions from 1917 until 1919. On Armistice night 1920 he was among a group of men who challenged members of the British Legion that were running amok in the town. A party of Devonshire Regiment soldiers came to the aid of the Legionnaires and in O' Brien's pub on Irish Street, they gave Byrne a severe beating from which he never properly recovered from. In the Civil War he was a member of the Republican forces which fought in the "Battle of Enniscorthy." Patrick Byrne died at his residence on the Ross Road in 1926 from Tuberculosis. He was 31 years of age.

Michael Cahill (The Shannon) Captain C Company. Michael Cahill joined the Volunteers at their inception in 1913. Early on the morning of the Rising he knocked on doors on The Shannon to rouse sleeping Volunteers. Before a H.Q. had been established in the Athenaeum, Cahill was placed in command of a party of Volunteers sent to the Turret Rocks to snipe on the R.I.C. barracks. Over the following days he was involved in securing supplies and manning outposts. On the Wednesday following the surrender he was arrested and deported shortly afterwards. Cahill was interned in Stafford Jail and then Frongach Camp before he was released in December. Cahill re-joined the Volunteers in 1917 and played a prominent role in their activities up until The Truce. He joined the National Army in 1922 and was an active participant in the "Battle of Enniscorthy" that July. For four days Cahill sniped from his vantage point on the Castle roof at the Anti-Treaty forces in St. Mary's Church. He also threw grenades at their positions elsewhere before surrendering. In later years he worked in Roches Malt factory on the Island Road and for a while in England. Michael Cahill died at his residence on The Shannon in 1952 aged 66.

Joseph John Cardiff (Duffry Street) C Company. Although Joseph Cardiff lived on Duffry Street, he joined The Shannon Company of the

Volunteers in 1915. At the time of the Rising he was employed as a bookkeeper for John F. Yates & Sons. Cardiff made his way to the Keegan house on Irish Street early on the morning of the Rising. Once there, he was given a rifle and was sent with the Company Captain Michael Cahill and a small party of Volunteers to the Turret Rocks, from where he fired at the R.I.C. barracks. After a half an hour of this, Cardiff was ordered to go to the Athenaeum and do an inventory of the Volunteers supplies. After this was completed he was placed on outpost duty on the Wexford Road. He spent a couple of hours there before he was moved to Clonhaston Cross. Cardiff slept in the Athenaeum on Thursday night. On Friday, Cardiff helped to commandeer supplies, firstly a bread van belonging to O' Connors of Wexford. Then he went to Donohue's yard for timber, saws and other tools. Once these tasks were completed, he was assigned outpost duty at St. Johns. On Saturday morning Cardiff was sent with an advance party to Ferns. There he helped secure the vacated R.I.C. barracks and patrol the village. He spent Saturday night in the barracks. On Sunday morning Cardiff accompanied a motorist who was lost to Enniscorthy. For the rest of the day he was on duty in the centre of the town. After the surrender he helped collect and hide munitions before returning to his home on Duffry Street.

Cardiff avoided arrest due to the personal intervention of his employer, who was a very influential man in the town. Cardiff re-joined on the resumption of the organisation in 1917 and served until The Truce. As well as being involved in several raids for arms, it was Cardiff who got the tip off about the large shipment of petrol which the Volunteers seized from the railway station in May 1920. In the course of his job Cardiff had cause to visit the R.I.C. barracks, (the building was owned by his employer) and on a couple of these occasions he overheard R.I.C. officers discussing forthcoming raids on Volunteer targets. Cardiff was able to inform his commanding officers and the targets of these raids were warned in advance and made themselves scarce. Joseph Cardiff died at the age of 77 in 1976.

John Carley (Old Church) C Company. John Carley joined the Volunteers at their inception in 1913. On the morning of the Rising he went to "Antwerp", there, he was instructed to go to Keegan's. On his arrival he was handed a rifle and then he lined up in formation with the other Volunteers to march to the Athenaeum. Carley was ordered with three other men under the command of Patrick Keegan to go to the roof of the Castle where they took up sniping positions. He remained there for 4 hours firing intermittingly at the R.I.C. barracks. Carley claimed to have fired approximately 50 rounds during this period in his testimony before the Military Service Pensions Board on the 5th of June 1940. The group then received orders to make their way to Lett's Corner at the bottom of Friary Hill, where Volunteers were under fire from the R.I.C. men who had locked themselves into the Bank of Ireland on the Abbey Square. Carley stated at his appearance before the Military Service Pensions Board on the 5th of June 1940, that he fired around 10 shots at the Bank. On Thursday evening he was on outpost duty at Clonhaston Cross until he was relieved at midnight. Carley spent all day Friday in the Athenaeum before sleeping that night in the Castle. On Saturday morning Carley was on outpost duty again at Clonhaston Cross before he returned to the Market Square to take part in a recruiting parade. On Sunday he was on guard duty on the corner of New Street. (Wafer Street) Once the surrender was announced Carley helped with the collection and disposal of arms. He took his own rifle home and managed to avoid arrest over the following days.

Carley re-joined in 1917 once the organisation was up and running and took part in the general Company activities up until The Truce. While working as a guard on the Dublin-Southeastern Railway he carried dispatches at least once a week between Enniscorthy and Wexford. On one occasion he carried two rifles and 4 boxes of ammunition aboard his train and dropped them off in Killurin where they were retrieved and used in an ambush. In later years Carley became the stationmaster in Camolin. John Carley died at the age of 91 in 1988.

John "Jack" Carroll (Irish Street) A Company. John Carroll was a member of Na Fianna Éireann before he joined the Volunteers in 1914. For the two years preceding the Rising he took a full part in all Company activities. After a parade during Holy Week, the company was instructed to muster with their weapons at headquarters at noon Easter Sunday and to bring enough rations for 24 hours. On the Sunday the Company drilled as normal and then marched to Vinegar Hill and around the town. When they returned to Mary Street they were dismissed and told to be ready for another mobilisation at short notice. Carroll was detailed to guard "The Dump" on Irish Street on Wednesday night. Early the following morning he mobilised with the rest of his Company and spent the following days manning outposts and raiding for arms and supplies. After the surrender he assisted with the concealment of arms and munitions and successfully evaded arrest. Carroll re-joined in 1917 and became Company O/C. For the next two years he participated in all Volunteer activities including raids for arms, providing security for the election workers during the 1918 General Election and the fight against conscription.

In 1920 his activities became more intense, these included the attack on the R.I.C. barracks in Clonroche, the burning of the R.I.C. barracks in Galbally and the raid for petrol at the railway station. In December 1920, an attempt was made on the life of a spy named Fredrick Newsome on the Market Square. Newsome fled, but in February the following year he was not as lucky. Carroll stated in his Witness Statement for the Bureau of Military History on the 20th of September 1955.

"In February 1921, I received orders from Joseph Cummins, who at that time was Brigade O/C, to execute Newsome. I decided to do the job myself. One night soon afterwards when in company with James Leacy, John St., both of us being armed (I had a .38), we carried out the execution order on Newsome when we met him at Slaney Place, Enniscorthy."

Three days later Carroll was arrested after the funeral of a local Volunteer Sean Moran from Church street, who had been killed by the Black and Tans in Drogheda, Carroll was not arrested for the killing of Newsome, but for unlawful assembly after bringing out the Company to honour their fallen comrade. He was sentenced to three months in Waterford Jail. At the outbreak of the Civil War, Carroll was one of the I.R.A. Volunteers based at their garrison at the courthouse. When hostilities broke out on the 2nd of July, he took up a position in the tower of St. Mary's Church from where he fired on the Free State positions on the Castle roof. After the surrender of the Free State soldiers four days later, they were allowed safe passage out of the town. When they returned in greater numbers, Carroll along with the other I.R.A. men went on the run. He was captured soon after in a neighbour's house and later detained in Gormanstown and Kildare before been released at Christmas 1923. John Carroll died on St. Patrick's Day 1974 at the age of 74.

Joseph Carroll (Irish Street) A Company. Joseph Carroll was John Carroll's older brother. He had also been a member of Na Fianna Éireann before joining the Volunteers. During the Rising his activities included sentry duty, blocking roads and raiding for supplies. After the surrender Carroll was arrested and deported shortly afterwards. He was interned in Stafford Jail until late summer. Carroll re-joined at the resumption in 1917. For the next two years he played his part in the various actions the Company took. In early 1921 he was arrested by members of the Devonshire Regiment and held at their headquarters (the courthouse) until July when The Truce was declared. Once the Civil War broke out Carroll was back in the courthouse as part of the I.R.A. forces who used it as their base. He took part in the "Battle of Enniscorthy" but went on the run once the Free State reinforcements came to take back control. Carroll was later arrested and detained in The Curragh until the end of the war.

Not long after, Carroll moved to England and settled in Coventry. In later years he would come home on holidays annually. Carroll applied for his

Military Service Pension twice and was deemed ineligible on both occasions. In early 1958 Carroll applied once again for his pension and yet again he was refused. However on this occasion he appealed the decision and won. That October he was notified he would receive his pension and that it would be backdated to 1949, the year the pensions amendment act came into force. On the 12th of December he received a lump sum and lodged it in his bank account on the 16th. On the 21st of December Joseph Carroll died at the age of 62.

Martin Carty (Slaney Street) A Company. Martin Carty became a member of the I.R.B. in 1909 and joined the Volunteers at their inception in 1913. He owned and ran a bicycle shop at number 1 Slaney Street. Prior to the Rising Carty's premises were used for meetings and the storing of weapons. From Easter Monday until the Wednesday evening he repaired over three dozen rifles and fixed bayonets to them. Carty also made keys which enabled the Volunteers to gain entrance to several hardware stores on the morning of the Rising, including Donohue's of Templeshannon, Hogan's of Castle Street and Greene's of Georges Street. (Rafter St.) On the morning of the Rising and with the help of a couple of Volunteers, Carty brought the weapons from his shop, which was less than a hundred yards away, to the Athenaeum. Seamus Rafter then ordered him to return to his shop and be on standby to repair any weapons brought there. Carty remained there until after the surrender. The following week he was arrested and shortly afterwards deported to Stafford Jail where he was interned until his release that August.

Once back home, Carty played an active part in the National Aid organisation, which sent food parcels to the Volunteer internees from Enniscorthy. In 1918 he helped with the printing of posters for the General Election and also continued to repair and store weapons. In November 1920, Carty was arrested by members of the Devonshire Regiment under the command of Captain Yeo and held for four days in the courthouse. He was severely beaten on numerous occasions and had his head shaved before he was paraded through the town. In April 1921 he received the same treatment and due to the stress of these events, his wife miscarried their son, Carty later stated that the soldiers had killed his son. After his last arrest he closed up his shop due to the fact that it was raided on a near daily basis. However, even after the closure Carty still received regular beatings on the street whenever he encountered soldiers or the police. Martin Carty died in 1957 at the age of 74.

Patrick Carty (Drumgoold) C Company. Patrick Carty joined the Volunteers in early 1914. At the time he was employed at the local quarry and had experience with Gelignite and blasting powder. In the following years up until The Truce he provided his expertise not only to his own Company but to other local Company's. On the morning of the Rising he assembled with the other Volunteers at the Keegan house on Irish Street. From there he was dispatched with the small *"sniping squad"* under the command of Michael Cahill to the Turret Rocks. Carty stated later before the Military Service Pensions Board on the 14th of May 1941, that he had fired five shots at the R.I.C. barracks. On Thursday afternoon he was on outpost duty at the Duffry Gate. He spent the night in the Athenaeum. On Friday, Carty accompanied Patrick Keegan to Cherryorchard and Clonhaston to collect Gelignite. They brought it back to the Athenaeum, where Carty was left in charge of it. On Saturday he went with Keegan to Edermine and set off explosives on the bridge, partially damaging it. When he returned he was detailed for sentry duty in the town centre. On the Sunday evening Carty was present in the Athenaeum for the surrender, after which he helped dispose of arms and munitions. He then went home to Drumgoold before he could be arrested. Patrick Carty died in 1949, he was 68 years of age.

James Cleary (Irish Street) Staff Captain A Company. James Cleary was a prominent member of the I.R.B. before joining the Volunteers in 1913. He worked as a blacksmith and had his own forge in Templeshannon. In the years prior to the Rising he used his skills to make hundreds of pike heads and all types of munitions. At the time of the

Insurrection he held the rank of Staff Captain. Cleary was one of the few officers in Enniscorthy who knew in advance the plans for the Rising. In the days leading up to it he made several trips to Wexford and the south of the county in an attempt to muster support from other Volunteer Company's. When word got back to the leaders on Wednesday night that two of Robert Brennan's envoys had been arrested in Wexford, Cleary and another Volunteer set off shortly after midnight to notify the leaders there that the Rising was beginning that morning. The two men returned to Enniscorthy as daylight was breaking.

Cleary joined with the rest of the Volunteers on Irish Street and then marched to the Athenaeum. After the H.Q. was established he took a position behind the Castle wall and fired at the R.I.C. barracks. For the remaining days of the Rising, Cleary spent most of his time in his forge manufacturing munitions. After the surrender he helped hide and move arms and equipment. On the Monday morning he helped Patrick Keegan clear "The Dump" on Irish Street of all munitions making material. Cleary was arrested a couple of days later at his forge and was deported shortly afterwards. He was interned in Woking Prison and then Frongach Camp before he was released in December. In 1917 Cleary re-joined the organisation and along with Keegan, recovered all the hidden arms and equipment. From this time up to The Truce he played an active role, along with participating in raids he continued in the manufacturing of munitions. Cleary made a special mould for buckshot which was sent to G.H.Q. in Dublin and was later used countrywide. During The Truce he made hand grenades and taught engineering classes. At the outbreak of the Civil War, he took the Anti-Treaty side and was involved in the "Battle of Enniscorthy". James Cleary died in 1975 at the age of 89.

Aidan Coady (Irish Street) A Company. Aidan Coady was one of four brothers who joined the Volunteers at their inception in 1913. He became a member of the I.R.B. shortly afterwards. On the first morning of the Rising he marched with the main body of men to the Athenaeum from Irish Street. Later that day while on patrol he encountered a couple of R.I.C. men in the vicinity of St. Johns Street and opened fire with his Lee Enfield rifle. No casualties were reported. On Friday, Coady marched with a column of Volunteers to Ferns. After they took over the vacant R.I.C. barracks, Coady was sent to commandeer food. When he returned he was placed on outpost duty on the Camolin Road. On Saturday, Coady spent the day felling trees and assembling roadblocks. While on Sunday he was once again on outpost duty, this time on the Enniscorthy Road. After word of the surrender, Coady returned to Enniscorthy and evaded arrest by going on the run for three weeks. He did not participate in anymore activities due to poor health. Aidan Coady died in St. John's Hospital in 1952. He was 59 years old.

James Coady (Irish Street) A Company. Another of the Coady brothers, James joined the Volunteers in 1913 and shortly after was accepted into the I.R.B.. In the years leading up to the Rising he participated in all of the Company's routine activities as well as some clandestine work such as following R.I.C. men as they patrolled the town. He helped make buckshot and other munitions in "The Dump" two or three nights a week. On the morning of the mobilisation Coady marched from Irish Street to the Athenaeum. A short while later he drove with Patrick Keegan and Seán Gallagher to Edermine. As they crossed the bridge and made their way down the Shannon Quay they were fired on from the R.I.C. barracks on the opposite side of the Slaney. They returned fire and continued on their journey unharmed. At Edermine they proceeded to lift planks off the bridge. They then raided a nearby house for arms. On Friday, Coady was detailed to Ferns where he spent the remainder of the Insurrection. His duties there consisted of sentry duty and the manning of outposts. Coady was arrested the following Friday and deported to England where he was held in Stafford Jail and then Frongach Camp. He was released in December. Coady re-joined in 1917 and continued with his routine Volunteer activities. He moved to Wexford in 1919 and joined a Company in the town. One night in 1920, Coady came across a drunk British soldier and took his revolver from him. After this he was a wanted man and had to go into hiding until The Truce. Coady had no involvement in the Civil War. James Coady died at the age of 62 in 1957.

John Coady (Irish Street) A Company. The eldest of the Coady brothers, John joined the Volunteers in 1913. On the morning of the Rising he marched with his Company to the Athenaeum. Later he was a member of the party tasked with blowing up the Boro Railway Bridge. They only succeeded in damaging one of its parapets due to inadequate ordnance. On his return to the Athenaeum Coady was ordered to go to the courthouse where the National Volunteers arms were stored and confiscate them. That evening he was on the Turret Rocks sniping at the R.I.C. barracks. The next day Coady was dispatched to Ferns where he spent the remaining days of the Rebellion. After the surrender he was arrested on Wednesday the 3rd of May and deported shortly afterwards. Coady was interned in Stafford Jail and Frongach Camp until his release in August. On his return to Enniscorthy he did not participate in anymore Volunteer activities.

In later years Coady worked as a self-employer carter for the Enniscorthy Co-operative Agricultural Society. In 1945 and now a widower, Coady had to retire due to heart problems. In 1947 he applied for the Special Services Allowance and in November he attended a medical examination in Dublin. The medical panel advised the Department that he was unable to work and was entitled to the allowance. By April the following year he had still not received the allowance. Brendan Corish T.D. wrote to the Department on the 29th of April stating.

"…. this man is grievously ill and in fact in danger of death. It is important in order to safeguard the interests of the dependants of this man that an early decision be reached on his application."

John Coady died on the 3rd of May aged 63, it would be three weeks later before the Department responded to Corish's letter.

"…that as Mr. Coady died before a decision was made on his claim, his death determined his claim and there is no provision under Section 7 of the Act under which any payment can be made to the next of kin. It is regretted therefore that no action can be taken in the matter."

Corish wrote back asking that under such special circumstances an ex-gratis payment to the dependents could be made. The department replied.

"…I regret I have no funds at my disposal out of which I could make an ex-gratis grant to the dependents of Mr. Coady."

Patrick Coady (Irish Street) A Company. Patrick Coady like his brothers joined the Volunteers in 1913 and the I.R.B. soon after. On the morning of the Rising he marched with his Company from Irish Street to the Athenaeum. He was then ordered to return to "The Dump" with a party of men to bring ammunition and supplies to the new H.Q.. Once completed he was tasked with cleaning the grease off pike heads. On Friday morning Coady was sent to guard the Provincial Bank at the bridge. In the afternoon he was posted to Mill Wheel Lane which was at the rear of the R.I.C. District Inspector's house. That evening he spent a few hours on sentry duty on The Duffry. On Saturday, Coady prepared the weapons for the Volunteer parade around the town. After the parade he went to Ferns and took up sentry duty at the top of the village before he was ordered to commandeer foodstuffs from Bolger's shop. Coady was then placed on guard duty at St. Mogue's Well on the Dublin Road. On Sunday he was ordered to march back to Enniscorthy in time for the surrender. On arrival he handed over his rifle and ammunition so they could be hidden. The next morning Coady was arrested. He was deported shortly afterwards and was interned in Stafford Jail for six weeks before he was released. On the reorganisation of his Company in 1917 Coady re-joined and took part in all general Company activities up until The Truce. He played no part in the Civil War. Patrick Coady died in 1958 at the age of 67.

Mark Colfer (Edermine) A Company. Mark Colfer joined the I.R.B. in 1911 and the Volunteers at their inception in 1913. On the morning of the Insurrection he marched with the rest of his Company to the Athenaeum where a H.Q. was established. At 11 a.m. Colfer and another Volunteer were sent on a scouting mission. They went by bicycle as far as Ferrycarrig. They travelled unarmed with the intention that if stopped they could plead their innocence. Once they approached Ferrycarrig they observed the bridge was held by British soldiers and the railway line was being patrolled by the R.I.C.. They turned back and returned to Enniscorthy where they relayed this information to their superior officers. Colfer then helped set up beds and cooking facilities in the Athenaeum. Later he was sent to Clonhaston Cross for outpost duty. On Friday, Colfer spent the day on sentry duty close to the Athenaeum. On Saturday evening he was sent to Davis's Mill for outpost duty while on Sunday morning he was detailed to Killagoley for the same. Colfer returned to the Athenaeum in the early afternoon. At 7 p.m. he was sent to help hold back the crowd at the top of Slaney Street as rumours of the forthcoming surrender spread. After the surrender he helped with the removal and disposal of arms and munitions before returning to his home in Edermine at 3 a.m. Monday morning. He was not arrested. Colfer re-joined the Volunteers in 1917 and served up until The Truce. He did not participate in the Civil War. Mark Colfer died in St. John's Hospital Enniscorthy in 1986 aged 92.

Thomas Connolly (Drumgoold) C Company. Thomas Connally was born in The Ballagh and joined the Volunteers not long after their formation. His service during the Rising included blocking roads and sentry and outpost duties. He was not arrested on its conclusion. Connolly re-joined in 1917 and served until the following year before he dropped out. Thomas Connolly died in 1975 at the age of 80.

Christopher Courtney (Ross Road) A Company. Christopher Courtney joined the Volunteers in 1914. At the time he was a staunch supporter and member of the G.A.A., having represented his county in both Provincial and All-Ireland Championships. In 1916 he held the rank of Sergeant in A Company. On the morning of the Rising Courtney reported to the Keegan house on Irish Street. From there he took two men and broke into Lar Codd's hardware shop on Main Street to search for weapons. On their return they were detailed to stop a goods train at the railway station. With Courtney in command, they stopped the train and brought its driver and fireman back to Keegan's. Once Courtney arrived at the new H.Q. in the Athenaeum he received his rifle and took up a position on Castle Hill from where he fired on the R.I.C. barracks. Later in the day he was placed on sentry duty on the Market Square, he would spend the entire night there.

On Friday afternoon Courtney continued his sentry duty on the Square. Later he raided any of the Public Houses which were opened, forcing them to close and removing any patrons who were on the premises. He spent Friday night in the Athenaeum. On Saturday morning Courtney went to Ferns in a lorry, staying for a few hours before returning to Enniscorthy. The rest of the day he was on sentry duty around the town. Courtney was present in the Athenaeum for the surrender on Sunday night, he left shortly afterwards and brought his rifle with him in order to hide it. He was arrested two days later and deported shortly afterwards. Courtney was interned in Stafford Jail and Frongach Camp until his release in early August. While in Frongach he made use of his profession, he was a barber, to cut the other prisoners hair. On his return his hairdressing business suffered badly due to his participation in the Rising. Nevertheless, he re-joined in 1917 and served up to 1919 before ill health took its toll on him and forced him to cease his activities. Christopher Courtney died in 1953 aged 74.

John "Jack" Courtney (Ross Road) A Company. A brother of Christopher Courtney, John Courtney was a member of the I.R.B. before he joined the Volunteers at their inception in 1913. His first duty on the morning of the Rising was to cut the telephone lines along the railway line heading towards Wexford. He cut the lines over a two-mile stretch. Once he returned he helped move munitions from Irish Street to the Athenaeum. When this was completed, Courtney was sent to Scarawalsh to erect roadblocks there. He remained there until approximately 2 p.m.. His next location was at Davis's Mill where he broke metal bars from a window so that from his vantage point he could cover two roads. He spent four hours there before returning to the Athenaeum for rest and food. Courtney spent Friday and Saturday on sentry duty on The Duffry, here he prevented anyone leaving the town who he thought looked suspicious. On Sunday while on sentry duty on the Ross Road, Courtney got into an altercation with a man attempting to leave the town in his car. (This dispute would lead to Courtney losing his job at the local Waterworks after the Rising when the man complained about him.) On Sunday night he was sent to Edermine where he was stopped by the advancing British troops. After searching him and finding him unarmed, the soldiers let him go. When he returned to town he hid his rifle and four others. Courtney was arrested the next day and deported a short time afterwards. He was interned in Stafford Jail, Wormwood Scrubs and Frongach Camp before he was released that August. On his return he lost his job at the Waterworks due to the motorist's complaint. Unable to find alternative employment, Courtney had to go to England for a period of time in order to support his family. John "Jack" Courtney died at his residence on the Ross Road in 1950, he was 75 years old.

John Courtney (Irish Street) C Company. John Courtney joined the Volunteers in 1914. At the outbreak of the Rising he was working in Arklow. He returned to Enniscorthy in the afternoon and immediately reported for duty to the Athenaeum. From there he was sent to the bottom of Slaney Street for guard duty. After been relieved there he was detailed to Friary Hill and later on, outpost duty at Brownswood. Courtney slept in the Athenaeum that night. On Friday he was placed on guard duty at the Gas Yard and after that on the Market Square. On Saturday morning Courtney took up sentry duty at the top of Slaney

Street and later on at Old Church Road. That evening Courtney participated in the recruiting parade around the town before marching to Ferns with the column of Volunteers under the command of Peter Galligan. In Ferns, Courtney was sent to the Camolin Road for outpost duty. On Sunday he was detailed for duty to the railway station at Milltown.

After news of the surrender came on Sunday evening, Courtney was ordered with the rest of the men to return to Enniscorthy. On his journey back the car in which he was a passenger broke down. They were instructed to remain with it until another vehicle could return to collect them. They remained with the car until daylight broke on Monday morning and then they dispersed. Courtney went to Ballymurtagh and hid four rifles there before going on the run. On the reorganisation of the Volunteers in 1917, Courtney joined the Monageer Company with whom he served with up until The Truce. He took the Anti-Treaty side in the Civil War and was captured and imprisoned until its conclusion. John Courtney died in 1971 at the age of 75.

William Courtney (Ross Road) A Company. A brother of Christopher and John "Jack" Courtney, William Courtney joined the Volunteers in 1913. On the first morning of the Rising Courtney was posted to the roof of the Castle from where he fired a number of shots at the R.I.C. barracks. For the remainder of the week, he was tasked with the transportation of munitions and supplies during the day and guard duty and patrol around the town centre at night-time. Courtney was arrested the day after the surrender and not long afterwards was deported. He was interned in Stafford Jail from where he was released after a couple of weeks. Courtney re-joined in 1917 and carried out general Volunteer activities. In 1918 he was among the party of 50 Volunteers sent to Waterford to help secure the Sinn Féin Election H.Q. during the Bye-Election. They also protected voters from intimidation at the Polling Station at Ballybricken. Courtney left the Volunteers in 1920 when he went to London at the request of a dying sister. On his return he re-joined but did not take part in any further activities. William Courtney died in St. John's Hospital in 1966, 50 years after the Rising and at the age of 81.

Greta Crosby (Taghmon) Cumann na mBan. Greta Crosby (nee Williams) joined Cumann na mBan in early 1916. In her statement dated the 25th of February 1938 she claimed to be one of the first members to report to the Athenaeum for duty. She also said she assisted in the raising of the Tricolour. For the next two days Crosby delivered dispatches, helped to commandeer food and materials and performed general services in H.Q.. On Saturday she was one of the women sent to Ferns to cook for the Volunteers there.

In the months following the surrender Crosby participated in the collection of money for the families of the interned Volunteers. She also sent food parcels to the internees. Crosby left Enniscorthy in 1918 and returned to her home in Taghmon. She reorganised the Cumann there and was also prominently involved in setting up branches in Glynn, Adamstown, Murrintown, Clongeen and Foulksmills. Her home and shop was used as a safe house for Volunteers on the run and was also a vital source of intelligence for the local Company. Crosby carried dispatches and ammunition on numerous occasions. Her home was raided by the military on a regular basis and on one occasion a Black and Tan threatened her with a bayonet. Her business began to suffer due to this constant harassment, but she still carried on until The Truce. In 1922 Crosby emigrated to the United States and settled there. Greta Crosby died in New Jersey in 1971 at the age of 77.

James Cullen (Irish Street) 1st Lieutenant A Company. James Cullen joined the I.R.B. in 1907 and the Volunteers at their inception in 1913. He mobilised on Easter Sunday under the impression the Rising was to take place that evening. His Company stood down after the news of Eoin McNeill's countermanding order was received. The Volunteers were then told to remain in a state of readiness for any emergency. It was not until Monday evening that Cullen learnt about the Rising in Dublin, he stated later that for the next two days confusion reigned. It was only the return of Peter Galligan from Dublin on Wednesday night that concrete plans were put in place. Cullen's main role during the Rising was to organise sentry and outpost positions, which he regularly visited. He also deployed men on scouting missions. On Sunday, Cullen went to Ballindaggin to order the Company there to stand down due to the imminent surrender. He went on the run after the surrender and was in Kiltealy when he heard of the arrests of the ordinary rank and file Volunteers. He decided to return and *"face the music."* Cullen was arrested on the 12th of May and deported shortly afterwards. He was interned in Woking Prison and Frongach Camp until his release on the 3rd of August, a date he would never forget for it was the day Roger Casement was executed.

In 1917 Cullen was appointed as a Company Captain and in 1918 he was promoted to Battalion O/C. He was arrested and jailed after Seamus Rafter's funeral for bringing out the Brigade in uniform to honour him. In 1920 Cullen was court martialled and stripped of his rank after being overheard discussing an ongoing operation. He still continued to play an active part including allowing the car he co-owned to be used in the killing of R.I.C. District Inspector Lea Wilson in Gorey. Cullen was jailed again for Volunteer activities in September 1920 and imprisoned until December the following year. After his release he ceased his activities and played no part in the Civil War. James Cullen died in 1968, he was 87 years old.

James "Jim" Cullen (Court Street) A Company. Jim Cullen joined the I.R.B. in 1911 and the Volunteers at their inception in 1913. On the first morning of the Rising he reported to the Athenaeum for duty. He was sent to Castle Hill and took up a sniping position there to fire on the R.I.C. barracks. After this Cullen was placed on sentry duty on Slaney Street and afterwards on Court Street. He spent his rest periods between his digs in Hayes's on Court Street and H.Q.. Cullen carried out sentry duty in various locations around the town over the remaining days. On

Sunday he escorted the R.I.C. District Inspector and his driver, who had brought Pádraig Pearse's surrender letter, to Mass in the Cathedral. Cullen was arrested a few days after the surrender and deported shortly afterwards. He was interned in Stafford Jail and Frongach Camp before his release in September. In 1917 Cullen moved to Kilkenny and joined a local Company there. In Cullen's later years he worked as a commercial traveller and moved to Dublin. He lost touch with his old comrades and was last heard of living in London in the early 1960's.

Patrick Cushen (Clonroche) A Company. Patrick Cushen joined the Volunteers in late 1915. On the first morning of the Rising he marched with the rest of the men from Irish Street to the Athenaeum, where he remained on post all day. On Friday he was again on post in the Athenaeum until the afternoon, then he was sent to Davis's Mill for a number of hours. On Saturday evening Cushen marched to Ferns with the column of Volunteers and took up duty there. On Sunday he returned to Enniscorthy on hearing the news of the imminent surrender. He was not arrested and returned to his home in Clonroche. Cushen took no part in any further activities until he joined the Clonroche Company in 1920, with whom he served up to The Truce. He was not involved in the Civil War. Patrick Cushen died aged 59 in 1958.

John Davis (St. John's Street) A Company. Originally from The Shannon, John Davis joined the Volunteers not long after their formation. Early on the morning of the Rising he was sent along with other Volunteers to Oylgate. Their mission was to set up an outpost to defend against any advancement of Special Constables or British military. Later in the day Davis went to Bree and carried out the same task. On Friday, Davis was a member of the advance party that went to Ferns. On his arrival he went to the railway station and proceeded to lift rails off the tracks, he then helped to cut telegraph lines in the area. With news of the surrender on Sunday, Davis returned to Enniscorthy. He was arrested a few days later and deported shortly afterwards. Davis was interned in Lewes Jail and Frongach Camp until he was released in December.

Not long after Davis re-joined in 1917, he was appointed as Captain of Engineers attached to Brigade Staff. His responsibility in this role included the manufacture of homemade gunpowder which was used to fill cartridges. In May 1918 while testing a new mix of powder in a field in Tomsallagh, a shotgun blew up in his face leaving him unconscious and covered in blood. Two Volunteers who were with him, had to bandage him up as best they could before they brought him to a doctor in Enniscorthy. Davis later stated that it was the same gunpowder mix that Seamus Rafter was killed by in September the same year. Late one night in October 1920, Davis's home on St. John's Street was raided by the R.I.C. and Black and Tans. They handed him a severe beating in front of his wife and children, whose screams alerted their neighbours. When the Tans left he was found unconscious with cuts and bruises all over his body.

In February 1921 the Tans returned, but this time they brought him with them to their headquarters in the courthouse. He was held there for three weeks and was beaten on a regular basis until the intervention of a doctor, who ordered that he be immediately transferred to hospital. Instead Davis was sent to Waterford Gaol and placed in its infirmary. After recovering, he was sent to Cork Jail and then Spike Island, from where he was released in December on compassionate grounds, his father was dying. Davis served as a member of the Republican police force, which was based in the courthouse, up to the outbreak of Civil War. After which he fought in the "Battle of Enniscorthy". Once the Free State Army regained control of the town, Davis went on the run and remained active up until the ceasefire. John Davis died at the age of 65 in 1953.

Michael Davis (Lower Church Street) A Company. Michael Davis was a younger brother of John Davis and joined the Volunteers on their formation in 1913. Having no job, he took up a full-time role with the organisation. His many duties in the years prior to the Rising included raiding for arms, delivering dispatches, manufacturing munitions and the digging out of rock at the back of Patrick Keegan's house in Irish Street during the construction of "The Dump". The week of the Rising Davis spent his time between Keegan's and Seamus Rafter's home. On the Thursday morning he was one of the Volunteers sent to mobilise the rest of the men. Davis then cut telegraph lines before taking up a sniping position outside the Post Office on the Abbey Square, from where he fired up to 30 rounds at the R.I.C. barracks. He spent the night in Keegan's. On Friday he was a member of a party of Volunteers who went to Edermine and partially destroyed the bridge, making it impossible for heavy traffic to cross. Davis then returned to "The Dump" where he remained until Sunday morning making munitions. That morning he raided a couple of local businesses for supplies that were running low.

After the surrender Davis was heavily involved in the collection and disposal of arms in several locations around the town and its outskirts. He then returned to the Keegan's house where he was arrested shortly afterwards. Davis was interned in Stafford Jail and then Frongach Camp before he was released in early August. On his return home he was immediately tasked with the recovery of hidden armaments and munitions. In September whilst transporting a quantity of gunpowder with two other Volunteers, there was an explosion at the Bloody Bridge, Milehouse Road. This explosion left Davis with severe burns. Fearing arrest, he was brought to a private house where a sympathetic doctor treated his wounds. He remained housebound for several months. From 1918 up until The Truce Davis played a prominent role in raids and operations throughout the district. When the Civil War broke out at the end of June 1922, he was a member of the Republican police force operating out of the courthouse. During the "Battle of Enniscorthy" in early July, Davis was in charge of communications between the I.R.A. units on both sides of the river. After the recapture of the town by the

Free State Army, Davis went on the run but by the middle of August had ceased his activities. Michael Davis died in Blackwater in 1946 aged 56.

Eugene Devereux (Georges Street) A Company. Eugene Devereux joined the I.R.B. in 1909 and the Volunteers at their inception in 1913. He worked as a bicycle mechanic. Early on the morning of the Rising he reported to the Athenaeum for duty. He was ordered to take up a position on the Market Square with his rifle to cover the windows of a building which was suspected of harbouring enemy snipers. Devereux remained there while other Volunteers broke down the door and searched the house. From there he was sent to Scarawalsh and Ballycarney to cut down trees and telegraph poles to make roadblocks. On Thursday evening an attack from the south of the town was expected, Devereux and another Volunteer were posted to a spot overlooking the Ringwood to keep watch. They remained there all night. After a brief rest when he returned to H.Q., Devereux was detailed to guard the weapons there and carry out any repairs necessary. On Saturday he was a member of a raiding party sent to Oylgate to search for arms and munitions. On his return he marched to Ferns with the column under the command of Peter Galligan. While on duty Sunday morning at the furthest outpost on the Camolin Road, Devereux intercepted the car containing Fr. Kehoe and D.I. Drake with Pádraig Pearse's surrender letter.

After the surrender was announced, Devereux was tasked with collecting a number of bicycles for the men to ride back to Enniscorthy. He was arrested several days later and deported shortly afterwards. Devereux was interned in Woking Jail and Frongach Camp until the beginning of August. From 1917 until The Truce, Devereux served as the district's gunsmith. Operating out of his own premises at 18 Georges Street, (Rafter Street) he repaired and concealed guns right under the nose of the military whose headquarters was up the street at the courthouse. Though he was raided several times no weaponry was ever found. Even after all this service Devereux would have his application for a Military Pension refused twice before finally receiving it in 1951. Eugene Devereux died at the age of 85 in 1968.

Thomas Devereux (Kilcotty) A Company. Thomas Devereux was from Kilcotty and joined the Volunteers in 1915. He was a member of a small unit attached to C Company. Although his unit did not mobilise on the Thursday of Easter Week, Devereux took it upon himself to go to Enniscorthy and join up with the rest of his Company. He spent the following days on sentry duty at various locations around the town. Upon the surrender he went on the run and did not return home until later in the year. In 1917 Devereux re-joined and was appointed section leader of the Kilcotty unit. Up until February 1920 he took part in all aspects of Volunteer activities. On February the 20th he was arrested and charged with unlawful assembly and the possession of a firearm. He was sentenced to six months in jail which he spent in Waterford Jail and Mountjoy. When the Civil War erupted Devereux chose the Anti-Treaty side and was frequently used as a scout and guide. He served in this capacity up until the ceasefire. A brother of Devereux fought and died in the Great War following a gas attack. Thomas Devereux himself died in 1962 at the age of 73.

James Donohoe (Ross Road) A Company. James Donohoe joined the Volunteers in 1914. On the morning of the Rising he assembled with the main force of Volunteers on Irish Street and marched to the Athenaeum. From there he was ordered to raid hardware shops for weapons and supplies. Donohoe was then placed on guard duty in the Athenaeum for the rest of the day and night. On Friday after a rest, he was sent on outpost duty to Clonhaston and after he was relieved, he returned to H.Q. and spent the night. On Saturday, Donohue was on guard duty at Mill Wheel Lane when his employer a Mr. John Bolger approached his position, when Bolger ignored his order to halt, Donohoe fired a warning shot over his head. (After the surrender the R.I.C. tried to get Bolger to press charges of attempted murder but he refused. However, Donohoe did lose his job.) The following day Donohoe was tasked with guarding the R.I.C. District Inspector, who had delivered Pádraig Pearse's surrender letter, and his driver in Bennetts Hotel for a short period.. After which he was sent on outpost duty to Red Pat's Cross from where he was recalled after the surrender. He was arrested a couple of days later and deported shortly afterwards. Donohoe was interned in Stafford Jail for a couple of weeks before he was released when the majority of Volunteers were transferred to Frongach Camp.

From 1917 until The Truce, Donohoe held several Officer positions within the organisation. In 1918 he led a party of Volunteers who held up the County Surveyor and his assistant in Tombrack and relieved them of a large quantity of Gelignite. In 1921 Donohoe used his position as signalman on the Dublin and South Eastern Railway to help plan the ambush of a train carrying British troops at Killurin. Donohoe was arrested about a month before The Truce and sent to Spike Island. Upon his release he continued to work on the railway and was transferred to Arklow. During the Civil War he chose the Republican side and was involved in several skirmishes with the Free State Army up until the ceasefire. James Donohoe died in Dublin in 1958 aged 61.

Richard Donohoe (St. John's Street) A Company. Richard "Dick" Donohoe joined the I.R.B. in 1912 and the Volunteers not long after their inception. In the years leading up to 1916 he played an active part in his Company's accumulation of arms and munitions. From Easter Sunday until the outbreak of hostilities on the following Thursday he spent most of his time at "The Dump" and on the town in a state of preparedness. Early on Thursday morning Donohoe was tasked with rousing the men. He was given four streets to mobilise. At around 6 a.m. he and another Volunteer were sent to the courthouse where rifles belonging to the National Volunteers were stored. While they waited for someone to come with a key for the building an R.I.C. constable came upon them. Donohoe would later claim before the Military Service Pensions Board on the3rd of March 1937 that he fired the first shot of the Insurrection at 6.40 a.m.

as a warning to the constable. The constable ran away only to return with five other officers. A gunfight then ensued which lasted approximately 10 minutes, Volunteer reinforcements arrived on the scene forcing the R.I.C. men to retreat. For the rest of the week Donohoe was involved in the setting up of roadblocks on the Wexford, Ferns, Newtownbarry (Bunclody) and Clonroche roads. After the surrender he helped with the concealment of arms. The following morning, Donohoe was arrested and brought to Waterford where he spent four days. He was then brought back to Enniscorthy and court-martialled. He was charged with.

Firing at the Police and taking part in armed resistance against his majesty the King.

Donohoe was sentenced to death and held in the R.I.C. barracks for two weeks before he was sent to Kilmainham Jail. There his sentenced was commuted to three years penal servitude and he was then transferred to Mountjoy before he was deported. Donohoe was interned in Dartmoor, Lewes, Portland and Pentonville Jails before he was released on the 17th of June 1917. Upon his return he re-joined his Company and took part in general activities up until The Truce. Richard Donohue died in St. John's Hospital in 1960, he was 78 years old.

James Doolan (St. John's Street) A Company. James Doolan was a member of the I.R.B. before joining the Volunteers at their inception in 1913. He worked as a plasterer and was working the week of the Rising. Each day after work he reported to "The Dump" and was deployed as a guard. Doolan was called out at 4 a.m. on the morning of the Rising. After been given a rifle he was sent to the Castle roof from where he fired intermittingly at the R.I.C. barracks over a six-hour period. He then reported back to the Athenaeum and was sent on outpost duty to Salville Cross. On the Friday Doolan was on sentry duty around the town while on Saturday evening he was a member of the contingent of Volunteers who marched to Ferns under the command of Peter Galligan. He spent Sunday on duty in Ferns before returning to Enniscorthy in the early hours of Monday morning after receiving word of the surrender. Doolan was arrested on Tuesday morning while on the town. He was later deported and interned in Stafford Jail and Frongach Camp before he was released in August.

After re-joining in 1917, Doolan's activities up until The Truce included scouting and the delivery of dispatches. In the weeks leading up to the Civil War he was a member of the Republican garrison in the courthouse. At the outbreak of the "Battle of Enniscorthy" in July 1922, Doolan was in the courthouse when it was attacked by Free State soldiers positioned in Lett's Brewery. Once the assault had been repelled, Doolan took part in the attack on the Castle. He took up a position in a house on Slaney Street from where he could fire on the Castle, however, the house was hit by a grenade which caused its roof to collapse. Escaping unscathed, Doolan went to a house three doors up the street which had a better view and continued firing. After the Free State reinforcements arrived and took back control of the town, Doolan went on the run until he was eventually arrested in Ferns the following April. He was brought to the Castle in Enniscorthy and detained there for ten days before he was released due to poor health. James Doolan died at his home in St. Aidan's Villas aged 68 in 1949.

Denis Doran (Hill View Terrace) A Company. Denis Doran joined the Volunteers at their inception in 1913. He was mobilised at 2 a.m. on the first morning of the Rising and was sent to raid for weapons in Donohue's hardware. Doran brought the weapons back to Irish Street on the back of an ass and cart. Once the cart was unloaded, he fell in with the rest of the men and marched to the Athenaeum. After a H.Q. had been established, Doran took up a sniping position on Castle Hill from where he fired upon the R.I.C. barracks. He then returned to the Athenaeum and was placed in charge of the ammunition room. At 10 p.m. he was posted to Reilly's Corner on Templeshannon to take up guard duty. He returned to H.Q. at 5 a.m. and slept for a few hours. Doran spent Friday around the town checking on the pubs. On Saturday, he was on sentry duty when he was sent for by Seamus Rafter. Rafter informed him that Denis O'Brien, who was in charge of transport, was exhausted and told him. *"We are promoting you in charge of transport to relieve Denis."* Doran said there was no proof of this but was adamant that he was in charge of transport and stores that night. On Sunday morning he was sent with an important dispatch to Ferns and was back in the Athenaeum by 5 p.m.. He remained there after the surrender and helped to clear the hall of munitions. Doran was arrested four days later and deported shortly afterwards. He was interned in Stafford Jail and Frongach Camp before he was released on the 23rd of December.

Though Doran re-joined in 1917 he never partook in anymore military operations. However, through his job as a solicitor's clerk he proved useful. In 1921 Doran was working in Newtownbarry (Bunclody) and had ready access to the R.I.C. barracks there. On several occasions he came across information of planned raids and arrests as well as troop movements. He passed this intelligence on via an intermediary named Mrs. Bolger. On another occasion after obtaining an official pass, he accompanied the same Mrs. Bolger to retrieve revolvers which were hidden in the grounds of Newtownbarry House. Denis Doran took no part in the Civil War and died in 1977, he was 85 years old.

Margaret Doran (Old Church) Cumann na mBan. Margaret Doran (nee Walsh) joined Cumann na mBan in 1914. In the months prior to the Rising she was engaged in making first aid kits. On the morning of the Insurrection she reported for duty to the Athenaeum at 7 a.m.. There she was ordered to assist in the setting up of a temporary hospital in the main hall. In order to accomplish this duty, Doran was sent with another member of Cumann na mBan to commandeer supplies from McDermott's shop on Castle Hill. Even though this shop happened to be in the line of fire between the Volunteers and the R.I.C. barracks, they still managed successfully to obtain the necessary supplies. Once the temporary hospital was completed, Doran was sent to the dining hall to serve the Volunteers. Over the following days she tended to two injured

Volunteers, one who had received a bad cut on his arm and another who was suffering from shock after a shotgun was discharged accidently beside him.

After the surrender Doran helped to load munitions into cars. Over the next few days her father Patrick and brother Thomas were arrested and interned for their involvement, along with her future husband Denis Doran. In the months following Doran collected food and packed it into parcels to send to the prisoners in Frongach Camp. In 1918 she helped during the General Election and marched with her Cumann at the funeral of Seamus Rafter. Doran continued with the routine activities of her Cumann up until The Truce. She played no role in The Civil War. Margaret Doran died in St. Francis's Hospital Dublin in 1953, she was 59 years of age.

Michael Doran (Kilcotty) A Company. Michael Doran worked as a shop assistant in the town when he joined the Volunteers in 1915 at the age of 16. He served all through the Rising in Enniscorthy and went on the run at its conclusion, losing his job in the process. Doran moved to Dublin in November 1916 and joined a Company there. By the time of The Truce he had been promoted to officer rank. Doran was the only officer in his Company who joined the National Army. Throughout the Civil War he served actively in the Bray area. In 1924 Doran left the army and returned to Enniscorthy. He opened a grocery shop at number 5 Main Street. However, by the beginning of 1927 his business was making a loss due to the high rent on the premises and other overheads. Doran was offered another premises to buy, he applied to the Military Pensions Office for five years of his pension in advance in order to purchase these premises. They refused, and by May 1927 Doran was living in Canada where he spent a year before moving to New York. Michael Doran lived in New York for the remainder of his life, he died there at the age of 82 in 1981.

Alexander Doyle (The Shannon) C Company. Alexander Doyle joined the Volunteers in 1913. In 1915 he accompanied Seamus Rafter to Dublin to collect a quantity of rifles. By the time of the Rising he had been appointed Company Captain. During the Insurrection he sniped on the R.I.C. barracks and carried out street patrol. On the Saturday he marched to Ferns with the column. Doyle served up until The Truce and then fought on the Republican side in the Civil War. Alexander Doyle died in Ferns in 1941 at the age of 73.

Andrew Doyle (The Shannon) C Company. Andrew Doyle joined the Volunteers in 1913. He marched with the main body of men from Irish Street to the Athenaeum early on the first morning of the Rising. From there he was detailed to the Turret Rocks where he took up a sniping position and opened fire on the R.I.C. barracks. After a couple of hours there, Doyle was ordered to go to Salville Cross for outpost duty. On his return to H.Q. in the afternoon he was instructed by Robert Brennan to guard the Bank of Ireland in the Abbey Square, which had two armed R.I.C. men locked inside. After a meal that night he slept under the stage in the Athenaeum. By 8 a.m. Friday, Doyle was on duty at the outpost on Clonhaston Cross, where he remained until midnight.

On Saturday he participated in the recruiting parade around the town before marching to Ferns that evening with the column of Volunteers under the command of Peter Galligan. Doyle did outpost duty that night and on Sunday morning he stood guard at Bolger's Corner. After the surrender he marched back to Enniscorthy and handed in his rifle and ammunition. Doyle was arrested on the 4th of May at his workplace and deported shortly afterwards. He was interned in Stafford Jail and Frongach Camp until he was released in December. Doyle re-joined in 1917 and took part in general Company activities up until The Truce. He did not take part in the Civil War. Andrew Doyle died in 1956 aged 69.

Andrew Doyle (Old Church) C Company. Andrew Doyle joined the Volunteers in 1914. He was mobilised early on the first morning of the

Rising and sent to block roads. Later he was posted to Vinegar Hill from where he claimed he fired on the R.I.C. barracks. (Military Service Pension Board interview on 12th of January 1937) Over the following days Doyle carried out sentry duty at the Gas Yard and at outposts at Drumgoold and Salville Cross. He was arrested four days after the surrender and deported shortly afterwards. Doyle was interned in Stafford Jail and Frongach Camp before he was released in early August. Doyle re-joined in March 1917 on the reorganisation. He worked as a self-employed carter and used his horse and cart to move arms and munitions for the Company. He also hid weapons at his house. Doyle took part in Company operations such as the large raid for petrol at the railway station and the raid at Davis's foundry for munition making equipment. He ceased all his activities prior to the Civil War. Andrew Doyle died at his home on the Rectory Road in 1951 aged 63.

Anthony Doyle (The Harrow) A Company. Anthony Doyle joined The Harrow Company of the Volunteers, which was attached to A Company, in 1914. On the first morning of the Rising, Doyle was placed on guard duty at the gates of Davis's Mill. In the afternoon he carried out sentry duty on The Duffry. Later that evening, he took up a sniping position on the Turret Rocks and fired on the R.I.C. barracks sporadically over a number of hours. Doyle then returned to the Athenaeum where he spent the night. On Friday and Saturday, he was assigned street patrol around the town before he was sent to Saville Cross on Saturday night for outpost duty. After the surrender Doyle evaded arrest and went on the run for three months.

He joined the Ferns Company in 1917 and participated in several of their operations over the following years, including the burning of Ardmine House in Courtown and the R.I.C. barracks at Clonevan Gorey. He was also involved in a gun attack on the R.I.C. barracks in Ferns. A month before the Civil War began and with tensions rising in Enniscorthy, Doyle went there and took up a position with the Republican police force based at the courthouse. When hostilities broke out on July 2nd he played an active part in the fighting. After the Republicans left the town on the arrival of the Free State reinforcements, he went on the run but was arrested on July 22nd. Doyle was at first imprisoned in Portobella Barracks in Dublin and then in Maryborough Jail. (Port Laoise) There he was involved in the setting of a fire after three Republican prisoners were apprehended while attempting to tunnel out. Doyle was sent to The Curragh Camp which the prisoners christened "Tin Town". Due to the poor conditions there, Doyle went on a hunger strike which lasted 27 days. He was finally released on the 23rd of December 1923. Anthony Doyle died in 1977 at the age of 83.

Charles Doyle (Ferns) Ferns Company. Charles Doyle was a member of the Ferns Company who marched to Enniscorthy on the first evening of the Rising. After spending the night there, he returned to Ferns on Friday and carried out sentry and outpost duty around the village up until the surrender on Sunday night. Doyle was arrested a few days later and deported shortly afterwards. He was interned in Wakefield Prison until the middle of July before he was released. On the reorganisation in 1917, Doyle joined the Volunteer Company in Ballycarney, which was attached to the Ferns Company. He played an active role in several of the Company's operations including raiding the British Revenue Office in Gorey, the attack on the R.I.C. barracks in Clonroche and the major raid for fuel at Enniscorthy railway station. After the latter raid, he helped distribute the fuel to individual units throughout the district. At the outbreak of the Civil War Doyle was a member of the Free State Army and served until the ceasefire. In 1924 Doyle emigrated to the United States where he spent 12 years before returning home. Charles Doyle died at his home in Woodlands Ferns in 1977 aged 80.

Daniel Doyle (Ross Road) A Company. Daniel Doyle reported to the Athenaeum from his house on the Ross Road at approximately 6 a.m. on the first morning of the Insurrection. From there he was sent to the Turret Rocks where he took up a sniping position overlooking the R.I.C. barracks. In his testimony before the Military Service Pensions Board on the 9th of February 1940, Doyle claimed to have fired three or four rounds over the short period of time he was there. After he was relieved, he was placed on guard duty at McCarthy's house on the corner of Mill Park Road and the Gas Yard Lane. This house had been evacuated and left open. Later Doyle was posted to Davis's Mill to relieve the Volunteers there. He spent the night at the Mill before returning to H.Q. for a few hours' sleep. On Friday, Doyle was placed on sentry duty at Lett's Brewery and from there he went to Salville Cross for outpost duty. That evening, Doyle and three other Volunteers were ordered to commandeer clothing from Bolger's Drapery on Georges Street. (Rafter Street) He spent the night at Davis's Mill once more. On Saturday, Doyle carried out guard duty at the McCarthy house again and later sentry duty at the bottom of Irish Street and the Island Road. From 11 p.m. until 2 a.m. he was on street patrol around the town. On Sunday morning Doyle resumed duty on Irish Street and from there was sent to the railway station. He was present in the Athenaeum for the surrender on Sunday night, after which he helped with the collection of arms.

Doyle was not arrested and went to work on Tuesday morning as normal, he was employed as a tailor in the Enniscorthy Asylum. However, following a hospital board meeting a week later, Doyle was dismissed from this position. He re-joined his Company in 1917 and carried out the general Volunteer duties which were expected of him. In 1918 he transferred to The Shannon Company. Doyle spent the Christmas Holidays at the courthouse after the 1918 General Election guarding ballot boxes. He also participated in raids for fuel and arms including one at the home of the County Sheriff in Lucas Park. Doyle served up until The Truce and played no role in the Civil War. Daniel Doyle died at his daughter's residence in Blackstoops in 1976 at the age of 82.

James Doyle (Ferns) Ferns Company. James Doyle joined the Volunteers in 1914. In the years leading up to the Rising he transported munitions from Enniscorthy to Ferns on numerous occasions. A few weeks prior to the Rising his brother Patrick, who was 1st Lieutenant of the Company, was arrested for attempting to smuggle rifles from Dublin to Ferns. Doyle marched with members of his Company to Enniscorthy on the Thursday afternoon when news that the town had risen was confirmed. After spending the night there, the Company returned to Ferns when intelligence warning of a British advance in the north of the county had been received. In Ferns, Doyle carried out all the orders that were issued to him which included blocking roads, cutting telegraph wires and outpost duty. After the surrender he was arrested and deported to Wandsworth Prison.

On the reorganisation of the Volunteers in 1917, Doyle re-joined and took part in the general activities of his Company for the next couple of years. In 1919 he emigrated to Liverpool and soon became an active and prominent member of the Liverpool I.R.A.. Doyle carried out several missions including the burning of warehouses and farms, attacks on known homes of members of the Black and Tans and a raid on the city's passport office. He also helped to smuggle weapons on to boats destined for Dublin. James Doyle died in Swansea, where he lived for many years, in 1954. He was 59 years of age.

James Doyle (Old Church) A Company. James Doyle joined the Volunteers in 1913. After the Company was stood down on Easter Sunday, he was ordered to report to "Antwerp" every evening after work. He did this for the next three nights. On Thursday morning Doyle reported to the Keegan house on Irish Street from where he marched with the main body of Volunteers to the Athenaeum. Once a H.Q. was up and running he was ordered along with another couple of Volunteers to search the premises of Mr. W. Armstrong in Templeshannon for weapons. They returned to the Athenaeum with two revolvers. Doyle was then posted to Templeshannon for sentry duty. That night he returned to H.Q. for a meal after which he bunked down for the night. On Friday, Doyle was once again sent to Templeshannon when information was received that some civilians were planning to loot shops. He remained on duty there for the day without any incident. After spending the night at H.Q., he was posted once again to Templeshannon, the reasoning behind this was that he was well known in the area and the civilians would be less likely to misbehave. On Sunday morning Doyle was placed on sentry duty at the top of New Street. (Wafer St.) He was relieved at 2 p.m. and spent the rest of the day around the Athenaeum. He was present for the surrender and afterwards helped with the collection of arms and munitions before going home. On Monday morning Doyle reported for work as usual but a few days later had to go on the run after the R.I.C. came looking for him there. Doyle played no further role in any Volunteer activities. In later years he moved to Yorkshire to work before returning home and settling in St. John's Villas. James Doyle died in 1970 at the age of 76.

James Doyle (Ballindaggin) A Company. James Doyle joined the Ballindaggin Company of the Volunteers on its formation in 1914. The Company was attached to A Company in Enniscorthy. On Easter Sunday 1916 they joined with their town comrades for their drills and parade around the town. They were there believing that an Insurrection was going to take place that evening. With mixed orders and confusion amongst the leadership, they were ordered to return to Ballindaggin to await further instruction. On Thursday when the word reached them that Enniscorthy had risen, the Company, comprising of about a dozen men, cycled to the town. Arriving at 4pm, they reported to the Athenaeum where they received orders from Seamus Rafter. They were ordered to return to Ballindaggin and hold the road from The Curragh, (where British troops were stationed) at Scollough Gap and furthermore patrol the roads leading to Enniscorthy. Doyle carried out these orders until the next morning when he was sent to Enniscorthy with a dispatch. When he arrived at H.Q. Rafter gave him additional orders, the Company were to hold up all cars on all roads in their area. Doyle was posted to Wheelgower Crossroads which had roads leading to The Curragh, New Ross via Killane and Gorey via Ferns and Newtownbarry. (Bunclody) He held this position until Saturday morning when he was again sent to town. This time Doyle received instructions from Patrick Keegan, who ordered that they close the pubs and post office in Ballindaggin and cut all the telegraph wires. Keegan also emphasised that the road from The Curragh must be held at all costs. After returning and not having slept since Wednesday night, Doyle went to bed for a few hours. He learnt of the surrender early on Monday morning when his brother returned from the town. He was not arrested in the aftermath.

In 1917 when the Ballindaggin Company reorganised, Doyle re-joined and was appointed Section Commander. At around the same time he became a member of the I.R.B.. Up until The Truce he played an active part in all types of operations including raids on County Council quarries for Gelignite, Loyalist homes for arms and lead, which was used in the manufacture of munitions. Doyle was involved in the capture of a spy also named James Doyle, whom he guarded on the day he was executed. He also acted as a scout for the Volunteers who killed R.I.C. District Inspector Lea-Wilson in Gorey. The assassins drove their car to Doyle's house where they cleaned up before he guided them over the Blackstairs mountains into Carlow. On one occasion Doyle was arrested by the Black and Tans in Kiltealy, he was beaten and robbed before he was released several hours later. On another occasion, during one of the many raids on his home by the military, Doyle was so savagely beaten he was left for dead in one of the outhouses. It was only for the intervention of a Dr. Kelly from Killane that he survived. During the Civil War Doyle chose the Republican side and participated in the "Battle of Enniscorthy". In the months that followed he was involved in road blocking and the carrying of dispatches between flying columns. James Doyle died at Wheelgower in 1962, he was 66 years old.

John Doyle (Ferns) A Company. John Doyle was a member of Na Fianna Éireann before he joined the Volunteers in 1915. On the morning of the Rising he reported to the Athenaeum after it had been taken over. He was instructed to go to the premises of A.J. Sutton on Georges Street (Rafter St.) to commandeer bed clothing. On his return he was placed on sentry duty outside of H.Q. After a period of four hours, he was relieved and went inside for a meal and a rest. That night Doyle was posted to the bridge to keep watch on the R.I.C. barracks. A couple of hours into this post he thought he saw someone near the barracks and fired two shots. There was no one there and he was ordered to report back to H.Q..

According to Doyle in his statement before the Military Service Pensions Board on the 4th of June 1940, once back in the Athenaeum he was brought in front of Seamus Rafter, Seamus Doyle and Robert Brennan, who all wanted him court-martialled. It was only on the intervention of Philip Murphy, who told them that he had given Doyle the order to open fire if he saw any activity at the barracks, that prevented them from doing so. After being reprimanded he was sent to the guard room to fill cartridges. On Friday morning Doyle was ordered to go to Earl's Shop on the Market Square to commandeer boots for the Volunteers. That evening intelligence was received that there was suspected communications between the R.I.C. barracks and the house of the District Inspector's on Mill Wheel Lane. Doyle was detailed to the garden of the Lett family home which overlooked the D.I.'s house. After spending four hours there he was relieved. Doyle observed nothing to give the intelligence any credence and returned to the Athenaeum. For the remainder of the week, he spent his time between sentry duty at H.Q. and street patrol on Castle Street and the Market Square. After the surrender Doyle evaded arrest and re-joined in 1917 at the reorganisation. He participated in all the general activities of the Company up until The Truce.

John Doyle died in 1968 in his 69th year.

Joseph Doyle (Monamolin) A Company. Joseph Doyle joined the I.R.B. in 1911 and the Volunteers at their inception in November 1913. On Easter Sunday he assembled with his Company in the expectation of taking part in an Insurrection. With the confusion of a lack of solid information, he was stood down but told to be ready for any eventuality. Doyle reported to "Antwerp" on the following three evenings after work.

He was summoned early on Thursday morning and fell in with the Volunteers who marched from Irish Street to the Athenaeum. After a H.Q. had been established there, Doyle was handed a rifle and took up a sniping position on Castle Hill to fire on the R.I.C. barracks. (In his statement to the Military Service Pensions Board on the 8th of February 1940, Doyle said he did not fire a shot.) After he was relieved he returned to the Athenaeum and helped organise accommodation arrangements for the Volunteers. That night he was sent out on patrol to check on various outposts and to make sure no civilians were on the streets. Doyle returned to H.Q. in the early hours of Friday morning and rested. When he reported back on duty he was posted to Coffey's Corner on the Market Square and stood guard there until the late evening. On Saturday morning, along with three other Volunteers Doyle occupied the Protestant Institute until they were relieved on Sunday morning. Once he reported back for duty on Sunday evening, Doyle was placed on guard duty in the vicinity of the Athenaeum. After the surrender he helped with the removal and loading of munitions. He then went to stay with relatives in the country in order to avoid arrest. Doyle returned to town a week later and played no further part in Volunteer activities. In later years Joseph Doyle owned and ran one of the most famous pubs in Enniscorthy. He died in 1964 aged 71.

Laurence Doyle (The Shannon) C Company. Laurence Doyle joined the Volunteers in 1913 when he was only 15 years of age. After been mobilised on the morning of the Rising, he was handed a rifle outside "The Dump" and sent with a group of Volunteers to the garden of the Mission House, which overlooked the R.I.C. barracks. Doyle remained there until 11 a.m. and in that time claimed to have fired five shots. (Military Service Pensions Board interview on the 9th of February 1940) After he was relieved Doyle reported to the Athenaeum to receive new orders. He was detailed to Clonhaston Cross for outpost duty. Later that evening, after having a meal, Doyle was placed on sentry duty at the corner of New Street (Wafer St.) and Lymington Road. He slept in the

Athenaeum that night. On Friday morning Doyle was on guard duty at "The Dump", while in the afternoon he was placed on sentry duty at the top of the Tan Yard Lane on Lymington Road. On Saturday morning he carried out guard duty at the railway station and then at the bottom of the Bohreen Hill before completing his days duty at the bottom of Munster Hill. For the third night in a row he slept in H.Q..

On Sunday, Doyle helped to keep Castle Street clear of people for the arrival of Fr. Kehoe and R.I.C. District Inspector Drake, who had the surrender letter from Pádraig Pearse. After they arrived Doyle was sent on outpost duty to Killagoley where he remained until the surrender. He returned to the Athenaeum and helped to pack away cartridges so they could be removed and hidden. Doyle evaded arrest over the following days. In March 1917 Doyle re-joined and served actively up to The Truce. He participated in such operations as the raids on the railway station for fuel, on Donohues for magnetos and Davis's foundry for materials for the manufacture of munitions. Doyle also took part in the attack on the Enniscorthy R.I.C. barracks the night before the Killurin train ambush. The purpose of this attack was to keep the police busy while the Active Service Unit who were to carry out the ambush passed through the town unnoticed. Laurence Doyle died on St. Patrick's Day 1954 at the age of 54.

Mary Ellen Doyle (Lower Church Street) Cumann na mBan. Mary Ellen Doyle joined Cumann na mBan in 1914. Her sister Brigid and brothers Thomas and Lawrence were also involved in the Rising. After reporting to the Athenaeum on the first morning she was placed in charge of the store. Her job entailed the issuing of rations to Volunteers going out on duty and keeping an account of all supplies. Doyle remained at this post throughout the week and after the surrender helped to clear out any supplies left over.

In the following months Doyle was elected as Secretary of the local branch of Cumann na mBan. She played a prominent role in collecting money for dependant families and sending food parcels to the imprisoned Volunteers. Doyle also helped to organise dances and propaganda concerts to raise funds for Cumann branches around the county. During the General Election of 1918 she canvassed for candidates and helped people register to vote who were sympathetic to the cause. The Sinn Féin Club was located close to where she lived, and in case of raids, Doyle kept any important documents belonging to it in her home. She also hid weapons in her house which were handed out to Volunteers when required for operations. On the occasions when Volunteers were arrested and sent for trial, Doyle would write and send threatening letters to prosecuting solicitors' and witnesses on behalf of the I.R.A.. After The Truce Doyle ceased her activity and played no role in the Civil War. Mary Ellen Doyle died at the age of 80 in 1969.

Mary Kate Doyle (Templeshannon) Cumann na mBan. Mary Kate Doyle (nee Murphy) was one of the founding members of Cumann na mBan in Enniscorthy. She was appointed Vice-President and Treasurer on its formation in 1914. During Easter Week Doyle was present in the Athenaeum from Thursday morning until the early hours of the following Monday. She helped to cook and organise sleeping arrangements for the Volunteers. In the months following the Rising, Doyle organised raffles and whist drives to raise funds for prisoner's dependants. From 1917 she travelled around the county helping to organise branches. In 1919 Doyle was elected Cumann Secretary and attended several council meetings in Dublin. She carried dispatches on several occasions and stored weapons in her home.

In 1920 Doyle was responsible for propaganda. In this role she received propaganda posters from London disguised as advertisements for women's undergarments. These posters were then put up all over the town. At the outbreak of the Civil War, Doyle chose the Anti-Treaty side and during the "Battle of Enniscorthy" cooked for Ernie O'Malley and his Tipperary column, who had taken over the Technical Institute in the Market Square. For the remainder of the Civil War she supplied various flying columns with food and clothes whenever the opportunity arose. Mary Kate Doyle died at the age of 77 in 1964.

Michael Doyle (The Shannon) C Company. Michael Doyle joined the Volunteers in 1913. Prior to the Rising he was employed in Donohue's hardware and was able to supply the Volunteers with a couple of hundred pike handles. After the split in 1915, Doyle with some others raided the house of one of the National Volunteers who had remained loyal to John Redmond and seized a quantity of rifles this man had been holding. From Easter Sunday, Doyle was in a state of readiness. For the next three days he reported to "Antwerp" every evening after work to help prepare for the impending Insurrection. On Thursday morning he marched with the main body of men from Irish Street to the Athenaeum. Doyle was placed on guard duty at the Munster and Leinster Bank on the Market Square. He remained there for four hours before he was relieved. He next carried out sentry duty at the bottom of Slaney Street. After two hours there, Doyle received orders to report to the corner of Castle Hill and Castle Street to take up a sniping position. He later stated before the Military Service Pensions Board on the 29th of November 1938, *"I fired a considerable number of rounds."* Doyle was then selected as a member of the party of Volunteers sent to blow up the Boro Bridge. They failed on this mission due to inadequate ordnance. On his return to H.Q. he had a meal and a rest.

On Friday morning, along with another Volunteer, Doyle was detailed to inspect all the outposts on the east side of the town. Later that night he took up post at Clonhaston Cross, where he remained until Saturday night. The reason for this was that Doyle was well known in this area and was ordered not to let anyone he did not know into the town. After resting on Sunday morning, Doyle guarded the R.I.C. officer who had brought Pádraig Pearse's surrender letter. He was then sent to Drumgoold until the surrender. Doyle returned to the Athenaeum and handed over his weapons which were then taken with the rest and secured. On the Monday morning he helped to clear roadblocks from the

Wexford Road, which was one of the stipulations of the surrender. Doyle was arrested the following Saturday and later deported. He was interned in Lewes Jail and Frongach Camp before he was released on the 23rd of December. On the reorganisation in 1917, he re-joined and played an active part in operations up until The Truce, including the raids on the railway station, the Enniscorthy Asylum and the attack on the Enniscorthy R.I.C. barracks. Doyle had no role in the Civil War. Michael Doyle died at the age of 71 in 1953.

Patrick and Thomas Doyle (Ballindaggin) A Company. Brothers of James Doyle, Patrick and Thomas Doyle joined the Volunteers in 1914 and both became members of the I.R.B. in early 1916. On the afternoon of the Rising they arrived at the Athenaeum with the rest of their Company. Not long after they were instructed by Seamus Rafter to return home and set up posts on roads leading to Enniscorthy. They remained on post until Saturday afternoon when they received word to accompany another Volunteer to Newtownbarry (Bunclody) in order to see if any British troops were assembling there. When they got there, they found no troops, but the R.I.C. barracks had been fortified with policemen who had vacated their own barracks in the area. They returned to Enniscorthy with this information and were then ordered to go to Ballindaggin and raise as many men as they could. On Sunday they held a meeting outside the Church at which the Parish Priest Canon Meehan advised the men there to join up. Nearly a hundred men did and were told to go home and be prepared to be called out at a moment's notice. Thomas Doyle then went to Enniscorthy to receive further orders; he was expected back that night but did not arrive until the following morning with the news of the surrender.

When the R.I.C. arrived back in Killane, Sergeant Peter McGlynn found a note on his desk in the barracks with the names of the Doyle's and three other Volunteers, who should be all arrested according to the note's anonymous author. McGlynn took the note to Canon Meehan who advised him to ignore it, thus the brothers avoided arrest. Sergeant

McGlynn would retire from the force shortly after the arrest of a number of uniformed Volunteers who paraded at Seamus Rafter's funeral in 1918. The Doyle's though in uniform were let go by McGlynn, who later told Patrick Doyle the reason for his retirement.

"…he was not going to fight against his own countrymen."

From 1917 up to The Truce, the Doyle home and land was a hive of activity. They had a munitions dump dug in a corner of a field which was never discovered during the many raids of their land. In 1918 at the height of the conscription scare, the Doyle's built a forge to manufacture pikes to arm the Volunteers if it was written in to law. After the shooting of R.I.C. District Inspector Lea Wilson in Gorey in June 1920, the five-man team who carried it out returned to the Doyle farm. Two of the men, Frank Thornton and Liam Tobin were from Dublin, Jack Whelan and Mick Sinnott from Enniscorthy and Joe McMahon was originally from Clare but now worked in Enniscorthy. On their arrival Patrick Doyle cycled to Enniscorthy to instruct James Cullen, the car's owner, to send a driver to take the car and two women to New Ross as cover.

However, once in town he found out that the R.I.C. already knew the car was missing and he returned home. As he approached Wheelgower Cross, which was 300 yards from his home, he saw a group of police and soldiers near the cross. He made it to his house unseen and readied "the Boys" for action should the soldiers approach. The soldiers and police instead took another road. In the following hours his brother James led the two Dubs over the Blackstairs and into Carlow. The three others made their way to Enniscorthy unimpeded and the Doyle's abandoned the car in Graiguenamanagh. In 1921 Patrick Doyle was appointed Quartermaster for the North Wexford Brigade. During the Civil War the brothers took the Anti-Treaty side.

Patrick Joseph Doyle (Templeshannon) A Company. P.J. Doyle joined the Volunteers in 1914. Upon the split in the organisation in 1915 he resigned and moved to Tullow. On Easter Monday he caught the train to Dublin and witnessed the start of the Rising. He returned to Tullow before cycling to Enniscorthy on Tuesday. On arrival that evening Doyle informed his former comrades of what he had seen in Dublin. At 3 a.m. on Thursday morning Doyle re-joined the Volunteers and was handed a rifle and a revolver. His first duty that morning was raiding for bedding and supplies. He was then detailed to raid the Magazine in Donohue's, where he had previously worked. After returning to the Athenaeum, Doyle was placed on sentry duty on the Lymington Road. On Friday morning he was involved in the seizure of ammunition from the premises of John M. Greene's on Georges Street. (Rafter St) Doyle spent the later part of the day on duty at the Gas Yard. For the rest of the weekend his time was divided between the Athenaeum and New Street. (Wafer St.) He was arrested a couple of days after the surrender and deported shortly afterwards. Doyle was interned in Stafford Jail from where he was released in the middle of June.

On Doyle's return he suffered with bad health, and it was not until November 1917 after moving to Carlow that he re-joined. He was appointed 1st Lieutenant in a Company there and for the next year played a part in all of its activities. In January 1919 Doyle moved to Kilcormac in County Offaly and established a Company there. As Captain of the Company, he organised and participated in numerous raids in the area as well as destroying the R.I.C. barracks in the village, after which the Company took over policing. On one occasion an ex-British soldier, who was causing trouble in the village, was arrested and brought in front of him. Doyle court-martialled him and administrated twenty lashes of a whip. The man caused no further trouble. By August 1920, Doyle's health problems had returned, causing him to withdraw from all activities. In later years P.J. Doyle opened and ran a successful grocery business in Dublin. He died in 1967 at the age of 80.

Richard Doyle (Irish Street) A Company. Richard Doyle joined the Volunteers in 1913. On the morning of the Rising he mobilised with the rest of his Company on Irish Street and marched to the Athenaeum. Over the following four days he carried out whatever orders that were issued to him, however he spent most of his time on sentry duty between Georges Street (Rafter St.) and New Street. (Wafer St.) Doyle was arrested four days after the surrender and deported shortly afterwards. He was held in Stafford Jail for a period of two weeks before he was released.

On his return to Enniscorthy Doyle immediately set to work on establishing an organisation to help the families of the imprisoned Volunteers. This was an onerous task since the majority of business owners in the town looked unfavourably on the Rising. While at the other end of the scale, the families of men fighting in the trenches in France were openly hostile. Nevertheless, Doyle proved successful and was able to help many families who were in dire circumstances. This organisation was then incorporated into the National Aid and Volunteer Dependent Fund which had its H.Q. in Dublin. Doyle re-joined the Volunteers in 1917 and served with them up until 1919. Richard Doyle died a month before the 50th Anniversary of the Rising in 1966 at the age of 85.

Seamus Doyle (Ferns) Brigade Adjutant. Seamus Doyle joined the Gaelic League in 1900 and became a member of the I.R.B. in Gorey in 1907. When he moved to Enniscorthy in early 1913 he transferred his membership. After Doyle joined the Volunteers he swiftly rose up the hierarchy and became a member of its National Executive. After the split in the movement approximately 60% of members in Enniscorthy remained loyal to the Irish Volunteers whilst the rest joined the National Volunteers. However, during the Rising several of these men joined up with their former comrades. After a concert held as part of a Commemoration for Robert Emmet in the Athenaeum in early March 1916, Pádraig Pearse, who was the guest of honour, told Doyle. *"Insurrection was near to hand."* The two came up with a code that Pearse would send once plans were finalised. On Holy Thursday morning Doyle received a message from Pearse which read.

Browns and Nolan tell me that they will have the books you require on the 23rd of July next. Remember three months earlier.

In this message Doyle understood the date for the Rising was the 23rd of April. A couple hours later another message arrived from G.H.Q. in Dublin which countermanded Pearse's order. Shortly thereafter a messenger arrived from Kilkenny to say that due to the message from G.H.Q. they would not be rising. At the time it had been planned that Wexford, Waterford and Kilkenny was to rise as one under the command of Captain J.J. "Ginger" O'Connell the future Deputy Chief of Staff of the National Army. That night Doyle went to Wexford and met with Brigade Commandant Seán Sinnott and Robert Brennan, where it was decided he should go to Dublin the next morning to clarify the situation. Doyle caught the morning train to Dublin on Good Friday and amongst the people he met with was Sean McDermott. McDermott had in his possession an order signed by Eoin McNeill directing O'Connell to proceed to Wexford and take command. McDermott told Doyle that McNeill had consented to the Rising taking place on Easter Sunday. Doyle returned to Enniscorthy and conveyed this news to his fellow officers. On Saturday morning the order was issued for all Volunteers to report for a parade on Sunday at midday with full equipment and rations, all outlaying Company's were to report later that afternoon.

When the Sunday Independent arrived in Enniscorthy with Eoin McNeill's countermanding order it plunged the leadership into chaos. The parade went ahead as planned but the men were ordered to stand down and hold themselves in a state of readiness for any imminent orders. Captain O'Connell and Dr. Dundon a Battalion O/C from Borris arrived in Enniscorthy, but they were none the wiser about the situation. Doyle went to Wexford to confer with Seán Sinnott, they agreed to postpone action and await developments. On Doyle's return to Enniscorthy there was a new message for him and Dr. Dundon, who had already returned to Borris. This message was from Pádraig Pearse and said the Rising was off. Early on Easter Monday morning Doyle went to

Borris with the message for Dundon. When he arrived at the Doctor's house he found Dundon and O'Connell in the sitting room with Miss Nancy Wyse-Power, who had travelled from Dublin with another message from Pearse. This message read.

We start at noon today. Carry out your orders. P.H. Pearse.

O'Connell said.

"I suppose we can tell Miss Power to tell them they cannot expect any help from us."

"No" Doyle replied.

"I cannot make any decision until I see my brother officers."

Doyle then returned to Enniscorthy, where the same message had been received. A meeting of the officers was called, which was also attended by O'Connell who had arrived from Borris. It was decided that Doyle and O'Connell would go to Wexford and meet with Sinnott and Brennan. Once there Sinnott told the two men.

"..in consequence of the conflicting orders he would have nothing to do with the matter."

They waited for the night train from Dublin and upon its arrival were told by railway men that the Volunteers had taken control of the city. Doyle and O'Connell returned to Enniscorthy in the early hours of Tuesday morning and found several officers waiting at "The Dump". O'Connell asked them not to make any decision until he returned, he wanted to go and find out what was happening elsewhere. He returned Wednesday evening with the news that no one else was going to turn out and he himself was not going to take any further action. He then left. Peter Galligan, who had just arrived back from Dublin informed them of James Connolly's order to hold the town, it was then decided to start operations early the next morning.

When news of the surrender in Dublin came on Sunday morning and after consultation with the British military command, Doyle accompanied Seán Etchingham to Dublin to meet Pearse in Arbour Hill Jail where the surrender was confirmed. On the following day Doyle surrendered with the rest of the leaders and was arrested. He was later court-martialled and sentenced to death which was commuted to penal servitude for five years. He spent parts of his sentence in Dartmoor and Lewes Jails before he was released from Pentonville in June 1917. On his return Doyle became more involved with the political side of the struggle and was elected twice to Dáil Éireann in 1921 for Sinn Féin and then in 1922 for the Anti Treaty Sinn Féin. Seamus Doyle died in 1971 in his 85th year.

Thomas Doyle (The Shannon) Captain A Company. Thomas Doyle was a member of the I.R.B. before joining the Volunteers at their inception in 1913. With Liam Mellows, he set up a branch of Na Fianna Éireann in the town and served as its drill instructor until late 1915. Doyle was employed as a sawyer in Donohue's, and with a couple of other employees, was responsible for the surreptitious manufacture of hundreds of pike handles prior to the Rising. From November 1915 up until Easter Week, Doyle attended officer classes twice a week under the tutorial of Peter Galligan. On the night of Holy Thursday he and his class were informed about the plans for the upcoming Insurrection on Easter Sunday and were sworn to secrecy. They mobilised with their Company on Easter Sunday and marched through the town before falling in at "Antwerp". There they were told to stand down but to remain ready to be called out at a moment's notice. On the following Thursday morning Doyle was called at 2 a.m. and told to round up the men, that they were going out. Along with a dozen or so he made his way to the Keegan house on Irish Street and marched to the Athenaeum. Once a H.Q. had been set up there, Doyle was appointed as Captain of the Guard. For the rest of the week he was responsible for outpost and sentry duty. Although based at H.Q. with the rest of the officers, he went out numerous times to inspect the outposts. On Friday morning while inspecting the men on the Castle roof, Doyle stated that he saw movement in one of the windows of the R.I.C. barracks, he picked up a rifle and fired one shot through it.

After the surrender Doyle went on the run for a couple of days, only returning home when he believed the arrests had ceased. He went back to work in Donohue's on the Thursday but was not long there before a group of R.I.C. men arrived and arrested him. They brought him and others to their barracks where they were held until 6 p.m.. At that time due to overcrowding, all the detainees were marched to the Athenaeum where they were placed in the custody of the Connacht Rangers. Doyle recalled the events in the Athenaeum in his Witness Statement for the Bureau of Military History on the 30th of November 1954. The Officer in charge allowed them to receive food from their relatives. On seeing this the Head Constable a man named Collins said.

"Let no more food into them because when they had us locked up in the barracks they would not let any into us."

The Officer in Charge replied.

"They are in my charge now and they can get all the food sent to them."

Later some of the R.I.C. men tried to throw their weight about and started to insult the Volunteers, upon hearing of this, the officer had them all removed from the building. That night one of the soldiers approached Doyle and asked him did he want a shave since they would be moving out the next morning. Doyle agreed to it, and afterwards the soldier asked him if he wanted to write a letter to a loved one. When he said yes the soldier got him a pen and some paper. Doyle wrote two letters, one to his father and another to his sister and gave them to the soldier. The soldier returned later with letters from them both which Doyle was extremely thankful for. He found out the soldier was an O'Sullivan from Cork. After he was deported Doyle was interned until late December in Frongach Camp.

Doyle joined The Shannon Company in 1917 and was appointed 1st Lieutenant. Shortly after he was reinstated in his old job at Donohue's. He resumed making pike handles and bomb parts up until the end of 1919 when he left to become a Bookmaker. In this new line of work he developed several relationships which helped him collect intelligence to pass on to the leadership, both at his premises and at racecourses throughout the country. In later years Thomas Doyle opened the Astor Cinema on Wafer Street, he died at the age of 70 in 1962.

Thomas Doyle (Lower Church Street) A Company. Thomas Doyle was a member of the I.R.B. before joining the Volunteers at their inception in 1913. His brother Lawrence was also a Volunteer, while his sister Mary Ellen was a member of Cumann na mBan. On the first morning of the Insurrection, he joined his fellow Volunteers on Irish Street and marched to the Athenaeum. From there Doyle was sent to a couple of hardware shops, including Donohue's, to raid for weapons. On his return he was ordered to Blackstoops for outpost duty with the instructions not to allow anyone entry or exit from the town. Doyle spent five hours there before he was relieved. After having a meal, he carried out sentry duty at various locations around the town before he was recalled to the Athenaeum to rest for the night.

On Friday, Doyle was among a party of Volunteers who were sent to the home of Lady Grey in Brownswood to commandeer her car and petrol. He spent the rest of the day on sentry duty. On Saturday he was placed on guard duty at the National Bank which was located across the road from the Athenaeum on Castle Street. That evening Doyle was a member of the party of Volunteers selected to go to Ferns under the command of Peter Galligan. On arrival there he went to the Post Office and found communications which alerted him to the assembly of approximately sixty R.I.C. men at Newtownbarry. (Bunclody) After Doyle passed on this information he dismantled the communications equipment and placed two Volunteers on the door of the post office. He then went to the railway station to help remove rails from the track. The following morning when the car containing D.I. Drake and the Parish Priest from Camolin arrived under the flag of truce, Doyle was ordered to escort it to Enniscorthy. On arrival at the Athenaeum the D.I. handed Robert Brennan Pearse's surrender letter. Later Doyle took the men to Bennetts Hotel in Templeshannon before escorting them back to Ferns. When the surrender was announced he returned to Enniscorthy and helped collect the arms and ammunition which were to be hidden. Doyle was arrested the following Tuesday and deported shortly afterwards. He was interned in Stafford Jail and Frongach Camp before his release in December.

In 1917 Doyle re-joined the Volunteers and was appointed as Captain. Following the funeral of Seamus Rafter in September 1918, at which he had led his company, Doyle was arrested and charged with.

Wearing illegal uniform and giving military words of command.

He was sentenced to six months in Cork Gaol. Three of which were spent in solitary confinement. He also went on hunger strike for a period. Doyle continued to serve after his release but ceased his activities in 1920. In later years Doyle worked as a Civil Servant in Dublin and applied for the Military Service Pension twice. He was refused on each occasion despite references from fellow officers, which included such statements as.

"I cannot understand how he did not get Easter Week Service." T.D. Sinnott. (25/4/1944)

"…certainly more entitled to a pension than some of the people claiming them." Phil Murphy. (13/5/1944)

"…I am prepared to give the above evidence on oath if required and I am further prepared to forgo my right to any pension which has been granted to me in the event of the above statements being disproved." Thomas Doyle, The Astor. (19/5/1944)

"…If his case does not warrant a pension for his services, no one in Enniscorthy should have qualified." Liam O'Leary. (May 1944).

Doyle received a letter from the Department of Defence on the 5th of October 1944 which stated,

...the additional evidence submitted by you and on your behalf has been carefully and sympathetically considered but it is not of a nature to warrant the minister to reopen your case.

Thomas Doyle reapplied a third time after the passing of the Military Service Pensions Amendment Act in 1949. He was finally awarded his pension on the 19th of June 1951. However, Doyle died suddenly at his home on Griffith Avenue on the 24th of September the same year. Thomas Doyle was 67 years old.

Thomas Doyle (Buckstown) Rocktavern Company. Thomas Doyle was from Buckstown which is located between Carnew and Gorey. He was a member of a the Rocktavern Company attached to the North Wexford Brigade. This Company had been decimated at the time of the Split with the vast majority of members joining the National Volunteers. Doyle arrived at the Athenaeum in Enniscorthy on Friday the 28th and was ordered by Seamus Doyle to take up a sniping position on the Castle roof. He remained there until the Sunday excluding rest breaks. Over that period he stated he did not fire any shots. After the surrender he made his way home and evaded arrest. In later years Thomas Doyle worked in forestry. He died in Glenageary, Dublin in 1962 at the age of 67.

Thomas Doyle (Ross Road) A Company. Thomas Doyle joined the Volunteers in 1913 and was also a member of the I.R.B. In 1916 he was employed in Seamus Rafter's shop and pub at the bridge. Prior to the Rising he delivered dispatches around the town for Rafter on numerous occasions. He also helped secure munitions in a room at the rear of the pub. On the first morning of the Rising, Doyle mobilised with the rest of the Volunteers at Keegan's on Irish Street and marched to the Athenaeum. From there he was sent to the bottom of Hospital Lane from where he could observe the R.I.C. District Inspector's house. In his testimony before the Military Service Pensions Board on the 2nd of March 1937, Doyle explained what happened while he was there. R.I.C. Constable Grace arrived to alert the D.I. of the Rebellion. Doyle called for him to halt and Grace opened fire with his revolver before retreating down Friary Hill. A short time after Grace returned with Sergeant Oliver and some other constables, shots were exchanged between the two groups for a short period before the R.I.C. men retreated down Friary Hill and back to their barracks. That night Doyle was placed on sentry duty at the bottom of Irish Street until he was relieved early on Friday morning.

After a brief rest in the Athenaeum, Doyle was sent on raids for ammunition to Armstrong's and Donohue's. Later he was sent to Kilcarbery to act as guard for the Volunteers who attempted to blow up the railway bridge there. On Friday night Doyle carried out guard duty at the Provincial Bank in Slaney Place. He spent the next day on sentry duty at various locations around the town. On Sunday morning Doyle was detailed for sentry duty at the top of Castle Hill, later in the day he was on outpost duty at St. John's Cross. After the surrender he helped to collect the arms that were later hidden.

On Tuesday morning the 2nd of May Doyle reported for work in Rafters. Shortly afterwards six R.I.C. men arrived and hauled him off to the barracks, where he was charged and tried for the shooting of Constable Grace. Sergeant Oliver and a Constable Armstrong gave evidence against him. Doyle was found guilty and sentenced to death along with Volunteer Dick Donohue who had been charged with the same offense. He was brought to Kilmainham Jail and spent two weeks there before his sentence was commuted to that of Penal Servitude. Doyle was then interned in Dartmoor, Lewes and Portland Jails before he was released from Pentonville in June 1917. On his release Doyle re-joined the Volunteers, but bar blocking a couple of roads, did not take part in any operations up to The Truce. The main reason for this was because Doyle was a married man, the leadership did not like to have men with any dependents placed in danger. During the Civil War he chose the Anti-Treaty side and fought on the first two days of "The Battle of Enniscorthy". Thomas Doyle died in 1955 at the age of 75.

Martin Dunbar (Ferns) Ferns Company. Martin Dunbar joined the Volunteers in 1914. In the weeks leading up to the Rising he spent most nights in a small cottage outside Ferns making buckshot. On the Tuesday of Easter Week, Dunbar along with the rest of his company set off for Enniscorthy with the belief the town had risen. On their way they met a dispatch rider who informed them that nothing had happened yet. They camped in Ballinahallin Wood before returning home in the early hours of Wednesday morning. When the word finally came on Thursday that the Rebellion had begun, Dunbar and approximately twenty members of his Company made their way to Enniscorthy. On arriving shortly before 5 p.m., Dunbar took up guard duty in the Athenaeum, where he spent the night. On Friday morning he was a member of a party of Volunteers who carried out raids for arms in the surrounding district. When he returned to H.Q. he was placed on sentry duty at the bottom of Irish Street. On Saturday, Dunbar was on duty at the Athenaeum until 5 p.m., then he took up outpost duty at the gates of the Enniscorthy Asylum on the Wexford Road.

At midnight he and the Volunteer with him received a message from H.Q., it informed them that intelligence had been obtained that the British Military was at Edermine. Dunbar and his colleague were ordered to open fire immediately if they encountered a British advance party. However, none arrived and the two of them were relieved at 5 a.m.. On his return to the Athenaeum, the word was that Ferns would be the British target. Dunbar set off on foot immediately and arrived in the village at 7 a.m.. Once there he reported to the R.I.C. barracks which the Volunteers had taken over as their H.Q.. Upon learning there was no imminent threat he went home to sleep; his home was close to the barracks. At 5 p.m. Dunbar reported back on duty and was placed on sentry in the village. After the surrender was announced and the men ordered back to Enniscorthy, Dunbar took a seat in the car behind Peter Galligan's. Less than halfway to Enniscorthy Galligan's car went off the road and over a ditch leaving a woman passenger and three Volunteers injured. Dunbar and another Volunteer, Thomas Barnes, drove to Newtownbarry (Bunclody) to fetch a doctor. By the time they returned with him and then went on to Enniscorthy it was nearly 6 a.m. They found the Athenaeum deserted so they went home to Ferns. Dunbar was arrested the following day and deported shortly after. He spent a month in Wandsworth Jail before he was released in June.

Dunbar re-joined in 1917 and took an active part in his Company's activities. He rose through the ranks and had become Battalion Adjutant before he was arrested in March 1921. He was imprisoned on Spike Island and in Maryborough Jail. (Port Laoise) until his release that December. Dunbar took the Republican side in the Civil War and in July 1922 participated in the burning of the barracks and courthouse in Gorey. In October Dunbar was arrested, he was held for a week before he was released due to ill health. Martin Dunbar died at the age of 81 in 1975.

Edward Dunne (Irish Street) A Company. Edward Dunne joined the I.R.B. in 1911 and the Volunteers in 1913. On the first morning of the Rising he fell in with the rest of his Company on Irish Street and marched to the Athenaeum. Once a H.Q. was up and running he was sent on sentry duty to the bottom of Irish Street. After spending a couple of hours there, he was recalled to the Athenaeum and ordered to take up a sniping position on Castle Hill. Dunne later stated (Military Service Pensions Board interview on the 21st of November 1939) that he fired several shots at the R.I.C. barracks from this position. Later on he was detailed to Blackstoops where he helped to man an outpost. For the next two days Dunne was on outpost duty at various locations including St. John's Cross and Blackstoops, he also carried out police patrol around the town centre. On Sunday morning he was on guard duty at H.Q., then at "The Dump", before he was recalled from the top of Irish Street for the surrender. Dunne avoided arrest the following day by hiding when the military came looking for him at his place of work in Buttles of Templeshannon. He went on the run and remained away for ten days before returning when things had settled down. Dunne re-joined in 1917 but only participated in the blocking of roads twice before The Truce. Edward Dunne died in St. John's Hospital in 1960 at the age of 82.

James Dwyer (St. John's Street) A Company. James Dwyer joined the Volunteers in 1913. At 4 a.m. on the morning of the Rising he was called to arms. He reported to Patrick Keegan's house on Irish Street and marched with the main body of men to the Athenaeum. Once a H.Q. had been established, Dwyer was sent to St. John's Street for sentry duty. On his return a few hours later, he helped six other Volunteers commandeer cooking equipment from the Protestant Institute on Church Street. They then went to Bolger's Drapery and took possession of overcoats and bedding which they brought to the Athenaeum. That night Dwyer took up post at Salville Cross and after he was relieved, returned to H.Q. to sleep. On Friday morning he unloaded a bread van belonging to O'Connor's Bakery of Wexford, which had been commandeered. Dwyer marched to Ferns as a member of the column of Volunteers under the command of Peter Galligan on Saturday evening. He slept in the R.I.C. barracks which had been vacated. On Sunday morning he was placed on guard duty at Ferns Castle for four hours and then was sent to The Palace. After the surrender Dwyer returned to Enniscorthy by car. He was arrested the following Tuesday and deported shortly afterwards. Dwyer was interned in Stafford Jail and Frongach Camp before he was released in August. He re-joined in 1917 but played no further role in any military operations. James Dwyer was 86 years old when he passed away in 1982.

James Dwyer (Tomnalosset) A Company. James Dwyer joined the Volunteers in 1914 and the I.R.B. shortly afterwards. On the first morning of the Rising, he marched with the rest of his Company from Irish Street to the Athenaeum. Once there he was instructed to take up a sniping position on Castle Hill. According to Dwyer's statement before the

Military Service Pensions Board on the 5th of June 1940, he fired approximately a dozen shots over a thirty-minute period at the R.I.C. barracks, the policemen inside returned fire. After he was relieved, he was sent with a party of Volunteers to take over Davis's Mill. Dwyer remained there until night-time, then, after some refreshments in the Athenaeum, he stood post at Clonhaston Cross until daylight. On Friday morning Dwyer was placed on outpost duty at Red Pat's Cross, where he remained for most of the day. After spending the night at H.Q., he took up sentry duty on the bridge for four hours on Saturday morning. In the early afternoon Dwyer was sent to Lymington Road. He stayed there until evening, then he was recalled to H.Q. and ordered to march to Ferns with the column of Volunteers. On Sunday Dwyer carried out sentry duty outside the village on the Dublin Road. After the surrender he returned to Enniscorthy and helped to clear the Athenaeum of weapons. Dwyer personally took possession of five rifles, three shotguns and four revolvers as well as two large bags of ammunition. It took him a few trips out to the country to hide these weapons. Once completed he went on the run and successfully avoided arrest.

In 1917 Dwyer re-joined and handed over the weapons he had hidden to the Company. At the 1918 Bye Election in Waterford, which was called after the death of The Irish Parliamentary Party leader John Redmond, Dwyer was a member of the party of Volunteers who travelled from Enniscorthy to provide protection for the Sinn Féin election team. He also played a part in some of the more prominent operations of his Company in the years leading up to The Truce, these included assisting in the escape of William Kavanagh from the local hospital in Enniscorthy, the attempted assassination of the spy Fredrick Newsome, (there was a successful attempt shortly afterwards) and the ambush of a train in Killurin where he fired a number of rounds. As well as these activities Dwyer acted as a scout for flying columns passing through the town, often providing them with provisions. Dwyer's final role was as a policeman in the town after The Truce, he served in this position until the

Free State Army took over the R.I.C. barracks in 1922. James Dwyer was aged 74 when he died in 1968.

John "Jack" Dwyer (Tomnalosset) A Company. A member of the Volunteers since 1914, John Dwyer was the younger brother of James Dwyer. In April 1916 he was working in Ballyregan. On Holy Saturday Dwyer received word to return to Enniscorthy the next day for mobilisation. He did so, but after the order to stand down was issued he returned to Ballyregan. On hearing the news the following Thursday that the town had risen, Dwyer set off on foot and walked the twenty odd miles to Enniscorthy. Upon his arrival at the Athenaeum Dwyer was handed a rifle and ten rounds of ammunition. He was then instructed to take up an outpost position on the main Enniscorthy New Ross road. He remained there until he was relieved at 10 a.m. on Friday morning. Dwyer returned to H.Q. where he rested for most of the day. That night he was detailed to Davis's Mill until Saturday morning. On Saturday evening Dwyer marched to Ferns with the column of Volunteers. The next day he was on outpost duty on the Dublin Road.

After the surrender, Dwyer returned to the Athenaeum and helped with the collection and concealment of weapons. He then went on the run and avoided arrest. Dwyer re-joined in 1917 and spent a considerable amount of time making buckshot and filling cartridges. Through a contact that he worked with in the County Council, he heard of a consignment of Gelignite was to be delivered to the quarry in Bunclody by the County Surveyor and his assistant. Dwyer passed this information on to Seamus Rafter who organised an ambush on the two men. Dwyer personally took part in raids for rate and excise books as well as the rescue of William Kavanagh from the local hospital. He was arrested on the 3rd of February 1921 and interned on Spike Island where he went on hunger strike, he was then sent to Maryborough Jail (Port Laoise) before he was released following The Truce. During the Civil War, although not a member of the Free State Army, Dwyer carried out intelligence work on their behalf which if had been discovered, would have placed him in great danger. John Dwyer died at the age of 69 in 1965.

Peter Dwyer (Tomnalosset) A Company. The oldest of the Dwyer brothers, Peter joined the Volunteers at their inception in 1913 and served in Enniscorthy and Ferns during Easter week. He was arrested a few days after the surrender and interned in Frongach until August. Dwyer rejoined in 1917 and took an active part in Company activities. By 1920 he had command of his own flying column.

On the 17th of February that year he was delayed in meeting up with the column for a raid for arms on a house in The Ballagh. Instead of waiting for him, the column went ahead with the raid. As the men entered the property, the woman of the house Mrs. Ellen Morris, aged 60 and the mother of fifteen, picked up a spade to try and stop them. One of the Volunteers, who was only eighteen at the time, shot her in the chest, mortally wounding her. Even though Dwyer was not present for the shooting, he was arrested four days later and sent to Mountjoy. Thirteen men went on trial in Wexford Assizes for the murder. The policeman investigating the case was R.I.C. District Inspector Percival Lea Wilson. Wilson had taken numerous statements regarding the killing but was shot dead himself in Gorey before he could give evidence. The eighteen-year-old was found guilty of the murder. Dwyer was released on the 28th of December 1920 and immediately joined up with a flying column. The following May he participated in the Killurin train ambush. Twelve months later and just weeks before the Civil War broke out, Dwyer joined the newly formed Garda Siochana and served with them until September 1923. Peter Dwyer died in 1950, he was 62 years old.

Michael Earle (Ross Road) A Company. Michael Earle was my Great Grandfather. He was a member of the I.R.B. for several years before he joined the Volunteers at their inception in 1913. In 1916 he was employed as a lorry driver for Davis's Mill. On the first morning of the Rising he reported for duty to the Athenaeum. He was detailed to the transport section owing to his driving capabilities. Earle was sent to Davis's where he commandeered a lorry. He then made several journeys across the bridge to transport weapons and supplies commandeered from Donohue's to the Athenaeum. On each occasion he came under heavy fire from the R.I.C. in the nearby barracks. Once finished this task, Earle transported men to set up outposts on the outskirts of the town. He helped with the felling of trees and the blocking of roads. Earle remained on call for the rest of the week, he drove men around the town to take up positions and brought the men they had relieved back to the Athenaeum. He slept in his lorry each night.

After the surrender on Sunday, Earle drove to Ferns to collect Volunteers and brought them back to Enniscorthy. On Monday he was instructed by his employer to prepare his lorry for use by the military to round up wanted Volunteers. Earle tinkered with the engine in such a way that the lorry broke down less than a mile outside the town. Realising they would come looking for him, he went on the run and stayed with relatives in Oulart for a fortnight. When he returned home he was dismissed from his job at Davis's. Earle played no further role in Volunteer activities, partly due to the fact he was a widower and the father of three children. Michael Earle died in 1939 at the age of 69.

James Ennis (Tomnalosset) A Company. James Ennis joined the Volunteers in 1914. On Easter Sunday he mobilised with the rest of his Company at "Antwerp" and took part in the parade around the town. After the order to stand down was issued, Ennis remained at "Antwerp" until the following Thursday morning. Then he joined the main body of Volunteers on Irish Street and marched to the Athenaeum. From there he was detailed for sentry duty at the top of St. John's Street and later, at the County Home. He slept in H.Q. that night. On Friday, Ennis was a member of the party of Volunteers ordered to commandeer coal for the Athenaeum from O'Neill's coal yard. The coal yard was located on the opposite side of the street from the Bank of Ireland on Mill Park Road. While in the process of getting the coal, the Volunteers came under fire from two R.I.C. men who had locked themselves in the Bank. Ennis returned fire, stating later he fired ten or twelve rounds. On Saturday evening he marched with the column of men under the command of Peter Galligan to Ferns. Once there, he was placed on outpost duty until news of the surrender came through. Ennis then marched back to Enniscorthy and handed in his rifle and ammunition. He remained on the run until the military and R.I.C. had ceased rounding up Volunteers. Ennis rejoined in 1917 and played a nominal role in Company activities up until The Truce. He did not participate in the Civil War. James Ennis died at the age of 72 in 1968.

Elizabeth "Lily" Ennis (Ferns) Cumann na mBan. Lily Ennis (nee Roche) joined Cumann na mBan in 1916. When the Volunteers came to Ferns during the Rising she cooked and set up sleeping facilities for them in the R.I.C. barracks. In the days following the surrender her house was raided on several occasions as the crown forces searched for her Volunteer brother. Over the next couple of years Ennis participated in flag days and church gate collections to raise funds for prisoner's families and later to buy arms for the I.R.A.. During the War of Independence she stored rifles in the rafters of her house and on other occasions in the hayshed in her yard. When the Civil War broke out Ennis chose the Republican side and was back cooking in the R.I.C. barracks during the fight in Ferns. After the ceasefire her family left Ferns due to the hostility shown to them for their support of the I.R.A.. Ennis settled in Enniscorthy and worked as a Mid-Wife in the town and district for many years. Lily Ennis died in her 83rd year in 1981.

Michael Ennis (Tomnalosset) A Company. Michael Ennis was an older brother of James Ennis. He joined the Volunteers in 1914 and became a member of the I.R.B. shortly afterwards. On the first morning of the Rising he reported to "The Dump" on Irish Street and helped convey munitions to the H.Q. which had been established in the Athenaeum. After this, Ennis was detailed for sentry duty at the town's

Gas Yard. While stationed there, he was fired upon from the R.I.C. barracks which was a distance of five hundred yards away. He returned fire but the distance was too great for his weapon.

On Friday morning Ennis was instructed to commandeer his employer's car and drive Denis Murphy to Dr. Dundon's (Volunteer Officer) residence in Borris with dispatches. On their way they were stopped by an R.I.C. patrol, they evaded arrest when Ennis claimed that Murphy was an insurance agent, and he was his driver. On his return he was engaged in transporting commandeered supplies to H.Q.. Ennis went to Ferns as a member of an advance party on Saturday afternoon and remained there until Sunday morning. When Fr. Kehoe of Camolin and R.I.C. District Inspector Drake arrived with Pádraig Pearse's surrender letter, Ennis was instructed to drive the men to Enniscorthy. He remained at H.Q. after the surrender and helped to collect weapons and ammunition for safe storage. Ennis was arrested at his place of employment the following Thursday and shortly afterwards was deported. He was interned in Stafford Jail and Frongach Camp before he was released on the 1st of August. On his return home Ennis was immediately dismissed from his job. He re-joined in 1917 but apart from protecting Sinn Féin officials in Waterford during the Bye-Election of 1918, his activities were routine up to The Truce. He played no part in the Civil War. Michael Ennis passed away in 1954 aged 61.

Seán Etchingham (Courtown) Brigade Commandant. Seán Etchingham joined the Enniscorthy Echo as a journalist on its foundation in 1902. As well as establishing a Gorey Branch of the Gaelic League, he was a prominent figure in the G.A.A., serving on county and national boards of the Association. Throughout the Rising Etchingham was responsible for the issue of travel permits. On the Sunday he accompanied Seamus Doyle to Arbour Hill Jail in Dublin to get confirmation of the surrender from Pádraig Pearse. He was arrested the next day and after being court-martialled was sentenced to death, (he joked at the time that it was his first offence) which was later commuted to five years penal servitude.

He was imprisoned in Lewes Jail and then Dartmoor from where he was released in June 1917 suffering from Tuberculosis. In March 1918 Etchingham was rearrested in connection with the so called "German Plot". Whilst in jail he was elected as a T.D. for East Wicklow. Upon his release, and with the War of Independence intensifying, he spent a considerable time on the run. In March 1921 Etchingham's home in Courtown was destroyed by the Black and Tans, while in May he was re-elected unopposed in the General Election. He took the Anti-Treaty side and spoke passionately against its introduction. In the General Election of June 1922, Etchingham was defeated by the Pro-Treaty candidate. With his health declining, Etchingham stepped away from politics. After spending several months in a nursing home in Dublin, Seán Etchingham returned to Courtown where he died on the 23rd of April 1923. He was 53 years old.

Patrick Farrell (Killagoley) A Company. Patrick Farrell was already a member of the I.R.B. when he joined the Volunteers in 1913. At the time he was employed in the Kynoch munitions factory in Arklow and only returned to Enniscorthy at weekends. On several occasions he stole small quantities of Gelignite from the factory and smuggled them home. This Gelignite was then used in the manufacture of munitions in "Antwerp" and "The Dump". On Easter Sunday, after his Company was told to stand down, Farrell went to "The Dump" and remained there preparing weapons and equipment until Thursday morning. He then marched with the rest of the Volunteers to the Athenaeum.

Farrell's first duty that morning was to accompany Patrick Keegan to visit sites for proposed outposts. On his return he took up a sniping position on Castle Hill where he came under fire from the R.I.C. barracks. After a brief period there he was summoned to H.Q. by Seamus Rafter. Rafter instructed him to set up a small armoury in one of the rooms of the

Athenaeum. Farrell made a list of the equipment he required to carry out this task. Volunteers then raided several hardware shops to obtain these items. Farrell spent the remainder of the week in this room repairing and sorting all the various weapons which had been seized in raids throughout the district.

Once the surrender was officially announced, Farrell helped clear the Athenaeum of all reusable weapons and munitions. He then went to "The Dump" and helped clear that out as well. They finished this with only an hour to spare before the British military entered the town on Monday afternoon. Farrell avoided arrest and re-joined in 1917. He continued to work at Kynoch's where he resumed his pilfering of Gelignite. Later he was involved in the establishment of the foundry in Corrageen, where he made buckshot and hand grenades. In 1920 Farrell carried out a demonstration of land mines that he had made for Cathal Brugha in Ballynaslaney. Farrell remained active up until The Truce and took no part in the Civil War. Patrick Farrell died in 1971 at the age of 91.

Marie Fitzpatrick (Church Street) Cumann na mBan. Marie Fitzpatrick (nee Moran) came from a staunch Republican family. She was a founding member of Cumann na mBan in the town and her parents and siblings were all involved in the Rising and the turbulent years which followed. On Easter Saturday Fitzpatrick was sent to Wexford with a dispatch for Robert Brennan, a task she would repeat on Easter Monday and the following Wednesday. On her return journey Wednesday evening she carried a large box of ammunition strapped to her bicycle. On the morning of the Rising Fitzpatrick reported for duty to the Athenaeum and was assigned the role of dispatch carrier. On Friday she went to Wexford with two dispatches and received news about British troop arrivals to bring back to H.Q.. Fitzpatrick had difficulty trying to make it back to Enniscorthy and ended up flirting with two soldiers at Ferrycarraig, she promised to meet up with them once they were off duty if they would let her through. For the remainder of the Insurrection Fitzpatrick remained at H.Q..

After the surrender her father and two brothers, Seán and William were arrested and deported. Her sister Sighle's house on Court Street was raided by police searching for her Volunteer husband Laurence Lynch. In her Witness Statement for the Bureau of Military History dated the 25th of January 1956, Fitzpatrick described the terrible consequences of this raid.

My sister had twin boys and when the police were raiding her house, thinking there was only one baby in the cot. When one baby was lifted out, a policeman pulled up the mattress and killed the other baby. Her husband had already been arrested.

In the following week Fitzpatrick received letters written from the leaders who had been sentenced to death to give to their families. With the exception of Seán Etchingham's letter, she found it easy enough to deliver them. When she attempted to board the train to Gorey in order to go to Etchingham's mother's residence in Courtown, she was stopped and told she was prohibited from leaving the town. Fitzpatrick was not a woman for half measures, so she walked to Courtown! While delivering the letter she was arrested and detained, but while the police went to make enquires she walked out and returned to Enniscorthy. At the end of May 1916 Fitzpatrick moved to Dublin and remained there until the end of the following year. Once back home in Enniscorthy she resumed her Cumann activities full-time. A secret cellar which lay beneath her father's shop was used to store weapons, Fitzpatrick would hand them out or deliver them on occasions when they were required. She was prominent in organising the so-called *Sinn Féin Post,* this was a system used to get dispatches sent from Dublin to individuals at risk of arrest. Throughout this period Fitzpatrick lived at home with her parents and their house and shop was raided and broken up on numerous occasions.

On the morning of Ash Wednesday 1921, the family received the devastating news that her brother Seán had been murdered by the Black and Tans in Drogheda, along with a local Alderman named Thomas Halpin. They had both been taken from their homes and shot multiple times. Their bodies were then dumped at the side of a road. In her Witness Statement Fitzpatrick gave details of what happened.

Seán was married and had a nine-month-old baby. His wife told us that Seán was on the run and that night he had just come in to say goodnight to the baby and herself when he was arrested. The officer told her to bring his breakfast in the morning to the barracks. She didn't know Mrs. Halpin but met her the next morning also going with her husband's breakfast. While they were waiting outside the barracks they heard about the murders.

When they brought her brother's remains back to Enniscorthy, they were informed by the police and military that there would be no funeral and that only a few people could attend the burial. However, on the day the town closed down and the streets were lined with men, women and children offering the family their respect and sympathy. In the aftermath many of the men were arrested and beaten. Fitzpatrick chose the Republican side in the Civil War and during the "Battle of Enniscorthy" she was in charge of a field hospital set up in a house on Court Street. Over the following months Fitzpatrick created a Cumann na mBan Active Service Unit with the purpose of delivering dispatches and ammunition to various flying columns. She was arrested in January 1923 and imprisoned for a month; upon her release she resumed her activities and continued right up until the ceasefire. Both of Fitzpatrick's parents died in 1924, her mother she claimed from a broken heart and her father as a result of all the hardship he had suffered in the preceding years. Marie Fitzpatrick died in 1958, she was 60 years old.

Patrick Fitzpatrick (Court Street) A Company. Patrick Fitzpatrick was the husband of Maria Fitzpatrick, he joined the I.R.B. in 1910 and the Volunteers in 1914. At 2 a.m. on the morning of the Rising he was sent by Seamus Rafter to Carley's Bridge and Wilton to rouse a couple of Volunteers. On his return he marched with the main body of men from Irish Street to the Athenaeum. Fitzpatrick took up sentry duty outside the new H.Q. until he was sent with a couple of Volunteers to Buttle's Bacon factory to commandeer a van. He then went to Hayes's of Greenmount and commandeered a car. After returning to H.Q. he was detailed with the same group of Volunteers to go to the Cookman residence in Monart and raid for arms. They were successful in obtaining a number of shotguns and revolvers along with a quantity of ammunition.

On Friday morning Fitzpatrick was a member of the party of Volunteers sent to Lady Grey's house in Brownswood to commandeer her car and petrol. This task took two separate trips and on both they came under fire from the R.I.C. barracks, Fitzpatrick later stated he returned fire. Save for one trip to Ferns on Sunday morning with a dispatch, Fitzpatrick carried out sentry duty and street patrols for the remainder of the week. He was arrested on the following Monday and deported shortly afterwards. Fitzpatrick was interned in Stafford Jail until he was released in early July.

Fitzpatrick re-joined in 1917 and took part in all the general activities of his Company. In 1918 he became Secretary of the newly formed Sinn Féin Club and spent the majority of his time at the club's premises which were located on Lower Church Street. Munitions were stored there and worked on by members of Cumann na mBan. The Club was destroyed by the Black and Tans in late 1919. During the Civil War Fitzpatrick served on the Republican side and carried out scouting and intelligence duties. Patrick Fitzpatrick died in March 1966, shortly before the 50th anniversary of the Rising. He was 79 years old.

James Forrestal (Ballindaggin) A Company. A member of the I.R.B. since 1910, James Forrestal joined the Volunteers in Enniscorthy in 1914. In early 1916 he returned home to live in Ballindaggin and joined the local Company. On Easter Sunday along with his Company he went to Enniscorthy under mobilisation orders. When the plans for an immediate uprising fell through he returned home and spent the next three days making buckshot and filling cartridges. Once word came through on Thursday that Enniscorthy had risen, he and his comrades cycled to the town and reported for duty at the Athenaeum. After spending a couple of hours there, Seamus Rafter ordered them to return to Ballindaggin and hold the road to Carlow, and thus The Curragh where British forces were stationed. Over the following days, Forrestal participated in the occupation of the village hall and post office as well as cutting telegraph wires and carrying out guard duty on various crossroads in the locale.

On news of the surrender he went to Bunclody and evaded arrest. In the later part of 1916 Forrestal organised house to house and church gate collections for the Prisoners Defence and Dependents Fund. In 1917 he re-joined and took part in the normal Company activities. At the funeral of Seamus Rafter in Ballindaggin in 1918, Forrestal provided the rifles used by the firing party for the salute over Rafter's grave, he then smuggled the weapons away to safety. Forrestal was appointed Brigade Adjutant in May 1921 and served as such until Spring 1922. At that time a gun he was testing exploded in his hand leaving him badly wounded and necessitating an operation. Forrestal had no involvement in the Civil War. James Forrestal died at the age of 80 in 1971.

John Franklin (St. John's Street) A Company. John Franklin was employed at the Gas Works when he joined the Volunteers in 1913, he was already a member of the I.R.B. Two months prior to the Rising he was involved in a successful raid for gunpowder and cartridges at Donohue's. He was mobilised on Easter Sunday and remained on standby for the entire week. On Thursday morning Franklin marched with the column of Volunteers from Irish Street to the Athenaeum. After the establishment of a H.Q. there, he was assigned to take up a sniping position on Castle Hill. At 9 a.m. R.I.C. District Inspector Hegarty and some of his constables attempted to reach the Post Office on the Abbey Square. Franklin and several other Volunteers fired on them and prevented them from succeeding. (Military Service Pensions Board interview on the 3rd of March 1937) He was relieved at midday. From then until Saturday evening Franklin was on sentry duty and street patrol about the town. On Saturday evening he marched to Ferns with the column of Volunteers and did not return until Sunday night after the surrender. Back at the Athenaeum he helped with the collection of weapons and ammunition. Franklin was arrested the following day and deported shortly afterwards. He was interned in Stafford Jail and Frongach Camp before he was released in early July.

On his release and return to Enniscorthy, Franklin was dismissed from his job at the Gas Works. He remained unemployed for over a year before obtaining work in The Co-op. He re-joined the Volunteers in 1917. While working at The Co-op, Franklin made a small dump behind the building to store arms. On the 22nd of March 1922, Franklin was arrested by Captain Yeo and members of the Devonshire's. His name was found on a list that had been confiscated off a captured I.R.A. officer. He was held for three weeks and while in custody was beaten on a regular basis. The military also used Franklin as a hostage, parading him around the town on the back of a lorry three times a week. Upon his release Franklin suffered from ill health due to the beatings he had received and took no further part in active duties. John Franklin died at the age of 49 in 1943.

Seán Gallagher (The Shannon) A Company. Seán Gallagher joined the Volunteers at their inception in 1913. There is not a lot of information about Gallagher's Easter Week service in the archives. What we do know is that on the first day of the Rising he took up a sniping position on the Turret Rocks and fired on the R.I.C. barracks. He also accompanied Patrick Keegan to Edermine that morning. From then we are unaware what he did until he marched to Ferns with the column of Volunteers on Saturday evening. He remained in Ferns until the surrender and then returned to Enniscorthy. Gallagher was arrested the following Sunday and deported shortly afterwards. He was interned in Wakefield and Frongach Camp before he was released in December.

Gallagher re-joined in 1917 and took part in general Volunteer activities. In 1918 he transferred to a Company in Carlow and was arrested for carrying illegal documents soon after. He was jailed for five years but was released in June 1919. Gallagher was appointed Commandant of the Carlow Brigade and took an active role in an attack on the R.I.C. barracks in Baltinglass in January 1920, after which he went on the run. The following September Gallagher was sent to Cavan by G.H.Q. in Dublin to help organise and train Company's in the county. He used the alias of Mulligan during this period. In April 1921 he was arrested for weapons possession and sentence to ten years. This sentence was under his assumed name, and he was released in January 1922. Gallagher enlisted in the National Army on its formation and played a prominent role in the "Battle of Enniscorthy" after the Civil War broke out. He was the commander of the Free State soldiers who occupied the Castle on the 30th of June 1922. It was between there and St. Marys Church that shooting suddenly erupted on the evening of Sunday the 2nd of July. The fighting was intense and lasted until the Wednesday evening. When the Free State soldiers in the old R.I.C. Barracks surrendered, Gallagher and his men soon followed and once their weapons were taken from them, they were given safe passage from the town.

After the Civil War Gallagher remained in the army until 1926. The following year he was appointed as Town Clerk of Enniscorthy and served in this position until 1939. In the early 1940's Gallagher moved to England and took up a position with the British Admiralty. Seán Gallagher died in Castle Bromwich, Warwickshire in 1965, he was 70 years of age.

Peter Galligan (Cavan) Vice Commandant A Company. Peter Galligan was sent to Enniscorthy in November 1915 by Tomas McDonagh following a fallout between the local leadership over the Volunteers attending dances. Company Commandant William Brennan Whitmore argued that the Volunteers should not be spending their money on such frivolous activity and instead should be using the money to buy weapons. Galligan handed his letter of introduction to Seamus Rafter who had replaced Whitmore as Commandant. He obtained a job in Bolger's on Georges Street (Rafter St.) under an alias. Shortly afterwards he organised an officer class for twenty chosen Volunteers. These classes were held in "Antwerp" on weekday evenings, at weekends Galligan brought the class to the country for practical work.

With confusion reigning on Easter Saturday, Galligan made his way to Dublin to try and learn the true facts of the situation. After he was told the Rising was off and then reading the order from Eoin McNeill in the Sunday Independent, he was convinced nothing was going to happen. On Easter Monday Galligan went to Dalkey with some friends and it was there he heard that things had kicked off in the city centre. He made his way to O'Connell Street and reported to an outpost, there, to his great surprise he found Brennan Whitmore in charge. Whitmore ordered an officer to accompany Galligan to the G.P.O. where he met with Pádraig Pearse, Joseph Mary Plunkett and James Connolly. Galligan received orders from Connolly that Enniscorthy was to be held. At the break of day on Tuesday Galligan left the G.P.O. on a bicycle for Enniscorthy. By nightfall he had reached Tinahely and rested for the night. He continued his journey on Wednesday and arrived in Enniscorthy that night. After briefing the officers, they came to the decision to mobilise.

On Thursday morning Galligan addressed the Volunteers assembled on Irish Street before the marched to the Athenaeum. After a H.Q. had been established there, Galligan was placed in charge of field operations. He organised outposts on the town's outskirts, had the banks closed and locked and confiscated the keys of many of the pubs. He remained at H.Q. throughout until word came on Saturday of a possible British military advance from Arklow. Galligan picked a column of fifty men and marched with them to Ferns. On their arrival they went to the R.I.C. barracks which was now the Volunteer H.Q. in the village. Some of the men were placed on duty while others were sent to the National School next door to rest. On Sunday morning when the car carrying Pádraig Pearse's surrender letter arrived, Galligan read the letter with some disbelief. He then ordered the car be escorted to Enniscorthy.

After Seamus Doyle and Seán Etchingham arrived back from Dublin that night with confirmation of the surrender, Galligan ordered his men back to Enniscorthy. Galligan was a passenger in the second last car to leave the village. When they came to a junction in the road, the driver took a wrong turn and drove the car over a ditch into a field, landing it on its roof. Galligan was unharmed but a member of Cumann na mBan and three Volunteers travelling with him were injured. He helped carry the woman to a nearby farmhouse and waited with her while some Volunteers went to Newtownbarry (Bunclody) to get a doctor. It was 8 a.m. Monday morning by the time Galligan arrived to find a deserted Athenaeum. A member of Cumann na mBan gave him the key to a house belonging to her brother-in-law for him to rest and hide in. Galligan remained there until Tuesday night then he set off for Carlow by bicycle. He stayed in Carlow until Thursday and then made his way via Mullingar to his home in Cavan, arriving on the Saturday. On the following Monday morning Galligan awoke to find his house surrounded by the R.I.C.. He surrendered immediately and was brought to Kilmainham Jail. There he was Court-martialled and sentenced to five years. He was then shipped to Dartmoor Prison and from there to Pentonville Jail where he was held until the following June. On his release Galligan moved back to Cavan and helped organise Company's there and in Leitrim up until The Truce. In later years he owned and operated a successful drapery shop in Dublin. Peter Galligan was 76 years old when he died in 1966.

James Garrett (Templeshannon) A Company. A native of Kilkenny, James Garrett joined the Volunteers in Enniscorthy in 1915 while employed as a shop assistant in Donohue's hardware. A couple of months before the Insurrection he passed on information to his commanding officers regarding a large shipment of gunpowder and cartridges which was due to arrive in the shop. A party of Volunteers intercepted the shipment at the railway and made off with it. Before marching to the Athenaeum on the first morning of the Rising, Garrett was ordered to go to Donohue's with a group of Volunteers and commandeer guns. On their return they stored the weapons in Keegan's.

After the H.Q. had been established at the Athenaeum, Garrett was a member of the firing party who fired three shots in salute after the Tricolour had been raised above the building. Later he was given a verbal dispatch and ordered to go to New Ross, this dispatch was to tell the Volunteers there to come to Enniscorthy. On Friday, Garrett was tasked with blocking the railway line on the Dublin side of the station. The next day he participated in raids for arms throughout the district and that night did outpost duty at Blackstoops.

On Sunday Garrett carried out sentry duty around the town until the surrender. He was arrested in Donohue's the following Tuesday and deported shortly afterwards. He was interned in Stafford Jail and Frongach Camp before he was released in September. On his return to Enniscorthy Garrett applied for his former job but was turned down. He then went home to Kilkenny. Garrett found work in Portadown in 1917 and joined the local Volunteer Company there. He served with this Company up to The Truce. James Garrett was aged 84 when he died in 1975.

James Gleeson (Gorey) Gorey Company. James Gleeson was one of six Volunteers who came to Enniscorthy under the command of Seán Etchingham. They arrived at "Antwerp" at 2 a.m. on the morning before the Insurrection began. The men remained there until the following morning, then they made their way to the Athenaeum once the action had begun. Gleeson remained at H.Q. until Saturday morning, then he was sent with a dispatch to Gorey, returning on Sunday morning. After the surrender he went on the run for a fortnight and evaded arrest. Gleeson re-joined in 1917 and served up until The Truce. At the outbreak of Civil War he chose the Republican side. James Gleeson died in 1977 in his 88th year.

Henry Goff (The Shannon) C Company. Henry Goff joined the Volunteers in 1914. On the morning of the Rising he marched with the main body of Volunteers from Irish Street to the Athenaeum. Goff served at various locations around the town before marching to Ferns on Saturday evening with the column of Volunteers. After the surrender he went on the run and avoided arrest. Goff re-joined in 1917 and took part in many raids across the district for arms. In 1918 he was a member of the party of Volunteers sent to Waterford to protect Sinn Féin officials and canvassers during the Bye Election.

Over the following years Goff participated in raids at the railway for petrol, Donohue's for magnetos and Davis's foundry where he worked, for materials used in the manufacture of munitions. As a result of the latter action Goff was arrested in early 1921 and sentenced to a year in jail. He was released that December. Goff joined the National Army in early 1922 and after completing training was placed in command of the barracks in Gorey. With tensions running high over the Treaty and just before the split in the army, Goff handed over a number of rifles and ammunition to the I.R.A. After the split he left Gorey and joined the I.R.A. garrison in the courthouse in Enniscorthy. Once the "Battle of Enniscorthy" broke out in July, Goff played an active part in the fighting. As the Free State Army retook the town, he was one of the I.R.A. men who set fire to the courthouse before escaping to the country. He went on the run for a couple of months before returning to take up employment. Over the last few months of the Civil War Goff passed on intelligence to various flying columns. He received this intelligence from a source in the Free State barracks. Henry Goff died in 1961 at the age of 62.

James Goodall (Maudlin's Folly) A Company. James Goodall joined the Volunteers in 1913. He reported for duty to the Keegan house on Irish Street at 4 a.m. on the first morning of the Rising and then marched with the main body of men to the Athenaeum. After a H.Q. was established, Goodall was ordered to go to the entrance of the Enniscorthy Asylum and take up outpost duty. After he was relieved, he returned to the Athenaeum and had something to eat before he was sent to Blackstoops for the remainder of the day. On Friday morning Goodall was detailed to the Wexford Road for outpost duty, that afternoon, he was placed on sentry duty on Main Street. Goodall took part in the recruiting parade around the town on Saturday afternoon before marching to Ferns with the column of Volunteers.

Once in Ferns he took up sentry duty at the top of the village. The next morning Goodall commandeered a car and brought it to the R.I.C. barracks in the village. He was then ordered to take up outpost duty on the Camolin Road. While there he encountered the car containing D.I. Drake and Father Kehoe with Pádraig Pearse's surrender letter. Goodall placed them under arrest and brought them back to the barracks, there he handed them over to Peter Galligan. He then returned to his post. After the surrender Goodall returned to Enniscorthy and handed in his weapon. He was arrested the following Tuesday and deported shortly afterwards. Goodall was interned in Stafford Jail and Frongach Camp before he was released in early July. Goodall re-joined in 1917 and participated in the general activities of his Company. When his brother was arrested in November 1920, Goodall resigned from his Company to look after their elderly mother. James Goodall passed away at the age of 83 in 1978.

Joseph Goodall (Maudlin's Folly) A Company. Joseph Goodall was James Goodall's younger brother. He joined the Volunteers at their inception in 1913. On the morning of the Insurrection he marched from Irish Street to the Athenaeum with the main body of Volunteers. After a H.Q. had been established he was sent to Georges Street (Rafter St.) on sentry duty. When Goodall was relieved he had something to eat in the Athenaeum and was then posted to The Duffry. From there he was sent to the top of Slaney Street before he finished his days duty on the outpost at Summerhill Cross. He slept in the Athenaeum that night. On Friday, Goodall spent the day on duty between St. John's Street and Friary Hill.

The following morning he was back on St. John's Street and later at Blackstoops Cross.

After he was recalled to H.Q. that evening, Goodall marched with the column of Volunteers to Ferns. On his arrival he was ordered to take up a position at the top of Ferns Castle where he remained until morning. Once relieved, he rested for a few hours in the R.I.C. barracks before returning to duty on the Camolin Road. After the surrender was announced, Goodall marched back to Enniscorthy and handed in his rifle and ammunition. He evaded capture by going on the run for three weeks before returning to his home.

In 1917 Goodall re-joined the organisation and for the better part of a year spent most evenings in "Antwerp" making munitions. Over the next couple of years he was involved in several raids for arms and equipment. Goodall was arrested on the 8th of November 1920 and charged with.

Driving a motor car for the wilful and unlawful murder of D.I. Lea Wilson at Gorey.

The car used for the killing had been left in Graiguenamanagh and Goodall's only role was collecting it and bringing it back to Enniscorthy. He spent over a year in Mountjoy before he was released in December 1921. At the outbreak of the Civil War, Goodall took the Republican side and fought in the "Battle of Enniscorthy". Later he was used as a driver to bring dispatches and supplies to various flying columns. Joseph Goodall died in 1980 at the age of 83.

Mary Grey (Tomduff) Cumann na mBan. Mary Grey was one of the first women to join Cumann na mBan on its formation in Enniscorthy in 1914. She reported for duty to the Athenaeum on the first morning of the Rising and was tasked with setting up beds and making stretchers. After this she was sent to the kitchen to help with the catering. Grey remained in the Athenaeum all night. On Friday morning she went home to rest and then reported back to H.Q. for several hours of duty before going home again that night. On Saturday Grey was placed in charge of laundry while on Sunday she carried out general duties until the surrender. In the years leading up to The Truce she participated in the routine activities of her Cumann and afterwards played no part in the Civil War. Mary Grey died in 1941 at the age of 63.

Harry Habernatty (The Shannon) C Company. Prior to joining the Volunteers in 1914, Henry Habernatty had been a Special Reserve in the British Army for four years. On the first morning of the Rising he took up a sniping position on the Turret Rocks overlooking the R.I.C. barracks. His orders were to only fire when fired upon and to try and preserve ammunition. From approximately 8 a.m. until mid-afternoon Habernatty stated he fired twelve to fourteen rounds (Military Service Pensions Board statement on the 21st of May 1936). He was relieved that evening and returned to the Athenaeum for something to eat and a rest. From then up until the surrender Habernatty's time was spent on outpost and sentry duties. After the surrender he reported back to H.Q. shortly after midnight and handed in his weapon.

Habernatty was arrested a few days later and deported shortly afterwards. He was interned in Lewes Jail and Frongach Camp before he was released in December. Once the Volunteers resumed in 1917 Habernatty re-joined and played a prominent role in activities up until The Truce. He raided for arms at Webster's of Finchogue, Hayes's of Greenmount, Kavanagh's of Drumgoold and Kings of Kilbride. He took part in raids for petrol at the railway, for magnetos at Donoghue's as well as munitions making materials from Davis's foundry. Although Habernatty could neither read nor write, he was well able to speak up for himself when he appeared before the Military Service Pensions Board in May 1936. Reading the transcript you cannot help but come away with the impression the board was deliberately trying to trip him up with their questioning. However, Habernatty was definitive in his answering regarding the duties he had carried out. Henry Habernatty died at the age of 74 in 1956.

Stephen Hayes (Court Street) Na Fianna Éireann. Stephen Hayes was just 13 years old when he reported for duty at the Athenaeum on the first morning of the Rising. There he was handed dispatches to deliver to various positions. After this he delivered food to the old R.I.C. barracks on Court Street, which the Volunteers had taken over and established a Republican police force under the command of Larry de Lacey. Hayes carried out this task for the duration of the Rising. On Friday he was sent on a scouting mission to the Killurin Road to verify intelligence that the British forces were using that route from Wexford. The intelligence was false.

Hayes was instructed to watch the homes of two prominent local business families, the Copelands and Earls in Monart on Saturday, to see if they were in contact with the authorities. After the surrender on Sunday night, Hayes was given a quantity of revolvers to hide, he brought them to his brother's house in Tomnalosset where they were stored until the reorganisation in 1917. In 1917 Hayes re-joined Na Fianna and by the summer of 1921 he was Brigade O/C. He took the Republican side during the Civil War and fought in both Enniscorthy and Ferns in July 1922. He was arrested later that month and imprisoned until the following June. Stephen Hayes died at the age of 72 in 1974.

James Healy (Irish Street) A Company. James Healy had been a member of the I.R.B. since 1911 when he joined the Volunteers at their inception in 1913. Healy was one of four volunteers assigned to lift rails off the tracks between Enniscorthy and Edermine at the Boro Bridge the night before the Rising. This was to prevent military reinforcements from arriving from Wexford once the Volunteers rose up the following morning. The men walked in twos, a short distance between them, Healy was at the front with William Boyne. As they proceeded to lift the rails, an R.I.C. patrol came upon them. A brief firefight erupted in which Healy later claimed to have fired five shots. He and his companion Boyne, bid a hasty retreat but one of the other Volunteers, John Tomkins, took a wrong turn and ended up being captured. The remaining three decided to go back to town and inform the leadership of what had happened. While crossing a field on their way back, Healy lost his footing and fell awkwardly, resulting in him breaking two of his ribs. His two comrades helped him to the local hospital beside the County Home, where he remained for over a week.

On the 6th of May the R.I.C. entered the hospital and dragged Healy from his bed and arrested him. With his ribs still not set properly, he was deported a short time later and was interned in Wakefield Prison and then Frongach Camp. Healy did not receive medical attention in either place, although in Frongach he was excluded from any chores. He was released the following December. Healy re-joined in 1917 but took no further role in any military activities due to ill health. James Healy died at his home in St. Aidan's Villas in 1956 aged 75.

Mary Ellen Hearne (Ross Road) Cumann na mBan. May Hearne (nee Murphy) joined Cumann na mBan in 1915. On the first morning of the Rising she was called from her house on the Ross Road and went to Keegan's, there she helped to hand out weapons to the assembled Volunteers. Hearne then followed the column to the Athenaeum. After a H.Q. had been established she was sent with a party of Volunteers to commandeer bedding and food. On her return, Hearne went to the kitchen and helped prepare meals for the men. After spending the night at H.Q. she was sent on Friday morning to commandeer fish and other foodstuffs. The following day she was sent with a dispatch and claimed she was fired upon by the R.I.C. in the barracks as she completed this task. Early on Sunday morning while in the Billiard room in the Athenaeum, Hearne was grazed on the neck by a rifle bullet which had been accidentaly discharged by a Volunteer. She remained at H.Q. after the surrender and helped to pack munitions.

In the following days before her Volunteer brothers, John and James Murphy Jr. were arrested, they told her where they had hidden their weapons and instructed her to remove them and hide them securely. One night three weeks later she went to the hiding place but discovered that she was unable to carry all the weapons and ammunition together. In all it took her three nights to remove everything to safety. Over the following months Hearne helped to raise funds for dependant families and sent food parcels to the prisoners. In 1918 she participated in concerts and plays which travelled the county to raise funds for the Volunteers. In 1919 Hearne suffered a serious illness which meant a lengthy stay in hospital and an inability to work for over three years. Due to these circumstances she ceased her Cumann activity. Mary Ellen "May" Hearne died in 1986 at the age of 89.

Thomas Hearne (Springvalley) A Company. Thomas Hearne had been a member of the I.R.B. before he joined the Volunteers in 1914. On Easter Sunday morning he went to play a Gaelic football match believing he would be taking up arms on his return. When he arrived back in the afternoon he learnt that the impending uprising had been cancelled. Seamus Rafter gave him a verbal message for an officer outside the district. Hearne cycled with this message and passed it on before arriving back later that night. He went to work as normal on Easter Monday but was called at 4 a.m. on Tuesday morning and told to report to Rafter. Rafter then gave him a verbal message to pass on to the Volunteer leader in New Ross, a man named Phil Lennon. The message was for the New Ross Company to be prepared to come to Enniscorthy at a moment's notice. Hearne cycled to New Ross armed with a revolver and passed on the message, but on his return journey the chain on his bike snapped. He did not make it home until late into the night.

On the first morning of the Rising Hearne reported to the Athenaeum, he was instructed to go on a scouting mission along the railway tracks to see if there was any sign of the British. After he reported back he had some breakfast and was then ordered to Castle Hill to take up a sniping position. According to his testimony before the Military Service Pensions Board on the 3rd of March 1937, Hearne observed two R.I.C. men attempting to leave the barracks and fired four shots at them, the men retreated back into the barracks. On Friday he was sent with the party of Volunteers assigned to blow up the Edermine bridge. Failing to do so, they felled trees and blocked both entrances to the bridge. Hearne then returned to the Athenaeum and spent the night there. For the rest of the weekend he was placed on guard duty at various locations and carried dispatches. Following the surrender Hearne escaped to the country and stayed there for three weeks.

Not long after he returned Hearne was arrested for the attempted murder of a Mr. Owens from Carley's bridge. He was held for three days before he was released. It had been a case of mistaken identity; it was actually Hearne's brother who had accidently shot at the gentleman. In 1917 Hearne went to England for several months. On his return to Enniscorthy he re-joined the Volunteers. From that time up to The Truce his activities were confined to delivering dispatches. Hearne took no part in the Civil War. Thomas Hearne died aged 69 at his home on the Ross Road in 1964.

Thomas Heavey (St. John's Street) A Company. Thomas Heavey joined the Volunteers in 1914. On the first morning of the Rising he was sent to Roche's Grain Store on the Abbey Square. From there he was able to observe the R.I.C. barracks on the opposite side of the Square while the Volunteers were establishing a H.Q. in the Athenaeum and snipers were taking their positions on the Turret Rocks. Heavey remained there until the firing broke out and then made his way to the Athenaeum. His next assignment that day was to take up sentry duty on St. John's Street. After he was relieved he returned to H.Q. and slept. The next morning a report was received at H.Q. that a group of R.I.C. men had gathered in the manor house at Borrmount. Heavey was instructed to go and investigate whether this report was true. He returned later to inform the leadership that it wasn't.

On Saturday along with another Volunteer, Heavey was sent on a scouting mission along the New Ross Road. They made it as far as the outskirts of Clonroche when they spotted an R.I.C. advance party from New Ross in the village. They watched for a short while before reporting back to the Athenaeum with this information. Heavey spent Sunday morning on sentry duty at the Duffry Gate, and after a break took up guard duty outside the Munster and Leinster Bank at the top of Slaney Street. While there, Heavey placed the manager of the Bank under arrest for being obstreperous with members of the guard. After the surrender he helped to load vehicles with weapons and ammunition that were then taken away and hidden. Heavey was arrested the following day and spent three weeks in Richmond Barracks in Dublin before he was released.

On the reorganisation in 1917 Heavey re-joined and was a regular participant in Company activities. During the General Election of 1918 he was sent to Wexford to help control the ex-British soldiers who were disrupting Sinn Féin rally's and trying to intimidate voters. In 1920 he participated in several raids including the one for petrol at the railway. Not long after this he was arrested by the Devonshire's and held in the courthouse for seven weeks. Upon his release he was involved in a raid on the Enniscorthy Asylum for Rate Books. After The Truce Heavey acted as a Republican policeman in the town and on one occasion, with another, arrested two robbers and tied them to the Cathedral's gates. At the outbreak of the Civil War he chose the Anti-Treaty side and joined the garrison in the courthouse on the 2nd of July 1922, the day the "Battle of Enniscorthy" began. Heavey fired on the castle from the roof of the courthouse the following day. When the town was retaken by the Free State Army, Heavey was prohibited by his senior officers from joining up with a column due to the fact he had a large family to look after. Once order had been restored in the town, Heavey lost his job and shortly after caught Pneumonia, he played no further part. Thomas Heavey died in 1956 at the age of 59.

Nicholas Hendrick (New Street) Na Fianna Éireann. Nicholas Hendrick was 15 years old when he reported for duty to the Athenaeum on the Thursday evening of the Rising. He was handed a shotgun and ordered to take up a position on the Shannon Quay to cover the R.I.C. barracks. Hendrick remained there until 4 a.m. Friday morning. On Friday he accompanied the party of Volunteers to Edermine on their mission to destroy the bridge there. Hendrick acted as a scout and look out at Borrmount Cross. On Saturday morning he helped commandeer milk and clothing, while in the afternoon he carried out guard duty on Court Street near D.I. Hegarty's house. For the remainder of the Rising, Hendrick acted as an orderly for Seamus Rafter. He was present in the Athenaeum for the surrender on Sunday night and avoided arrest over the following days due to his young age.

Hendrick joined The Shannon Company in 1917 and participated in general Volunteer activities. In 1918 Hendrick was sent to Waterford for the Bye- Election and later that year to Wexford for the General Election. In between these two events he carried dispatches for Seamus Rafter to and from New Ross on a number of occasions. In 1919 Hendrick participated in several raids for arms. The following year he was shot in the hand by a comrade when he accidentally discharged his revolver. After The Truce Hendrick played no further role. Nicholas Hendrick died aged 71 in 1972.

William Hendrick (New Street) A Company. William Hendrick was the older brother of Nicholas Hendrick.. He joined the Volunteers in 1914. On the first morning of the Insurrection he marched with the main body of men from Irish Street to the Athenaeum. While the H.Q. was being established, he took up guard duty at the top of Castle Hill. Later, along with another Volunteer, Hendrick was instructed to go to Lett's Brewery at the bottom of Friary Hill for sentry duty. While there they exchanged fire with the R.I.C. men barricaded in the Bank of Ireland. On Friday, Hendrick spent the day on outpost duty at Salville Cross. That night he accompanied Peter Galligan as he inspected outposts at various locations. Hendrick was a member of the party of Volunteers who occupied the Protestant Institute on Church Street on Saturday morning. He remained there until the following morning. After resting in the Athenaeum, Hendrick returned to duty on Sunday evening and took up a sentry position on the corner of the Market Square and Georges Street (Rafter St.). He was recalled to H.Q. for the surrender and then he helped with the collection and disposal of weapons. Hendrick was arrested the next day and deported shortly afterwards. He was interned in Stafford Jail and Frongach Camp until he was released in August.

Hendrick re-joined in 1917 and participated in the general activities of his Company. He was sent to Waterford and Wexford during the two separate elections of 1918. A butcher by trade, Hendrick had contracts with the Enniscorthy Asylum and the County Home. On several occasions he used this premise to transport arms on his horse and cart to various locations. After The Truce he played no further role in any military activities. William Hendrick died at Parkton Nursing Home on New Year's Eve 1959; he was 62 years old.

Annie Heneghan (Duffry Street) Cumann na mBan. Annie Heneghan (nee Cardiff) joined Cumann na mBan in 1915. On the first morning of the Rising she reported for duty to H.Q. at the Athenaeum. She was assigned to the dressing station and remained there all day. On Friday she helped in the kitchen and later that day went to Ferns with other members of her Cumann. Heneghan cooked and cleaned at the R.I.C. barracks in the village until the surrender on Sunday. In the years following the Rising, Heneghan took part in the routine activities of her Cumann as well as participating in concerts to raise funds. She also carried out election work in 1918. Throughout the years 1920-1921 her house was raided regularly as the Black and Tans searched for her Volunteer brother Joseph Cardiff. After Volunteers were arrested and imprisoned in the courthouse, Heneghan cooked and brought food to them on a daily basis. In the summer of 1921 she had to cease all her activity due to illness. Annie Heneghan died in 1944 at the age of 44.

William Hiney (Templeshannon) C Company. William Hiney served in both Enniscorthy and Ferns during Easter Week 1916. However there is not a lot of information in the archives about what duties he carried out. What we do know about Hiney is that he re-joined in 1917 and played an active role in several of his Company's major operations, such as the raid for petrol at the railway, the raid for magnetos at Donohue's and the attack on the R.I.C. barracks in Enniscorthy. Hiney also participated in the raid for munitions material and equipment at Davis's foundry and was involved afterwards in transporting said material to the foundry in Corrageen. From late 1920 until 1922 Hiney acted as the primary driver for Brigade H.Q.. After The Truce he joined the National Army at Beggars Bush and served throughout the Civil War. William Hiney moved to Drogheda and died there in 1964 aged 67.

Matthew Holbrook (The Shannon) A Company. Matthew Holbrook had been a member of the I.R.B. for a number of years before he joined the Volunteers at their inception in 1913. For three weeks prior to the Rising he was at "The Dump" on a daily basis making buckshot. On Wednesday evening, the day before the Insurrection, Holbrook was sent to Wexford with a verbal dispatch to the leaders there "...*to have the fellows ready.*". (Military Service Pensions Board interview on the 10th of May 1937) After the mobilisation on the Thursday morning he played a leading role in the organising and transfer of munitions from "The Dump" to the Athenaeum. Holbrook claimed to have fired on the R.I.C. barracks from the vantage point of Bennett's Hotel on the Saturday, as well as doing outpost duty throughout the period. After the surrender Holbrook and a few others brought a large quantity of weapons and munitions to an undisclosed location in the country. They spent two days there burying and concealing these items before returning to the town. Holbrook was arrested the next day and deported shortly afterwards. He was interned in Stafford Jail and Frongach Camp before he was released in December.

After the reorganisation in 1917, Holbrook handed the weapons he had hidden over to Patrick Keegan greased and cleaned. During the War of Independence he was appointed Brigade Captain of Engineers and was responsible for the munition's factory in Corrageen. Along with carrying out those duties, Holbrook played an active part in military operations as well, which included the ambush of a military train at Killurin. At the outbreak of Civil War, Holbrook joined the Republican garrison in the courthouse and participated in the "Battle of Enniscorthy." After the Free State Army retook the town, Holbrook joined a flying column headed by Robert Lambert. He was arrested at the end of August 1922 and imprisoned until Christmas 1923. Matthew Holbrook died in his 80th year in 1954.

Patrick J. Howlin (Killagoley) A Company. Patrick Howlin worked as an office clerk in Donohue's hardware when he joined the Volunteers in 1913. On the first morning of the Rising he reported for duty to the Athenaeum at 8 a.m.. His first assignment of the day was to transfer munitions from "The Dump" to the newly established H.Q.. He was then sent on outpost duty. On Friday morning Howlin was detailed to the Dublin Road for outpost duty, that evening he was sent to the Wexford Road for similar duty and spent the night there. After resting on Saturday morning, Howlin marched with the column of Volunteers to Ferns that evening. He returned to Enniscorthy on Sunday evening and was present for the announcement of the surrender in the Athenaeum. Afterwards he helped with loading the munitions that were taken away and hidden.

Howlin evaded arrest and helped with organising aid for the men interned and their families up until that Christmas. He re-joined in 1917 and continued with the general activities of a Volunteer. He also assisted with the political side of the movement. In April 1919 Howlin was appointed Battalion Quartermaster. He was involved in the raid on the railway station for petrol and the burning of the R.I.C. barracks in Blackwater in May 1920. The following month, the car that Howlin co-owned with James Cullen was used for the assassination of D.I. Lea

Wilson in Gorey. A few weeks after that killing he had to resign as Quartermaster due to ill health.

Howlin would never fully recover his health and over the next decade would be bedridden for a significant amount of time every year. After been diagnosed with Tuberculosis, Howlin went to a Sanatorium in Davos Switzerland in 1931. The cost of which was funded by himself and relatives in Ireland and America. He remained there for sixteen months. On his return, Howlin was broke and could only work intermittingly. He applied for the Military Service Pension in August 1935 and was awarded it on the 20th of July 1938. Unfortunately Patrick Howlin had died exactly a month previously on the 20th of June. He was 50 years of age.

John Hughes (The Shannon) C Company. A member of the Volunteers since 1914, John Hughes spent every night from Easter Sunday to the morning of the Rising at "Antwerp". Early on Thursday morning he went to Irish Street and joined the Volunteers assembled outside the Keegan house and marched with them to the Athenaeum. His first duty that day was outpost duty at Drumgoold Cross. He spent several hours there before he was ordered to take up a sniping position on the Turret Rocks. Over the course of an hour Hughes fired five to six rounds at the R.I.C. barracks across the river. (Military Service Pensions Board interview on the 29th of November 1938) He then returned to Drumgoold Cross and resumed outpost duty. Later that evening he helped to fell trees for use as roadblocks. On Friday, Hughes spent the day on sentry duty between Drumgoold Cross and Templeshannon. After participating in the recruiting parade around the town on Saturday evening he marched to Ferns with the column of Volunteers. Once there he took up guard duty at the Volunteer H.Q. in the abandoned R.I.C. barracks.

Following the surrender Hughes returned to the Athenaeum late on Sunday night. He helped with the collection and loading of arms and munitions before going on the run and avoiding arrest. In 1917 Hughes re-joined his Company and took part in all general Volunteer activities up to The Truce. When the Civil war broke out he chose the Republican side. Hughes was stationed in Bennetts Hotel throughout the "Battle of Enniscorthy". He fired several times at Free State soldiers on the roof of the Castle and at the former R.I.C. barracks which was their H.Q.. Hughes left the town after the Free State Army regained control but had to return home a few days later due to ill health. He had no further service. John Hughes died at his residence on the Rectory Road at the age of 68 in 1941.

Joseph Hyland (The Shannon) C Company. Joseph Hyland joined the Volunteers in 1913, he was already a member of the I.R.B.. On the first morning of the Insurrection he went from "Antwerp" to Irish Street and took up guard duty in the Cathedral grounds overlooking "The Dump" at the back of the Keegan house. He remained there until 10 a.m. when he was sent to the Wexford Road to help build roadblocks. Once finished there, Hyland took up outpost duty at Clonhaston Cross from where he was relieved at midnight. After carrying out a couple of hours guard duty at the top of Castle Hill he slept in the Athenaeum. On Friday, Hyland was tasked with blocking roads and raiding for arms in the Ballycarney area. He spent Saturday blocking roads between Blackstoops and The Moyne before raiding for arms in Kiltrea and Templescoby. After the column of Volunteers left for Ferns that evening, Hyland carried out street patrol around the town. On Sunday he was placed on outpost duty at Blackstoops and later at Davis's Mill. He was recalled to the Athenaeum after the surrender and given five rifles to look after. (Hyland kept these rifles until 1919, then he handed four of them over, greased and cleaned to Patrick Keegan.) Hyland evaded arrest and re-joined in 1917. He carried out general Volunteer activities up to The Truce and did not participate in the Civil War. Joseph Hyland died aged 82 in 1957.

Matthew Hyland (Drumgoold) C Company. Matthew Hyland joined the Volunteers in 1914. On the morning of the Rising he marched with the main body of men from Irish Street to the Athenaeum. From there he was sent to Red Pat's Cross for outpost duty. He remained there for a few hours before he was ordered to go to the Turret Rocks and take up a sniping position. According to his testimony before the Military Service Pensions Board on the 29th of November 1938, Hyland fired approximately a dozen rounds at the R.I.C. barracks over a two-hour period. He was then sent to Drumgoold Cross for outpost duty. On Friday, Hyland commandeered coal from O'Neill's yard on the Mill Park Road and flour from Davis's Mill. The following day he was on guard duty at various locations around the town. When the surrender was announced on Sunday night, Hyland was recalled from the corner of Georges Street (Rafter St.) and Church Street to the Athenaeum. He handed in his rifle and then waited around outside for a while before going home. He was arrested later in the week and deported shortly afterwards. Hyland was interned in Lewes Jail before he was released in July. Hyland re-joined in 1917 and participated in Company activities up to The Truce. He was not involved in the Civil War. Matthew Hyland died in 1965 at the age of 69.

Patrick Johnson (Templeshannon) C Company. Patrick Johnson joined the Volunteers at their inception in 1913. He went from "Antwerp" to Irish Street on the first morning of the Rising and marched with the main body of Volunteers to the Athenaeum. From there he was ordered to go to St. John's Cross and assume guard duty. After several hours there Johnson was detailed to the Turret Rocks and took up a sniping position. A couple of hours later he was sent to commandeer a boiler from Lambert's hardware for use in the kitchen of the Athenaeum. Afterwards he delivered messages to the outposts at Blackstoops and Bellefield. Johnson spent Friday on outpost duty at Davis's Mill and then at Killagoley. On Saturday he took part in the recruiting parade around the town before marching to Ferns with the column of Volunteers under the command of Peter Galligan. Once there, Johnson was assigned sentry duty in the village. After the surrender he returned to Enniscorthy and handed in his rifle. He evaded arrest and re-joined in 1917. Up until The

Truce he participated in general Volunteer activities. Patrick Johnson died in 1959 at the age of 77.

James Jordan (Ballindaggin) A Company. James Jordan joined the Volunteers in 1913. During Easter Week he lifted rails from the tracks, cut telegraph wires, raided for arms and fired a shot at the R.I.C. barracks. Jordan was arrested on the 4th of May and deported shortly afterwards. He was interned in Stafford Jail before he was released in August. In 1917 Jordan joined the Ballindaggin Company and participated in several operations including the attack on Clonroche R.I.C. barracks and the burning of the barracks in Killane. During the Civil War he served with the Free State Army. James Jordan died in Monbeg, Ballindaggin in 1944 aged 68.

Michael Jordan (Market Square) A Company. Michael Jordan joined the Volunteers in February 1916. On the first morning of the Rising he marched with the main body of men to the Athenaeum. From there along with another Volunteer he was sent to the homes of Samuel Armstrong and Dr. Boyce on the Mill Park Road to raid for arms. They succeeded in obtaining some rifles, revolvers and shotguns before returning to the Athenaeum. Jordan then went to his father's shop on the Market Square and commandeered some cheese and tea. He then raided Val Murphy's shop which was also on the Square for clothing. (When he had been released from detention after the Rising his father would not let Jordan into the house until he got a receipt from Murphy for the clothing taken. His father then wrote a cheque for twenty-five pounds to reimburse him.) On Thursday night Jordan was assigned sentry duty at the top of New Street. (Wafer St.)

Between guard duty on the Friday, outside the Protestant Institute and the Provincial Bank, Jordan raided for bedding in Greene's of Georges Street (Rafter St.) He finished his day on sentry duty at the top of Slaney Street. On Saturday Jordan was sent to see the Reverend Mother in the Mercy Convent to ask for her permission to take over their laundry, which overlooked the R.I.C. barracks on the opposite side of the river. The Reverend Mother replied that she would need to get permission from her Mother Superior in Wexford, but she would prefer if they did not. On Sunday morning Jordan was on sentry duty on The Duffry and after a rest he was posted to the bottom of Irish Street where he remained until (as he said in his statement before the Military Service Pensions Board on the 5th of June 1940) *"a little fellow came around with a bugle and we went back then to the Athenaeum around half nine."* Jordan went to his father's shop and retrieved some empty tea chests so they could be filled with ammunition and taken away. He was arrested the following Tuesday and released a fortnight later due to his age.

Jordan re-joined in 1917 and carried out general Volunteer activities. In 1918 he was involved in the Elections in Waterford and Wexford. While working in his father's pub in 1920, he entered into conversation with some British soldiers who ended up selling him revolvers and ammunition. Jordan passed these guns on to the I.R.A.. During the Civil War he chose the Republican side, although he did not participate in any military activities, he supplied food to the garrison in the courthouse throughout the "Battle of Enniscorthy." Over the following months he was able to pass on information he overheard about proposed raids on certain houses from Free State soldiers in his pub. Michael Jordan died a week before his 71st birthday in 1969.

Sarah Jordan (Court Street) Cumann na mBan. Sarah Jordan (nee Walsh) joined Cumann na mBan in 1915. On the first morning of the Rising she reported for duty to the Athenaeum. Her first task was to help assemble beds for a temporary hospital. After completing this she was assigned to the kitchen to cook, which she did for the rest of the week. After the Volunteers were arrested and imprisoned, Jordan helped to raise money for their families through collections, raffles and flag days. In 1918 she took part in concerts and plays which travelled the county to raise funds for the Volunteers. In 1920-1921 Jordan supplied food and cigarettes to the Volunteers held prisoner in the courthouse. During the

"Battle of Enniscorthy" in July 1922 Jordan fed members of the Republican forces in her own home. In the aftermath she organised and sang in concerts in Clonroche, Gussrane, and Ballindaggin to raise money for them. She gave up her activities in late August 1922 due to ill health. Sarah Jordan died at the age of 62 in 1956.

Patrick Kavanagh (St. John's Street) A Company. One of the oldest members of his Company, Patrick Kavanagh was a member of the I.R.B. for several years before joining the Volunteers in 1913. On the night before the Rising he was on guard duty outside "The Dump" on Irish Street. After the mobilisation he was sent to the Turret Rocks and took up a sniping position, he remained there until 3 p.m.. On Friday, Kavanagh raided for arms at several locations and helped build roadblocks on the Wexford and Newtownbarry (Bunclody) roads. He used his horse and cart on Saturday to transport munitions and supplies. Kavanagh spent Sunday in the vicinity of the Athenaeum until the surrender. On Monday he helped clear the Wexford road at the request of Canon Murphy. Kavanagh was arrested and deported shortly afterwards. He was held in Stafford Jail until he was released at the end of June.

On his return to Enniscorthy Kavanagh was instructed to look after munitions stored in a dump at the Milehouse. While carrying out these orders along with a couple of other Volunteers, one of whom was Michael Davis, there was an explosion near the Bloody Bridge as they moved some of the explosives. Kavanagh's hands, chest and face were badly burned. Unable to be brought to hospital due to the circumstances of the incident, Kavanagh was nursed at home where he remained bedridden for three months. When Kavanagh recovered he was only fit to transport munitions with his horse and cart. During the War of Independence the Black and Tans raided his house and yard, they brought his horse out on to the street and beat it to such an extent Kavanagh had to have it put down. Patrick Kavanagh died in the County Home aged 73 in 1942.

William Kavanagh (Ferns) Ferns Company. William Kavanagh was 18 years old when he took part in the Easter Rising. His primary activities that week included sentry duty and the carrying of dispatches between Enniscorthy and Ferns. After the surrender he was arrested and later deported. Kavanagh was interned in Wandsworth Detention Centre and Frongach Camp before his release that December. In the following years Kavanagh played a prominent role for both his Company and the North Wexford Active Service Unit. In September 1920 he was arrested and imprisoned for four months in the Enniscorthy courthouse, where he was beaten on a regular basis. Owing to the injuries he received, Kavanagh had to be moved to the local hospital. A couple of nights later he made a daring escape with the help of some local Volunteers. (including brothers James and John Dwyer from Tomnalosset.)

Kavanagh was involved in the executions of three spies, the Skelton brothers from Booladurragh and James Morrisey from Marshalstown. He also took part in an attack on an R.I.C. patrol in Ferns on the 4th of April 1921 and the ambush of a military train in Killurin the following month. In early 1922 Kavanagh joined the National Army and by the time the Civil War broke out at the end of June, he was stationed in Kilkenny. He was involved in a firefight with the I.R.A. there and was promoted to 1st Lieutenant for *bravery under fire*. Kavanagh was then detailed to Wexford and was involved in a skirmish at Wellington Bridge which left him wounded. He resigned from the Army at the end of 1923 but re-enlisted the following summer, only to be dismissed before Christmas for alleged loyalty to the I.R.A.. William Kavanagh died at the age of 76 in 1974.

Ellen Keegan (Irish Street) Cumann na mBan. Ellen Keegan joined Cumann na mBan in 1914. In the years prior to the Rising she kept watch while "The Dump" was being constructed at the back of her uncle's house at number 10 Irish Street. She also fed the men who were working there and helped dispose of the surplus earth and clay. Once "The Dump" was up and running, Keegan helped to manufacture munitions. Throughout the Rising she continued this work. After the surrender she moved all leftover materials two doors down to number 12 Irish Street where she lived.

In the following months Keegan was a member of the fund-raising committee set up for the prisoner's dependents. She organised raffles, flag days and jumble sales amongst other initiatives. Throughout the War of Independence her home was a safe house for volunteers on the run and was also used to store weapons. Keegan carried dispatches on a regular basis between flying columns. She also cooked food which was brought to the Volunteers held in the courthouse. During the "Battle of Enniscorthy", Keegan tended to the fatally wounded Volunteers Maurice Spillane from Hospital Lane and Paddy O'Brien from Dublin. She prepared Spillane's body so it could be waked. Although on the Republican side, Keegan also treated wounded Free State soldiers. In the months that followed she carried dispatches and food to various flying columns around the district. Keegan was never arrested because as she said in her sworn statement before the Advisory Committee on the 2nd of June 1938.

"Gallagher said he knew us too well."

Keegan was referring to Seán Gallagher who was a Commander of the Free State troops in the town at that time. Ellen Keegan died in 1964 at the age of 77.

Patrick Keegan (Irish Street) Brigade Q/M. The younger brother of Teresa and Ellen Keegan, Patrick Keegan was one of the most senior members of the I.R.B. at the inception of the Volunteers in 1913. Soon after, he set about obtaining as many weapons as possible in his role as Quartermaster. In 1914 he established a munitions factory at the rear of number 10 Irish Street, the home he shared with his Uncle Tom. Alongside the factory, he and his *special party of Volunteers* dug out an underground cavern at the back of the yard which was used to store the materials and weapons that were seized in many of their raids. This became known as "The Dump". Keegan organised a group of Volunteers who were assigned to the manufacture of munitions on a daily basis for the next two years. Their endeavour was such a success that they supplied some Company's in Dublin with material at the personal request of Pádraig Pearse. On Easter Sunday after the leaders had received Eoin McNeill's countermanding order, they established a temporary H.Q. in Keegan's house as all the war material was stored there in preparation for the Rising.

On the commencement of hostilities, the Volunteers who gathered at Keegan's were each handed a weapon and after been addressed by Peter Galligan, marched to the Athenaeum and set up a H.Q. there. Keegan's many activities over the following days included firing on the R.I.C. barracks, the attempt to blow up the bridge at Edermine, commandeering supplies and equipment and responsibility for "The Dump". After the surrender, along with Seamus Rafter, Keegan had to be persuaded not to continue with a guerrilla campaign. Keegan took charge of the collection and disposal of all the reusable weapons and munitions at the Athenaeum. He then moved all the weapons and material from "The Dump" itself. This job was completed with only minutes to spare before the British military arrived on the Monday afternoon. Keegan was arrested and deported shortly afterwards. He was interned in Stafford Jail and Frongach Camp before his release on the 23rd of December 1916.

On the reorganisation in 1917, Keegan took a leading role. He re-established "The Dump" and organised many raids for arms and materials. After the funerals of Seamus Rafter and Volunteer Thomas Stokes in 1918 he was the only member of the Brigade Staff to evade capture. From 1914 to 1919 he served at various intervals as Brigade Quartermaster, 1st Lieutenant and Captain of A Company, Commandant and Brigade Commandant.

Keegan met Michael Collins, at Collin's request, in the Mansion House in Dublin on the 21st of January 1919, the night of the first Dáil sitting. The next day they met again to discuss the plans Collins had for him. Initially Collins wanted Keegan to remain in Dublin and set up a foundry, but Keegan informed him of his intention to return to Enniscorthy. Then Collins decided to send him to Liverpool, to take charge of a mission to run guns from Brest in France through Liverpool and then on to Dublin. Keegan went to Liverpool but after three weeks there the plan had fallen apart. He was about to return home when Collins ordered him to take the next boat to New York and contact Liam Mellows.

From the time he arrived in New York until February 1921, Keegan followed Mellows orders, he collected arms and stored them before smuggling them onboard whatever ship he was working on to bring them across the Atlantic. He made at least a half a dozen crossings. By July 1921 Keegan was working under the command of Harry Barton and on the 13th of that month he loaded 495 Thompson machine guns on a vessel bound for Ireland. Unbeknownst to them the operation was under the surveillance of the American authorities and the shipment was seized. Keegan was now a wanted man, he had to go on the run for several months before finally making it back to Enniscorthy at the end of April 1922.

Once home, Keegan took the Republican side opposed to the Treaty and joined the garrison in the courthouse. At the outbreak of the Civil War he fought in the "Battle of Enniscorthy". After the Free State Army regained control of the town, Keegan joined up with a flying column. Over the next couple of months he returned to the town at night on several occasions, to snipe at the Free State soldiers in the Castle. He was arrested at the end of September and imprisoned until December 1923. Keegan left for America shortly afterwards and did not return until November 1934 with his wife and three children. Patrick Keegan died in 1953 at the age of 60.

Teresa Keegan (Irish Street) Cumann na mBan. Teresa Keegan was Ellen and Patrick Keegan's older sister. She joined Cumann na mBan in 1914. Like her sister she helped out as "The Dump" was being constructed at the rear of her uncle's house on Irish Street, she kept guard and disposed of the excess earth and clay. Once it was up and running she assisted with the manufacture of munitions. Throughout Easter Week Keegan remained at "The Dump" filling cartridges and running lead, after the surrender she helped to clear it out. Over the following years Keegan played a prominent role in her Cumann. After Seamus Rafter was severely injured in an explosion at his premises in August 1918, Keegan helped nurse him during the day while her sister nursed him at night until he passed away. In the Spring of 1920 Keegan was appointed as Captain of her Cumann, she organised her women to make and sterilise bandages and first aid kits which were then distributed to the various flying columns around the district. During the "Battle of Enniscorthy" Keegan was based at the Technical Institute on the Market Square, where she cooked for the Republican side. Following their evacuation from the town she continued to assist the flying columns throughout the district until the ceasefire. Teresa Keegan died at the age of 79 in 1968.

Josephine Kehoe (Court Street) Cumann na mBan. Josephine Kehoe (nee Hayes) joined Cumann na mBan in 1915. She reported to the Athenaeum for duty on the morning of the Rising and remained there until the surrender. Her duties consisted of cooking and helping to set up a temporary field hospital. In the months following the surrender Kehoe raised funds for the prisoner's dependants. She carried out the routine activities of her Cumann up until September 1919 when she married Patrick Kehoe, a future T.D.. Josephine Kehoe died in 1937 aged 38.

Michael J. Kehoe (New Street) Na Fianna Éireann. Michael Joseph Kehoe joined the Volunteers in 1914. After a branch of Na Fianna was established in the town he became Captain of the Slugadh (Company). In the period leading up to the Rising, Kehoe and the members of Na Fianna were used by Patrick Keegan as scouts and lookouts. Keegan later wrote in a letter to the Military Service Pensions Board on Kehoe's behalf dated 30th of July 1940.

"…it was he and his unit that were the eyes and ears of the raiding party and munitions workers that operated under my command."

On Easter Sunday Kehoe and a comrade were sent on a scouting mission to the Bree and Edermine area by Seamus Rafter to watch for R.I.C. movements. On the following Tuesday and Wednesday he was tasked with guarding weapons which had been brought to the town from Gorey by Seán Etchingham, these weapons were stored in "Antwerp". On the first morning of the Rising, Kehoe reported for duty to the Athenaeum. His first assignment was to scout close to Oylgate for any troop or police movements. On his return to H.Q. he was tasked with writing out passes granted for the people of the town who needed to leave for a valid reason. On Friday, Kehoe went to various outposts to deliver and collect dispatches. From then up until the surrender on Sunday night, Kehoe's time was spent in and around the Athenaeum except for when he slept in his own house on New Street (Weafer St.). After the surrender he helped with the collection of arms and ammunition. He was not arrested on account of his age.

In the weeks that followed, Kehoe along with members of his unit retrieved weapons that had been hastily dumped after the surrender, this included from the Slaney. These weapons were then cleaned and stored away safely. Kehoe also helped out with the Programme for National Aid for the prisoners and their families. He travelled around the Districts helping to organise new branches of Na Fianna. Kehoe left Enniscorthy in September 1918 to go to college in De La Salle, Waterford, where after two years of study he qualified as a primary school teacher. Kehoe continued to serve when he returned to Enniscorthy on his holidays by taking up an intelligence role. Through contacts he had in the post office, Kehoe was able to obtain up to date information about planned troop deployments and raids. He was active in this role until The Truce. Michael Joseph Kehoe died at the age of 78 in 1977.

Patrick J. Kehoe (Clonhaston) A Company. Patrick J. Kehoe was the husband of Josephine Kehoe. On hearing the news of the Rising in Enniscorthy, Kehoe, who lived three miles from the town, made his way to the Athenaeum. Once there he was sent on street patrol around the town. Later that night he carried out sentry duty at the bottom of Hospital Lane. The following day acting on his own suggestion, Kehoe was given permission to leave the town with another Volunteer in order to try and gather intelligence of what was happening elsewhere. They also planned to ask the Wicklow Company's to block the railways in their area. The two men left on bicycles and went to Shillelagh first and then Avoca and Wicklow, where they arrived on the Saturday evening. In each location they met with several people who acted with great indifference and who did not want to get involved. By the time they returned to Enniscorthy early on Monday morning, everyone had left the Athenaeum. Kehoe was arrested at his home the following day and deported shortly afterwards. He was held in Stafford Jail until June. In later years Patrick Kehoe served as a T.D. and as a Senator. Patrick J. Kehoe died in 1959 aged 79.

James Kelly (Ferns) Ferns Company. James Kelly was a member of the I.R.B. before joining the Volunteers in 1914. During the Rising he served in Enniscorthy and Ferns, carrying out sentry and outpost duty at several locations. He was arrested shortly after the surrender and deported. Kelly was interned for three months before he was released from Frongach Camp in August. He re-joined his Company in 1917 and participated in all its general activities.

Throughout the years 1919 and 1920, Kelly was involved in several raids for arms and on one occasion was wounded in the hand by gunfire. In March 1921 Kelly joined the North Wexford flying column. The following month, while making a clandestine visit to his fathers' home in order to change his clothes, the house was surrounded by the Black and Tans. As Kelly attempted to escape out a side window he was wounded by a rifle shot. He managed to evade capture despite being chased for over two miles. Kelly made his way to Gorey where he was treated by a local doctor sympathetic to the movement. On the 7th of May that same year Kelly and his column ambushed a R.I.C. cycle patrol near Inch which left one policeman dead and another badly wounded. Kelly continued to make munitions throughout this period and by the time of The Truce had been appointed Lieutenant in Charge of Engineers. During The Truce period Kelly visited various camps to instruct Volunteers in the use and manufacture of explosives.

When the Civil War broke out Kelly was a member of the Free State Army garrison based in the former R.I.C. barracks on the Abbey Square. During the "Battle of Enniscorthy" in early July, he was wounded while trying to defend the barracks.. Kelly resigned from the army in August that year in order to go work on his father's farm. The farm had fallen into disrepair over the previous few years due to his absence. Although now he was a civilian, Kelly left the army with the understanding that he was willing to take up arms again should circumstance dictate. James Kelly passed away at the age of 79 in 1973.

John J. Kelly (Ferns) Ferns Company. John J. Kelly joined the Volunteers in April 1914. During the Easter Rising he was on duty in both Enniscorthy and Ferns. He was arrested on the Wednesday following the surrender and deported shortly afterwards. Kelly was interned in Wakefield Prison and Frongach Camp before he was released in August. In 1917 Kelly was heavily involved in the reorganisation of the Company in Ferns and held the position of Section Leader.

By 1920 Kelly held the rank of Vice-Commandant of the Third Battalion North Wexford Brigade. In March the same year he was involved in the attack on the R.I.C. barracks in Clonroche, while in June he acted as one of the scouts in the operation to kill D.I. Lea Wilson in Gorey. The following March Kelly was appointed second in command of the North Wexford Flying Column with the rank of Captain. He participated in the attack on a R.I.C. patrol and barracks in April, and a month later, the Inch ambush which resulted in the death of a R.I.C. Constable. Kelly's father's house was burned to the ground in retaliation for his actions by the Black and Tans. After The Truce he joined the National Army and served with them throughout the Civil War. John J. Kelly died at the age of 64 in 1954.

John P. Kelly (Kilpierce) A Company. A member of the Volunteers since August 1914, John P. Kelly reported to the Athenaeum at 9 a.m. on the first morning of the Rising. From there he was sent to the old R.I.C. barracks on Court Street where the Volunteers had established their own police force. Kelly's role for the duration of the week was policing duty. This involved patrolling the streets, making sure shops had enough foodstuffs, preventing these shops from being looted and enforcing the closure order on the Public Houses. After the surrender Kelly went home at 2.30 a.m. on Monday morning. He was arrested nearly two weeks later on the 13th of May but was released the following morning. Afterwards he played no further role. John P. Kelly died in Luton in 1959 aged 68, while visiting his daughter who lived there

Margaret King (Brownswood) Cumann na mBan. Margaret "Peg" King was a younger sister of Richard F. King and she joined Cumann na mBan in 1914. In the weeks before the Rising she was in "Antwerp" three to four nights a week filling cartridges and making first aid kits. The week prior to the Insurrection King delivered dispatches to her brother and to Robert Brennan from Seamus Rafter. In return Brennan gave her ammunition to bring to Enniscorthy. On the first morning of the Rising King reported for duty to the Athenaeum at 7.30 a.m. where she helped prepare food. On Friday she was sent to Wexford with a dispatch, while on Saturday evening she went to Ferns. In Ferns King helped to commandeer food supplies for the H.Q. which had been set up in the vacated R.I.C. barracks. After the surrender she was a passenger in Peter Galligan's car which crashed on its return to Enniscorthy. King was badly injured and was treated in a nearby house by a doctor who had been summoned from Newtownbarry. (Bunclody) It took King a full year to recover from her injuries.. Once her health was okay, she returned to Cumann service and continued until April 1919. Margaret "Peg" King died in 1968 at the age of 75.

Richard F. King (Brownswood) Captain A Company. In 1912 along with three others, Thomas Doyle, Patrick Fitzpatrick and William Murphy, Richard F. King founded a group in Enniscorthy with the goal of *working for the complete independence of Ireland*. They called themselves The Irish Brigade and by the time they merged with the Volunteers in early 1914 they had approximately twenty-five members. Once the Rising began, King was placed in charge of all scouts and worked out of the Athenaeum for the week. He was one of six signatories to a letter received by the commander of the British forces in Wexford, Colonel French, requesting permission for Seán Etchingham and Seamus Doyle to go to Dublin and confirm Pádraig Pearse's surrender order.

After the surrender King was sentenced to death, this was later commuted to five years penal servitude. King served his time in Dartmoor and Lewes Jails before he was released from Pentonville jail in June 1917. After his release King was involved in Election work for Sinn Féin and operated out of an office on Frederick Street in Dublin. In the years up The Truce, King claimed to have carried out secret missions to England and Scotland on behalf of Michael Collins, Arthur Griffith and Cathal Brugha. He also claimed to do likewise for Austin Stack in counties Donegal, Galway and Kerry. King played no role in the Civil War and in later years worked as a Fisheries Inspector. Richard F. King died at his residence in Arklow in 1938 aged 47.

Peter Kinsella (Ross Road) A Company. Peter Kinsella was a member of the I.R.B. for several years before joining the Volunteers in 1913. On the morning of the Rising his first task was to take up guard duty on the corner of Irish Street. He was then detailed to take up a sniping position on the Castle roof from where he stated he fired one shot at a window in the R.I.C. barracks. (testimony before the Military Service

Pensions Board on the 3rd of March 1937) He slept in the Athenaeum that night. On Friday, Kinsella was on outpost duty at The Moyne before returning to the roof of the Castle for half the night. On Saturday he spent the day on duty once again at The Moyne. Seamus Rafter assigned him to guard duty at the Athenaeum on Sunday and Kinsella was present there for the surrender. He handed in his weapon and evaded arrest over the following days.

Kinsella re-joined in 1917 and participated in the general activities of his Company. In 1918 he was one of the Volunteers sent to Waterford to protect Sinn Féin officials during the Bye-Election. The following year he constructed a small arms dump at his home following fears that a dump at The Malt House on Island Road, where he worked, had been compromised. From then, Kinsella played a peripheral role in Volunteer activities up to The Truce. He had no involvement in the Civil War. Peter Kinsella died at the age of 71 in 1947.

Robert Kinsella (Ferns) A Company. A member of the I.R.B. since 1910 and Captain of his local hurling team, Robert Kinsella joined the Volunteers in 1914. On the Tuesday of Easter Week, Kinsella set out with his Company for Enniscorthy under the impression that the town had risen, only to receive word on the way that all was quiet. After spending the day in Ballinahallin Wood the Company returned to Ferns.

After a few false starts, word was finally received on Thursday that Enniscorthy had risen. Kinsella and some of his comrades made their way to the town. He was placed on guard duty at various locations around the town over the following two days before returning to Ferns on Saturday evening. That night Kinsella acted as a guard for the Volunteers who were felling trees and making roadblocks. He was arrested in the days following the surrender and deported shortly afterwards. Kinsella was interned in Wandsworth Prison and Frongach Camp before he was released in August. Prior to the Rising Kinsella had been employed at the Kynoch munitions factory in Arklow. Upon his release he learnt he had lost his job due to his involvement in the Insurrection. He re-joined his Company in 1917 and participated in several operations up until The Truce including raids for rate books, burning of a vacated R.I.C. barracks and the attack on the barracks in Ferns. Kinsella joined the National Army in April 1922 and served with it until April 1924. Robert Kinsella died at the age of 89 in 1973.

Michael Kirwan (Killagoley) A Company. Michael Kirwan joined the Volunteers in 1916. In the weeks leading up to the Rising he carried out guard duty at "The Dump" on numerous occasions, including the Wednesday night before it started. On the first morning of hostilities he helped transport munitions from "The Dump" to the Athenaeum. At midday he was a member of a party of Volunteers sent to the railway yard to raid for shotgun cartridges. That night Kirwan carried out sentry duty on the bridge until 6 a.m. Friday morning. After resting at H.Q., he was placed on sentry duty on Lymington Road for the afternoon. Later that night he was sent to Vinegar Hill Lane on outpost duty, he remained there until 8 a.m. Saturday morning. After resting, Kirwan was placed on guard duty at Volunteer police headquarters on Court Street. From midnight until 9 a.m. Sunday he was on sentry duty at the railway station. Kirwan was off duty until 8 p.m. Sunday night, then he took up guard duty in the Athenaeum until the surrender. He evaded arrest.

Before the reorganisation of the Volunteers in 1917, Kirwan was appointed to a squad of men responsible for the cleaning and preparing of weapons which had been dumped after the Rising. Once the Company was up and running he helped in the manufacture of munitions. In 1918 Kirwan was a member of the honour guard at Seamus Rafter's wake and funeral, after which he acted as a guard on the homes of Company officers wanted for their part in the militarisation of the funeral. Over the Christmas Holidays Kirwan helped guard the ballot boxes that were stored in the courthouse. In 1919 he was appointed Company Adjutant. In January 1920, Kirwan's home was raided and a notebook containing the names of the members of his Company was seized, along with a copy of a play titled *"The Spirit of 16"* which the Company were hoping to put on to raise funds. Kirwan was sentenced to two months in jail along with the month he was held for before his trial. While in jail he was promoted to Adjutant 1st Battalion Wexford Brigade, this was due in part to the suspension of several officers after the killing of Mrs. Morris in The Ballagh during a botched raid for arms. After his release Kirwan was involved in some major operations, including the attack on the R.I.C. barracks in Clonroche in April 1920 and the big raid for petrol at the railway station the following month. Kirwan acted as a scout and guard for the men who killed D.I. Lea Wilson in Gorey that June. In July he commandeered lorries in Enniscorthy for a raid on Pierce's foundry in Wexford, the lorries were used to transport old artillery shells from World War One to Adamstown.

During this period Kirwan was appointed as a senior police officer. He was responsible for the implementation of the Belfast Boycott at the railway station. This was a controversial policy backed by the provisional government and involved the destruction of any goods which arrived at the station from the North that were on a prohibited list. In September Kirwan planned the abduction of the spy James Doyle from Ballycarney and served at his court-martial and execution. In October 1920 Kirwan was arrested and charged for writing dispatches found in the possession of Edward Balfe. He was sentenced to two years in jail. In November 1921 along with Balfe, he escaped from the jail in Kilkenny. He stayed on the run for over a month.

Kirwan joined the Republican garrison in the courthouse in March 1922 and was there when the Civil War erupted at the end of June. On the evening of the 2nd of July, the first evening of the "Battle of Enniscorthy", Kirwan was badly wounded while sniping from the steeple of St. Mary's Church. He was brought to Enniscorthy hospital before he was transferred to the general hospital in Wexford. Shortly after his discharge on the 17th of August, Kirwan was arrested. He was imprisoned until December 1923. Michael Kirwan died at the age of 77 in 1976.

Ita Larkin (The Shannon) Cumann na mBan. Margaret "Ita" Larkin (nee Forrestal) joined Cumann na mBan in 1914. On the first morning of the Rising Larkin reported to the Athenaeum for duty at 7 a.m., she remained there until after the surrender, save going to Mass on the Sunday morning. Her tasks included making bandages and cooking. For three weeks after the surrender Larkin offered safe harbour to three Volunteers in her home, they hid in the fields by day and slept inside at night. In the following months she helped to raise funds for the prisoner's families and sent food parcels to the prisoners. Larkin took part in the routine Cumann activities until 1919 when she got married and moved to Tullamore to live. Ita Larkin died in 1966, she was 72 years old.

James Leacy (Court Street) A Company. James Leacy was a member of Na Fianna Éireann before becoming a Volunteer in April 1916. Prior to the Rising he acted as a scout for Patrick Keegan and his raiding party. On several occasions Leacy borrowed the horse and cart belonging to his employer (without his knowledge) to move material to and from "The Dump". On the first morning of the Insurrection he marched to the Athenaeum with the main body of Volunteers. After a H.Q. had been established, Leacy took up a sniping position at the top of Castle Hill. According to his statement before the Military Service Pensions Board on the 2nd of March 1937, he fired approximately 15 rounds over the period of time he was there After been relieved Leacy had something to eat before going to the Protestant Institute on Church Street for guard duty, he remained there until 2 a.m. the following morning.

On Friday afternoon Leacy was sent with two dispatches, one to Boolabawn and the other to The Leap. After returning he was instructed to bring some of the countrymen who had arrived and volunteered to serve, to their assigned posts. For the remainder of the weekend Leacy was on duty around the Athenaeum. After the surrender he assisted with the collection and removal of arms, finishing this task at 7 a.m. Monday morning. He successfully avoided arrest. In 1917 Leacy re-joined and participated in general Volunteer activities. He was a member of the party of Volunteers sent to Waterford for the Bye Election in early 1918. In 1919 Leacy was involved in a series of raids for arms including at the homes of the Jameson Davis's at Killabeg, the Hayes's of Greenmount, Major Ryan's at Edermine, the Richards's of Solsboro and Captain Alcock in Wilton. In 1920 Leacy took part in the raids for petrol at the railway station, for magnetos at Donohoe's and munition material from Davis's foundry. He was also involved in the attack on the R.I.C. barracks in Clonroche. In February 1921 along with Volunteer John Carroll, Leacy was responsible for the killing of the spy Fredrick Newsome in Slaney Place.

Leacy joined the National Army at Beggars Bush in March 1923. After completing his training he was sent to the barracks in Kilkenny. Upon the split in the army over the Treaty, Leacy sided with the Republicans and was a member of the group of soldiers who absconded with seventy-five rifles and thousands of rounds of ammunition. He returned to Enniscorthy and joined the garrison in the courthouse. During the "Battle of Enniscorthy" he fired on the Free State soldiers in the Castle from a house on Slaney Street. After the Free State Army regained control of the town, Leacy joined with a flying column and went on the run. In the months of July, August and September, he returned to the town on several nights to snipe on the Castle from the Nun's field. Leacy avoided arrest throughout the Civil War and only laid down his arms at the announcement of the ceasefire. James Leacy died in 1974 a month shy of his 73rd birthday.

John Leacy (Templeshannon) A Company. John" Jack" Leacy was a member of the I.R.B. before joining the Volunteers in 1913. On the first morning of the Rising he marched from Irish Street to the Athenaeum with the main body of Volunteers. From there he was assigned a sniping position on the Castle roof. Before the Military service Pensions Board on the 8th of December 1937, Leacy stated he fired a dozen or so times at the R.I.C. barracks from this position. From Thursday afternoon to the

Saturday evening he carried out sentry duty around the town. Leacy marched to Ferns with the column of Volunteers under the command of Peter Galligan on Saturday night. In Ferns he carried out guard duty at several locations around the village. After the surrender was announced on Sunday night, he returned to Enniscorthy. While at work the following day, Leacy was arrested and later deported. He was interned in Stafford Jail and Frongach Camp until his release in December. Leacy re-joined in 1917 and took part in the general activities of his Company. In 1919 he moved to Wexford for a job and joined a local Company. In July 1920 he was involved in the raid on Pierce's foundry for large artillery shells. After that Leacy played no further role in any significant operations, nor did he participate in the Civil War. John "Jack" Leacy died in Wexford hospital aged 55 in 1945.

Laurence Leacy (Court Street) A Company. Laurence Leacy was an older brother of James Leacy. He was a member of Na Fianna Éireann before joining the Volunteers in 1915. On the first morning of the Rising he reported for duty at Irish Street and marched to the Athenaeum with the main body of Volunteers. Once an H.Q. had been established, Leacy was assigned to the transportation section. For his first duty he was ordered to commandeer a motor car. Successful in this task, he then used this car to transport men to and from various locations as well as delivering commandeered goods back to H.Q.. Leacy was engaged in these activities for most of Thursday and Friday. On the Saturday morning he drove to Ferns with arms and dispatches and then returned to the Athenaeum. In the afternoon he transported men who raided several houses in the country for arms.

After the surrender on Sunday night Leacy was instructed to go to Ferns and bring Peter Galligan back to the Athenaeum. On the way back Leacy used a bye road he was unfamiliar with; he took a wrong turn which resulted in him driving the car through and open ditch and landing it on its roof. Leacy and a member of Cumann na mBan, Margaret King were badly injured and needed immediate medical treatment, two other

Volunteers were also hurt. A Doctor was brought from Newtownbarry (Bunclody) and a priest from Ferns, in fact the priest anointed the injured. Leacy was confined to bed for several days and managed to evade arrest. However, as a result of his injuries he was unable to work for a considerable time. Leacy re-joined in 1917 and beside making munitions occasionally, his main role was as a driver. Several times a week he drove various officers around the county to meetings. He also transported men to Clonroche for the attack on the R.I.C. barracks in April 1920.

On the 11th of November 1920, Leacy was arrested and charged with the murder of D.I. Lea Wilson in Gorey the previous June. His only role was giving the car to be used in the killing the once over. He later stated he wasn't aware of the mission. Leacy was imprisoned in Mountjoy Jail until February 1922. On his return to Enniscorthy Leacy worked as a hackney driver and acted as a part-time driver for the Republican garrison in the courthouse. During the "Battle of Enniscorthy" he drove a lorry delivering sandbags and barbed wire to wherever they were required. For the remainder of the Civil War he offered his car and services and was regarded as a trusted Volunteer to call on. Laurence Leacy died at his residence on St. Johns Street in 1952 aged 53

Owen Leacy (Duffry Gate) A Company. Owen Leacy was already a member of the I.R.B. when he joined the Volunteers at their inception in 1913. He marched with the main body of men to the Athenaeum from Irish Street on the first morning of the Insurrection. Leacy was assigned a sniping position on Castle Hill from where he fired a half a dozen shots at the R.I.C. barracks. (Military Service Pensions Board interview on the 2nd of March 1937) Later that day he was placed on guard duty outside "The Dump". On Friday morning Leacy was sent to the Wexford Road for outpost duty. That night he was at Davis's Mill, where he remained until Saturday morning. Leacy was a member of the column of men who marched to Ferns under the command of Peter Galligan on Saturday evening. He carried out sentry duty in the village throughout the time he was there. After the surrender on Sunday night Leacy returned to

Enniscorthy and handed in his weapon. Over the following days he was successful in avoiding capture. Leacy re-joined his Company in 1917 and participated in their general activities before resigning in 1918 due to ill health. He played no further role in any operations up to and including the Civil War. Owen Leacy died in St. Martin's Hospital, Bath England in 1946 at the age of 59.

Sheila Lynch (Court Street) Cumann na mBan. Sheila "Sighle" Lynch (nee Moran) joined Cumann Na mBan in 1915. She came from a staunch Republican family who lived on Church Street. In the days prior to the Rising, rifles and ammunition were stored in her matrimonial home on Court Street, which was situated opposite the old R.I.C. barracks. Throughout the Rising her home was used to feed and accommodate the Volunteers who were stationed in the old barracks after it was taken over and used as the H.Q. for the Republican police. On Saturday night Lynch went to Summerhill to the outpost there to make sure the men had food. On the Monday following the surrender she let Peter Galligan and another Volunteer stay in her house to avoid capture. Galligan stayed in the house until Tuesday and then left for his home in Cavan on a bicycle.

Lynch's husband was Volunteer Laurence Lynch, who was arrested and interned after the Rising. While searching for him a few days after the surrender, soldiers killed one of their twin infant sons when they turned over his cot, they did not realise there was a second baby in it. In the years up to The Truce Lynch held a senior position in her Cumann, her home was used to store weapons on many occasions, she also assisted with the propaganda side of the conflict. Tragedy befell her family once more in 1921 when her brother Seán was murdered by the Black and Tans in Drogheda. Sheila Lynch died in 1974 at the age of 84.

Michael Maguire (St. John's Street) A Company. Michael Maguire joined the Volunteers in 1913. On the evening of Easter Sunday he was sent with a dispatch to Ballindaggin by Seamus Rafter. Maguire marched from Irish Street to the Athenaeum with the main column of Volunteers on the following Thursday morning. Along with another Volunteer, Maguire was then sent on a scouting mission along the railway as far as Edermine. They returned at 2 p.m. and reported all was quiet. After resting, he acted as an orderly in H.Q. until 10 p.m., then he was sent by himself on the same scouting mission. Maguire arrived back at H.Q. at 2 a.m. and reported directly to Seamus Rafter.

After receiving intelligence early on Friday morning that the British military were advancing from Arklow, the leadership instructed Maguire and another Volunteer to cycled to Ferns and assess the situation. When they arrived at a crossroads on the outskirts of the village they were greeted by a small crowd who informed them that the R.I.C. had vacated their barracks and were heading for Gorey. The two Volunteers cycled as far as Camolin but did not catch a glimpse of the retreating policemen. They returned to Ferns and waited for the advance party to arrive. Once they had, Maguire and his comrade cycled back to Enniscorthy to let H.Q. know the advance party had arrived safely and what the general situation in the village was. On Friday afternoon Maguire was detailed with a small party of Volunteers under the command of Patrick Keegan to go to the Enniscorthy Asylum. While travelling down the Shannon Quay they came under fire from the R.I.C. barracks on the opposite side of the river. Maguire returned fire as the car sped down the Quay to safety. Once at the Asylum they commandeered an Electrical Standard and brought it to John Breen at the Rock Factory for him to try and make a trench mortar. That night Maguire was sent by Peter Galligan to collect reports from outposts at Salville Cross, Springvalley and The Shannon.

On Saturday, Maguire was sent back to Ferns with a dispatch for Seán Gallagher, he remained in the village until the following morning. When he returned to Enniscorthy he was put on outpost duty. That afternoon he was placed on guard duty in the Athenaeum and was present there for the surrender. Afterwards Maguire helped with the collection of weapons and was personally tasked with transporting some rifles to a safe house in Knockroe near New Ross. He managed to evade arrest over the following days and weeks. After re-joining in 1917 Maguire took part in all the regular Volunteer activities. By 1920 he had been appointed Lieutenant, however, this was to be short lived after his name was discovered in a notebook belonging to a fellow officer. Maguire was ordered to go on the run and spent the following months up to The Truce as a member of various flying columns. In that period he was involved in such operations as the attack on the Clonroche R.I.C. barracks, the ambush at Inch of an R.I.C. patrol which left one policeman dead, and another seriously wounded.

Maguire was also involved in failed attempts to kill an R.I.C. Sergeant in Newtownbarry (Bunclody) and the despised Captain Yeo of the Devonshire Regiment in Enniscorthy. After The Truce Maguire joined the National Army in early 1922. At the outbreak of the "Battle of Enniscorthy" that July, he was stationed in the former R.I.C. barracks on the Abbey Square which was the Free State Army's H.Q.. After the surrender of the Free State, Maguire held the white flag aloft as the soldiers left the barracks. He resigned from the army at the end of the same month and played no further role.

Like many of his comrades, Maguire applied for the Military Service Pension for his roles in the Easter Rising and War of Independence, (he did not claim for the Civil War in his belief that he did not deserve it) and like so many of his colleagues he was refused his pension. He appealed the decision and was refused again, only for it to come to light in 1944 that he had been mistaken for a Michael Maguire from Templescoby who had served in the National Army from June 1922 until December 1923. In righting this wrong, Maguire was awarded his pension and it was backdated to 1934. Michael Maguire died at the age of 60 in St. John's Hospital in 1957.

James Maher (The Shannon) A Company. James Maher joined the I.R.B. in 1911 and the Volunteers in 1913. From Easter Sunday night to the following Wednesday night he was in "Antwerp". At around midnight on Wednesday he was summoned to Keegan's on Irish Street, there he was instructed to accompany another Volunteer to Knockmarshal and Tomnalosset. They went by bicycle and called at five houses belonging to Volunteers and told them to report for duty. On his return Maher marched with the main body of men to the Athenaeum. After a H.Q. had been established there, he took up a sniping position at the top of Castle Hill. In his testimony before the Military Service Pensions Board on the 21st of November 1939, Maher stated he fired four shots from there at the R.I.C. barracks over a period of a few hours. After Maher was relieved, he was sent to Lett's Brewery at the bottom of Friary Hill. There he came under fire from the R.I.C. men locked inside the Bank of Ireland on the Abbey Square. He returned fire and remained at this location until evening. On Maher's return to the Athenaeum, he was ordered to commandeer bedding from Bolger's Shop on Georges Street. (Rafter St.) On Friday morning Maher went to Davis's Mill with rations for the guards on duty there.

In the early afternoon he went in one of three carloads of Volunteers to Edermine. Once there, he helped to fell trees and block roads, he was back in the Atheneum by 6 p.m.. After having something to eat, Robert Brennan instructed Maher to take charge of an office on the top floor that was used as an armoury. There the Volunteers handed in their weapons before going to sleep and Maher handed them out to those who were going on duty. On Saturday morning he inspected outposts with an officer and that evening went to Ferns by car with two other officers. The officers observed the situation there before they drove back to Enniscorthy. On Sunday Maher spent the day on outpost duty at Red Pat's Cross before returning to H.Q. at 5.30 p.m.. He remained there for the surrender and then helped with the collection of weapons. He took four rifles and three bandoliers full of ammunition to hide. Maher stayed at the home of a cousin in the town for a couple of weeks while the military were rounding up the Volunteers and successfully avoided being detained. Maher re-joined in 1917, and along with his general

Volunteer duties he was primarily engaged in carrying dispatches several times a week all over the district. In April 1920 he was assigned to the Republican police in the town and served in this role until The Truce, after which he resigned and played no further part. James Maher was 71 years old when he died in St. John's Hospital in 1959.

William Mahon (Irish Street) A Company. William Mahon joined the Volunteers in 1913 and the I.R.B. shortly afterwards. On the first morning of the Rising he was detailed to the corner of Georges Street (Rafter St.) and the Market Square. While there he heard gunfire coming from the direction of the courthouse, he made his way up Georges Street and joined the Volunteers who were exchanging gunfire with the R.I.C. at the top of Friary Hill. Mahon fired several times at the policemen before they retreated down Friary Hill and back to their barracks. On Friday he took up a sniping position on the Turret Rocks and fired sporadically on the barracks over several hours. For the remainder of the week Mahon was on night duty at outposts and slept in the Athenaeum during the day. He was present for the surrender and successfully avoided capture afterwards. Mahon re-joined in 1917 and took part in the general activities of his Company. His last involvement was in May 1920, when he participated in the large raid for petrol at the railway station William Mahon died at the age of 75 in 1971.

Patrick McGrath (Fairview Terrace) A Company. Patrick McGrath joined the I.R.B. in 1908 and the Volunteers at their inception in 1913. In the years prior to the Rising, he was involved in the manufacture of munitions at "The Dump". Reports began circulating a month before the Insurrection that the R.I.C. were going to arrest Seamus Rafter. McGrath and a couple of other Volunteers were assigned to protect Rafter and make sure the R.I.C. did not get near him. On the first morning of the Rising, McGrath was placed on sentry duty on the Market Square. After a few hours there, he joined a raiding party which commandeered a motor car and several weapons at various houses in the district. On

Friday morning he was detailed to Davis's Mill, where he was employed, and took up an observation post high in the building. McGrath remained there until Saturday when he accompanied a couple of officers to Ferns to gauge the situation there. He returned to the Athenaeum that night. On Sunday, McGrath held various posts around the town until he was recalled to H.Q. for the surrender. Afterwards he helped collect and load weapons and other materials. He was arrested the following Tuesday and deported shortly afterwards. McGrath was interned in Lewes and Woking Jails before he was released from Frongach Camp at the end of August.

On his return to Enniscorthy McGrath was told by his employer, in no uncertain terms, that his job had been filled. In 1917 he helped with the reorganisation of the movement, but due to a lack of employment and with a wife and family to feed, he moved to Dublin to obtain work. McGrath got a job at the Dock Milling Company on Barrow Street in the city. Shortly after he transferred to the Emerald branch of the I.R.B. and then became a member of B Company Third Battalion Dublin. From then up to The Truce he was an active participant in his Company.

McGrath's most significant action occurred on the night of the 16th of March 1921. That day six volunteers who had been captured during an ambush two months previously, were executed in Mountjoy Jail. After curfew that night a party of Black and Tans attempted to raid the H.Q. of McGrath's Company on Great Brunswick Street (now Pearse Street), however the Volunteers were waiting for them. A bloody battle ensued (according to his Statement for the Military Service Pension on the 5th of December 1935, he fired several rounds) which lasted approximately five minutes. At its conclusion seven people lay dead, two Volunteers, two Black and Tans and three civilians. The Volunteers made their escape through the backyards and gardens on the street and no arrests were made.

During the Civil War McGrath chose the Republican side but had no part in the fighting due to a lack of weapons. Instead he used his role as a chargehand in the Dock Milling Company to provide a safe place for those members who were militarily active to rest and hide. He also reported on the activities of the Free State forces in the area. McGrath carried out these activities up until the ceasefire. Afterwards he found employment once again hard to find and he emigrated to the United States in 1927. McGrath returned to Enniscorthy in 1934. Patrick McGrath was my Great Grandfather, he died in 1969 at the age of 88 in Enniscorthy.

John J. McGuire (Ballinakill) A Company. John J. McGuire had not long turned seventeen when he officially became a Volunteer during Easter Week. For the first two days of the Rising he was detailed to the transport section. He was present at raids to commandeer motor cars for the use of Volunteers. His duties included passing on orders to the drivers and reporting to his superior officer when the cars returned. On Saturday evening McGuire marched to Ferns armed with a pike as a member of the column of Volunteers under the command of Peter Galligan. After resting in the National School he was handed a rifle and took up sentry duty in the village at 3 a.m.. On news of the surrender he marched back to Enniscorthy on Sunday evening. McGuire was arrested the following Tuesday and was sent to Waterford and then onto Dublin before he was released three weeks later.

McGuire re-joined in 1917 and was involved in the regular Volunteer activities. During the attack on the R.I.C. barracks in Clonroche on the night of April 20th, 1920, McGuire was one of the handful of riflemen engaged in firing on the barracks. Later that summer he was involved in an attack on the R.I.C. barracks in Baltinglass. McGuire joined the Active Service Unit in October 1920 at its inception and participated in all the operations of this unit, including sniping at the R.I.C. barracks in Enniscorthy, Clonroche and Ferns, the fatal ambush at Inch of a R.I.C. cycle patrol and the burning of Ardmine House near Courtown. Following The Truce McGuire joined the National Army at Beggars Bush in February 1922. From there he was sent to the barracks in Kilkenny. In April following the split in the army, McGuire was one of a group of approximately thirty-five soldiers who absconded with a large quantity of rifles and ammunition from the barracks. McGuire returned to Wexford and took up a position as a Republican policeman in Gorey. In July after the outbreak of the Civil War, he was involved in the capture of Ferns from the Free State Army. The village was retaken shortly afterwards when McGuire and his colleagues surrendered. He was arrested and imprisoned until 1924. John J. McGuire died aged 86 in 1985.

Thomas Francis Meagher (Irish Street) A Company. Thomas Francis Meagher joined the Volunteers in 1914. Following the split in the organisation in 1915, Seamus Rafter instructed him to remain inconspicuous and use his job in the post office as a source of information. He was appointed Intelligence officer for the Company. By steaming open R.I.C. dispatches from Dublin he was able to inform Rafter what the forces orders were. On the first morning of the Rising Meagher helped carry ammunition from "Antwerp" to the Athenaeum. He then went to the post office and disabled the phone system. For the remainder of that day he was placed on sentry duty. On Friday he helped commandeer bedding and food for the H.Q.. Meagher went to Ferns on Saturday; he was on outpost duty Sunday on the Camolin Road when the car carrying Pádraig Pearse's surrender letter was let through. With news of the surrender Meagher returned to Enniscorthy and was present in the Athenaeum to hear the leaders speak. Afterwards he helped with the collection and disposal of arms. Meagher was arrested early the following week and deported shortly afterwards. He was interned in Stafford Jail and Frongach Camp. While at the Camp he received a letter informing him of his dismissal from his job at the post office owing to his Volunteer activities. He was released in December.

After re-joining in 1917 Meagher worked full time at the manufacture of munitions under the command of Patrick Keegan. In 1918 he was one of the uniformed Volunteers who fired a salute over the grave of Seamus Rafter. A few days later he was arrested and charged with.

"wearing uniform and firing volleys over the grave of James Rafter."

He was jailed for a month. In the summer of 1919 Meagher received word from an old colleague in the post office that his name, along with the names of two other Volunteers, was on a list requesting their immediate arrest. From then until The Truce Meagher was on the run.

Meagher was a founding member of the North Wexford Active Service Unit in October 1920. One of the first operations of this unit was an attempted ambush on a military supply truck at Ballycarney. In December the unit decided to attack the R.I.C. barracks in Newtownbarry (Bunclody). In preparation five members of the unit went into the village on a reconnaissance mission. One of the group, Ned Murphy, went into Kelly's pub to meet with an informant. After he entered the pub he was accosted by an R.I.C. Constable by the name of William Jones. Murphy pulled out his revolver and shot Jones in the chest, killing him. Meagher heard the shot and ran towards the pub, he met Murphy on his way out and after a brief discussion they made their escape.

Another of the operations Meagher participated in was the ambush of an R.I.C. cycle patrol at Inch, one officer was killed and another wounded. Afterwards Meagher confiscated the dead and wounded men's weapons, the wounded man, a Sergeant, asked for his help, Meagher later recalled the incident in his Witness Statement for the Bureau of Military History dated April 12th, 1955.

"The Sergeant asked me to put a bandage on him and as a soldier I did."

After The Truce Meagher joined the National Army at Beggars Bush in 1922. From there he was sent to Kilkenny and was one of the soldiers who absconded with rifles and ammunition that April. On his return to Enniscorthy, Meagher was appointed as a member of the Republican police and was stationed at the courthouse. At the outbreak of Civil War he took part in the "Battle of Enniscorthy". For two days Meagher sniped at the Free State soldiers in the Castle from the steeple of St. Mary's Church. Before evacuating the town after it was retaken, he helped set fire to the courthouse. Meagher was arrested that October but was released by a former comrade from 1916 before he could be sent to Dublin. He continued active service up until Christmas, then with his health failing, he laid down his arms and returned to civilian life. Thomas Francis Meagher died at the age of 72 in 1958.

Brigid Moore (Lower Church Street) Cumann na mBan. Brigid Moore (nee Doyle) joined Cumann na mBan in 1915, her sister Mary Ellen was also a member. On the first morning of the Rising two boys called to her house at around 7 a.m. with orders for her to report to the Athenaeum. When she arrived she was instructed to go to the kitchen and help with the cooking. Moore would remain in the Athenaeum until Sunday; the one exception was when she went home to get rosary beads and prayer books to give to Volunteers going to Ferns. On Sunday afternoon Moore and another woman volunteered to go to Ferns to assist the women there. She remained there until the surrender and then she returned to the Athenaeum. In the following months Moore sent food parcels to the Volunteers who were imprisoned including her brother Thomas Doyle, another brother Laurence also served but he evaded arrest. She married in 1918 and her activity ceased except for on one occasion in 1919 when she looked after a box of revolvers and ammunition belonging to her brother Thomas for several months. Moore did this against the wishes of her new husband, who had been a Redmondite. Brigid Moore died in Parkton Nursing Home in 1966, she was 78 years old.

Brigid C. Moran (Church Street) Cumann na mBan. Brigid Christina Moran joined Cumann na mBan in 1914. In the weeks prior to the Rising she made over one hundred first aid kits. On the first morning of the Insurrection she reported for duty at the Athenaeum at 7 a.m..

Moran was placed in charge of setting up a temporary hospital there and with the help of other members of the Cumann readied beds and first aid kits. After this was done Moran went to the District Hospital and arranged to have an area in the emergency ward prepared for any casualties. This area consisted of two beds with their own medical supplies. The following night Moran helped treat a seriously wounded Volunteer at H.Q. who had been shot accidently while out on patrol. She accompanied him to the hospital where he would remain for several months. On Saturday evening Moran went to Ferns in charge of four others to set up a first aid station in the R.I.C. barracks, which was now the H.Q. of the Volunteers in the village. She remained there until they received the order to return to Enniscorthy after the surrender. Moran was in the convoy of cars when the car containing Peter Galligan crashed injuring four people including one of the Cumann members, Margaret King. Moran helped treat the injured and then brought Galligan and one of the Volunteers to her sister Sheila's house on Court Street for them to rest and hide.

In the months following she raised funds and organised events for the prisoner's and their dependants. Moran lived with her parents on Church Street over her father's tailor shop, beneath the shop there was a secret cellar. The cellar had a small entrance which only Moran, her sister and youngest brother could fit through. This cellar was used to store rifles, revolvers and ammunition from 1917-1921. Moran used to hand out the weapons when required and take them back afterwards. The week before the attack on the Clonroche R.I.C. barracks in April 1921, the explosives used in the attack were stored in this cellar. In the reprisals after the attack the cellar was discovered by the Black and Tans who then broke up her parent's shop and home.

By the time of the "Battle of Enniscorthy" in July 1922 the cellar was back in use. Moran made several trips to remove boxes of ammunition from it while under fire from the Free State soldiers in the Castle. These boxes were brought to Larkin's on The Duffry. Moran also acted as a medic for those few days and helped prepare the body of Volunteer Paddy O'Brien, (who was from Dublin and who had been shot dead along with local Volunteer Maurice Spillane on Friary Place on the last day of the fighting) so he could be waked. For the next few months Moran helped out however she could but by Christmas she had to cease her activities due to ill health. Brigid Christina Moran died in 1956, she was 64 years old.

James J. Moran (Friary Place) Lieutenant A Company. James Moran was a member of the officer class which Peter Galligan established in November 1915. Prior to Easter Week Moran helped with the manufacture of munitions and trained Volunteers belonging to Company's outside the town. On the first day of the Rising he was promoted to the rank of Lieutenant and served in both Enniscorthy and Ferns. Moran was arrested shortly after the surrender and deported. He was interned in Stafford Jail and Frongach Camp from where he was released in December. On the reorganisation of the movement he rejoined and participated in the general activities of his Company until he emigrated to the United States in 1919. James Moran settled in Chicago and died there aged 71 in 1960.

Michael Moran (Friary Place) Lieutenant A Company. A younger brother of James Moran, Michael Moran joined the Volunteers in 1914 and the I.R.B. shortly afterwards. Like his brother he was also a member of the officer class instructed by Peter Galligan. Moran worked as a clerk in the Enniscorthy Co-op and was able to use his position to learn of sales of material which would be beneficial to Patrick Keegan and his munition team. Moran passed this information on and then those homes and premises were raided. On the first morning of the Rising Moran marched from Irish Street to the Athenaeum with the main body of Volunteers. After a H.Q. had been established he was appointed as a Lieutenant and sent to take up duty at the bridge with four men under his command. After been relieved that evening he returned to H.Q. and carried out relief duty in the guard room.

On Friday morning Moran received information that a large quantity of ammunition had been shipped by rail to Enniscorthy from Arklow. With a dozen men in tow, he searched the railway stores and all the wagons there to see if there was any credence to this intelligence. They came up empty handed. From then until the surrender, Moran was tasked with making sure that no food in any of the shops left the town. He was also placed in charge of outposts at The Moyne and Greenville among others and he inspected these regularly. Moran was arrested at the Co-op on the Tuesday following the surrender and deported shortly afterwards. He was interned in Stafford Jail before he was released at the end of May. After his release he was dismissed from the Co-op.

While unemployed Moran helped to found *The Liberty Club* and became its first secretary. This club was used as a cover for the reorganisation of the Volunteers in 1917 and would later be known as the Sinn Féin Club. He found work in Donohue's and was a useful source of information for raids on its premises. Moran stepped away from the movement to get married in 1919 and played no further role.

On the 29th of November 1938 Moran appeared before a Military Pension Tribunal. On the day he was feeling unwell having recently been hospitalised on two separate occasions due to stomach problems. The Referee on the day was unsympathetic, noting in a memo.

This applicant appears to be stupid and confused on his recollection on what actually happened.

Moran was not a stupid man; in fact he owned and ran his own hardware business at the time. After been refused the pension and losing his appeal against the decision, Moran received a form for a service medal in May 1944 which he had not applied for. Returning the form he wrote a scathing letter on the 17th of May to accompany it. Some excerpts follow.

"I appeared before the Tribunal and must say the Referee was most insulting, the reception I received was more in keeping with a criminal appearing before a

criminal court Judge than a man who had spent the best part of his life in the service of his country, and I may tell you it was well for the Referee that my health was as it was otherwise I would have smashed his face for his insulting remarks."

"I had taken certain pride in being associated with the 1916 movement but from that morning I never have or never will talk of 1916 or anything connected with it."

"Nor did I ever anticipate a pension when I was working for the cause that was dear to me. However P.G. I shall see that my children shall never find themselves in the same humiliated position."

Michael Moran died at the age of 62 in 1953 having been awarded a Military Service Pension two years previously.

Denis Murphy (The Harrow) A Company. Denis Murphy was a member of the I.R.B. before he joined the Volunteers at their inception in 1913. Prior to the Rising he was a member of Patrick Keegan's munitions manufacturing team. During the Insurrection his main role was in the armoury at H.Q., he handed out supplies to the Volunteers as required. On Friday morning he went with a dispatch to Borris in a car driven by Michael Ennis. After the column of Volunteers marched to Ferns on Saturday evening, Murphy carried out relief duty at a few outposts when called upon. He was arrested a couple of days after the surrender and deported shortly afterwards. Murphy was interned in Stafford Jail and Frongach Camp before he was released in August.

On the reorganisation in 1917, Murphy was appointed as Company Adjutant and by late 1918 had been promoted to Brigade Adjutant. His primary activities up to The Truce was organising the manufacture of munitions. Murphy chose to take the Republican side of the Civil War and helped to block roads and dig trenches. On one occasion while felling a tree he was badly injured and put out of action for several weeks. After the Civil War Murphy had to close the clothes shop which he owned in

Enniscorthy due to a lack of business, the reason for this he believed was down to his activities during the Civil War. Murphy moved to Liverpool shortly after and worked as an ice-cream seller and then as a gravedigger. Denis Murphy was 63 years old when he died in Liverpool in 1954.

Felix Murphy (The Shannon) Sgt. Major A Company. A member of the Volunteers since their inception, Felix (Philip) Murphy held the rank of Sergeant Major in A Company. He was at "Antwerp" early on the morning of the Rising when Peter Galligan instructed him to proceed to "The Dump". Once there he helped with the distribution of weapons to the Volunteers before they marched to the Athenaeum. Murphy was then ordered by Seamus Rafter to gather a few men together and cut telegraph lines, this he did on the railway bridge and at Brownswood. On his return to the town Murphy went to the railway station, where he was employed, to wait on the train which brought men from Wexford to work in the Kynoch's munitions factory in Arklow. Murphy stopped the train on its arrival and had the engine put in a siding. All the workers onboard were ordered to get off and walk back to Wexford. Murphy then spent a short period of time on the Turret Rocks, from where he fired four rounds at the R.I.C. barracks. (Military Service Pensions Board interview on the 5th of June 1940) Murphy returned to H.Q. around midday and reported his activities to Seamus Rafter, who then along with Seán Etchingham and Robert Brennan promoted him to the rank of Captain.

Murphy then set about organising Volunteers for various outposts including Clonhaston, Drumgoold and Brownswood. After this he placed sentries on Old Church, Templeshannon and the courthouse. For the next three days this was his sole job, he inspected each post up to ten times a day to hear reports and summon relief. When the car containing D.I. Drake and Father Kehoe arrived at the Athenaeum on Sunday, Murphy relieved them of the white flag they were carrying. Later after the surrender was made official, he helped collect weapons which had been left around the town and brought them back to the Athenaeum. Once finished he went on the run for ten days only to be arrested in his bed on his return and deported shortly afterwards. Murphy was interned in Wakefield Prison and Frongach Camp before he was released in December. On his return he was dismissed from his job at the railway station. Murphy re-joined in 1917 but due to his unemployment status had to leave Enniscorthy in March 1918 to find work. In later years he opened a successful grocery and provisions shop in Athlone. Felix (Philip) Murphy died in Portiuncula Hospital, Ballinasloe in 1958 at the age of 72.

Felix Murphy (Irish Street) A Company. Felix Murphy joined the Volunteers in 1913. Over the next couple of years he helped make munitions two to three nights a week. At daybreak on the first morning of the Rising he was instructed to commandeer a car at the Hayes residence in Greenmount. On his return he was detailed to outpost duty at St. John's Manor. On Friday, Murphy was sent to the Turret Rocks where he took up a sniping position. He stated before the Military Service Pensions Board on the 8th of December 1937 that he fired approximately fifteen rounds at the R.I.C. barracks over the period of 4 hours.. Murphy finished his day on sentry duty at the bottom of Irish Street. On Saturday morning Murphy was on sentry duty at Maudlin's Folly and after he was relieved, marched to Ferns with the column of Volunteers. In Ferns he carried out guard duty until he was recalled to the Athenaeum after the surrender. Murphy helped with the collection and disposal of weapons before going home in the early hours of Monday morning. He evaded arrest and played no further role in any Volunteer activity. In later years Murphy was employed by Wexford County Council as a shoemaker in St. John's Hospital. Felix Murphy died in his 73rd year in 1963.

James Murphy (Carley's Bridge) Lieutenant A Company. A member of the I.R.B. for several years, James Murphy was one of the first men to join the Volunteers in 1913. He was appointed as a Sergeant by Seamus Rafter and helped to drill new recruits. Murphy was also a member of Patrick Keegan's group that raided for materials to manufacture munitions in the years leading up to the Rising. Murphy's first task on the morning of the Insurrection was to go to the Turret Rocks with a rifle. His orders were to open fire on any R.I.C. men attempting to go outside their barracks. He remained there until evening and then returned to the Athenaeum. From there he was sent to Edermine for outpost duty. On Friday morning Murphy was a member of a raiding party sent to seize arms in Kiltrea, Killane, Rathnure and Monart. On his return he was promoted to Lieutenant. Murphy then carried out street patrol around the town centre to prevent the looting of shops and to stop people demanding goods in the name of the Irish Republic. On Saturday he was detailed to Davis's Mill where he remained until he was recalled to the Athenaeum for the surrender on Sunday night. After which he helped with the collection of weapons. Murphy was arrested a couple of days later at his residence in Carley's Bridge and deported shortly afterwards. He was interned in Woking Detention Centre and Frongach Camp before he was released in late July.

Murphy re-joined in 1917 and participated in the general activities of his Company. In 1918 he was a member of the party of Volunteers sent to Waterford for the Bye-Election. At the end of that year he left Enniscorthy and moved to Clifden in County Galway. Murphy joined a fledgling Company there and helped train them. He carried dispatches and arms between Clifden and Galway on numerous occasions. Murphy was one of four Volunteers who destroyed the Clifden Coastguard Station on the night of the 8th of August 1920 after intelligence had been received that it was going to be used by the military. Murphy left Clifden and emigrated to the United States a couple of months later. James Murphy died in Brooklyn, New York in 1955, he was 69 years old.

James Murphy (Ross Road) A Company. James Murphy joined the Volunteers in 1914. On the first morning of the Rising he marched from Irish Street to the Athenaeum with the main body of Volunteers. From there he was sent to the Market Square to take up sentry duty. While there he heard gunfire coming from the direction of the courthouse. Murphy ran up Georges Street and came across some Volunteers engaged in a gun battle with a group of R.I.C. officers near the top of Friary Hill. He offered supporting fire for the Volunteers before the R.I.C. men made their way back to their barracks. Murphy then resumed his duty on the Square. At 8 p.m. that night he was detailed for guard duty at the bridge, he remained there until 8 a.m. the following morning. After resting in the Athenaeum, Murphy next returned to duty at the Gas Yard on Friday evening. On Saturday he marched with the column of Volunteers to Ferns, he carried out sentry duty in the village until he was recalled to Enniscorthy after the surrender on Sunday night.. Murphy was arrested the next day and deported shortly afterwards. He was interned in Stafford Jail and Frongach Camp before he was released at the end of July.

Murphy re-joined in 1917. At the time he was employed in Seamus Rafter's pub and carried dispatches for him to Ferns a few times a week. In 1918 after the General Election he helped guard the ballot boxes at the courthouse over the Christmas Holidays. In May 1920 he took part in the major raid for petrol at the railway station. Murphy was arrested in February 1921 and held in the courthouse. He was released a week later after catching double pneumonia due to the ill treatment he received at the hands of the military. In 1922 Murphy joined the Republican police and served in the garrison at the courthouse. When the Civil War broke out he took part in the" Battle of Enniscorthy". He sniped at the Castle from the Turret Rocks for two days. After the Free State Army retook the town, Murphy went on the run and hid in Galbally for a number of days before returning home. In the following months he carried dispatches for various flying columns before finishing up prior to the ceasefire. James Murphy died in Wexford Hospital in 1962 at the age of 67.

James Murphy (St. John's Street) A Company. James Murphy was a member of the I.R.B. for several years before he joined the Volunteers in 1913. After the split in the movement in 1915 and acting on the orders of Seamus Rafter, Murphy led a raid on the premises of Michael Kelly on Georges Street (Rafter St.) for weapons. Kelly had stayed loyal to the

National Volunteers and was holding a quantity of rifles which Rafter now believed belonged to the Irish Volunteers. Murphy and his men forced their way in and retrieved the weapons without much of a struggle. He was also involved in the landing of arms at Ballyconnigar the same year under the command of Seamus Doyle. During the Rising, Murphy carried out street patrols around the town centre and guard duty at the Gas Yard. He also took part in several raids for weapons throughout the district. After the surrender he evaded arrest. In 1917 he re-joined and participated in the regular activities of his Company. Murphy worked in the Enniscorthy Co-op during this period and stored a number of weapons there without the knowledge of his employer. He remained a Volunteer until The Truce and then dropped out. James Murphy died in 1951 at the age of 64.

John Murphy (Ross Road) A Company. John Murphy joined the Volunteers in late 1914. On the morning of the Rising, he was one of the men who stopped the 4.20 a.m. train at the railway station and removed the driver and guard. Later that morning he exchanged gunfire with an R.I.C. constable named Cahill on the Mill Park Road. The policeman successfully made his way to the barracks on the Abbey Square. (testimony before the Military service Pensions Board on the 29th of October 1936) Murphy was then detailed to commandeer bedding and food for H.Q.. For the remainder of the week he was on outpost duty at several different locations. After the surrender Murphy helped to return bicycles, that had been commandeered for Volunteer scouts, to their rightful owners. Murphy was arrested on the 13th of May and deported shortly afterwards. He was interned at Wakefield Prison and Frongach Camp until December.

Murphy re-joined in 1917 and took part in the general activities of his Company. The following year he was sent to Waterford for the Bye-Election and to Wexford for the General Election. On one occasion in 1919 he encountered a drunk British soldier and relieved him of his rifle. In 1920 Murphy participated in both the attack on the R.I.C. barracks in

Clonroche and the raid for petrol at the railway station.. The following May he was a member of the party of Volunteers who sniped on the Enniscorthy R.I.C. barracks the night before the Killurin train ambush. After The Truce Murphy joined the Republican garrison in the courthouse in April 1922. When the Civil War erupted he played an active part in the "Battle of Enniscorthy", sniping on the Castle from the Nun's Field and helping to build barricades. As the Free State Army retook the town and the courthouse was set alight, Murphy was sent to inform the men who were on outpost duty the news. On his return to town he was arrested, however, was released the following day by a sympathetic Free State officer with whom he had fought alongside during the War of Independence. In later years Murphy was employed as a tailor in the County Home. John Murphy died at his residence on the Ross Road aged 92 in 1985.

Kate Murphy (New Street) Cumann na mBan. Kate Murphy (nee Murphy) joined Cumann na mBan in 1914. For the duration of the Rising she cooked for the Volunteers in the Athenaeum. After the surrender she helped with the collection of weapons and then went home. Over the following months Murphy assisted in raising funds for the prisoner's dependants and sent food parcels to the prisoners themselves. While working at various houses during the War of Independence Murphy was able to pass on information to the Volunteers about weapons stored in these houses. The houses were then raided. On one occasion she personally walked out of a house with two rifles. During this period her husband Philip was employed as the caretaker of the Showgrounds, and they lived in a house on the grounds. On numerous occasions on the run Volunteers would call at night-time to rest and be fed. Kate Murphy died in 1969, she was 78 years old.

Martin Murphy (Templescoby) A Company. One of the oldest Volunteers, Martin Murphy was 55 years old when he took part in the Easter Rising in 1916. Previous to joining the Volunteers he had been a long-time member of the I.R.B.. For the first two days of the Insurrection, Murphy helped load and unload materials at the Athenaeum, while on Saturday he was tasked with filling cartridge cases. He was present in the Athenaeum for the surrender and evaded arrest a couple of days later, thanks to the intervention of a prominent local businessman. Martin Murphy died at the age of 78 in 1939.

Matthew Murphy (Ferns) Ferns Company. Matthew Murphy joined the Volunteers in 1913. At the time of the Rising he was a section leader in the Ferns Company. When he arrived at the Athenaeum on the Thursday, Seamus Rafter placed him in charge of four Volunteers and sent them to the entrance of the Enniscorthy Asylum to take up outpost duty. Later that night Murphy took up a position on the Turret Rocks which enabled him to cover the R.I.C. barracks, his orders were to only open fire if the police attempted to leave. On Friday he returned to Ferns on compassionate leave to visit with a dying aunt. He remained there until after the surrender and then returned to the Athenaeum. There he was given three rifles and a shotgun to bring away and hide. Murphy was arrested the following Tuesday at the forge where he worked as a blacksmith. He was deported a short time after and was interned in Wandsworth Prison for six weeks before he was released.

Murphy re-joined in 1917 and his activities up to March 1921 included the attack on the Clonroche R.I.C. barracks, the burning of the barracks in Clonevan, raids for mail and the manufacture of munitions. He was arrested in March 1921 and interned on Spike Island until that December. Murphy joined the National Army in 1922 and fought in the "Battle of Enniscorthy" in early July. He resigned from the army in 1923 and joined the newly formed Garda Siochana, with whom he served with until 1946. For the majority of this time he was based in Stepaside, Dublin. After retiring Murphy worked part-time for the Department of Agriculture as an Inspector at Dublin Port. Matthew Murphy died in Dublin at the age of 93 in 1979.

Michael Murphy (The Shannon) A Company. Michael "Rasher" Murphy was already a member of the I.R.B. when he joined the Volunteers at their inception in 1913. In the months preceding the Rising he was involved in the manufacture of munitions at "The Dump" as well as taking part in raids on Donohue's and the railway stores for materials. For the first three days of Easter Week Murphy worked as a cabinet maker before standing guard at "The Dump" for two hours each night. After he had been mobilised early on Thursday morning, Murphy was sent to the Turret Rocks to take up a sniping position. He fired several times on the R.I.C. barracks before he was relieved at midday. Murphy's next task was to take up outpost duty at Solsboro. He finished his days duty standing guard on the Old Church Road. On Friday he was sent back to Solsboro where he helped to block roads. Later Murphy was a member of a party of Volunteers detailed to commandeer foodstuffs for H.Q.. From then until the surrender on Sunday night, he was on street patrol around the town centre. After the surrender Murphy helped bring weapons and materials to Patrick Keegan's house on Irish Street. There he was given a number of rifles and ammunition to hide, which he did in his mother's house. He successfully evaded arrest.

Murphy re-joined in 1917 and played a prominent part in the reorganisation of The Shannon Company, of which he was appointed as 2nd Lieutenant. In the following years he participated in raids for petrol at the railway, magnetos in Donohue's, bomb making materials at Davis's foundry and for Rate Books at the Enniscorthy Asylum. Murphy was also one of the Volunteers who sniped on the R.I.C. barracks in Enniscorthy the night before the Killurin train ambush in May 1921. After The Truce Murphy performed police work for a short period. He took no part in the Civil War. In 1937 Murphy's wife died leaving him with eight children. In order to provide for them he went to work in Sheffield for a number of years. He returned to Enniscorthy in the late 1950's. Michael "Rasher" Murphy died in 1972 at the age of 76.

Michael Murphy (Killagoley) C Company. A member of the Volunteers since 1913, Michael Murphy marched with the main body of men from Irish Street to the Athenaeum on the first morning of the Rising. From there he took up a sentry position at the top of Castle Hill where he remained for several hours. In the afternoon Murphy was sent to Salville Cross. When he was relieved he returned to the Athenaeum and after a short rest was detailed to Davis's Mill. Murphy was employed at the Mill and was able to allocate Volunteers to the best vantage points to watch the roads. He stayed at the Mill until 8 a.m. the following morning. On Friday afternoon Murphy was sent on outpost duty to Clonhaston. Saturday morning he was on sentry duty on The Duffry for four hours. According to his testimony before the Military Service Pensions Board on the 9th of February 1940, he was then posted to the Turret Rocks from where he later claimed to have fired ten shots at the R.I.C. barracks. Later that night Murphy was placed on sentry duty on the Island Road until the early hours of Sunday Morning. After resting at H.Q., Murphy spent Sunday afternoon on street patrol around The Shannon before he was recalled for the surrender. Murphy evaded arrest by going on the run for several weeks and afterwards had no further involvement with the Volunteers. Michael Murphy died in 1970 in his 83rd year.

Patrick Murphy (Ferns) Ferns Company. Patrick Murphy joined the Volunteers in 1914. At the time of the Easter Rising he was a section commander in the Ferns Company. Murphy set off with his Company for Enniscorthy on the Tuesday of Easter Week, only to receive word on the way that nothing had yet occurred in the town. The men set up camp at Ballinahallin Wood on the outskirts to await developments. Late that night instructions came for them to return to Ferns. After new orders were issued on Thursday morning and were confirmed, the members of the Company who had not gone home (about twenty men) made their way to Enniscorthy. Murphy was armed with a pike but at the Athenaeum was issued with a rifle. For the next two days he carried out sentry duty around the town centre. On Saturday evening Murphy returned to Ferns and the following morning he commandeered tools from Bolger's hardware to fell trees and make roadblocks. In the afternoon he was placed on outpost duty. After the surrender was announced Murphy returned to the Athenaeum and helped with the collection of weapons. He was allowed to keep his rifle which he hid in his father's house. Murphy was arrested the following week and deported shortly afterwards. He was interned in Wandsworth Prison and Frongach Camp before he was released in December. Murphy re-joined in 1917 but the only activities he was involved in was drilling and parades, he took no part in any operations. Patrick Murphy was 79 years old when he passed away in 1970.

Patrick Murphy (Ballycarney) A Company. Patrick Murphy joined the Volunteers in 1913. On the first morning of the Rising he marched with the main body of men from Irish Street to the Athenaeum. His first duty of the day was to obtain a boiler and cooking utensils. Murphy then went to the Manse with a couple of other Volunteers to inform the Priests of what was happening. In the afternoon he was placed on sentry duty at the top of Irish Street and later that night on guard duty at the entrance to the Athenaeum. Murphy spent Friday morning on sentry duty on The Duffry, while in the afternoon he was on duty in the guard room at the Athenaeum. That night he accompanied a couple of officers as they inspected outposts. At around midday on Saturday Murphy was sent to Ballindaggin with a dispatch. While there he helped Volunteers cut telegraph lines and take down poles. He spent the night there at an outpost. When he returned to Enniscorthy early on Sunday morning he had a brief rest before he was sent to Davis's Mill. He was recalled from the Mill for the surrender.

Murphy was arrested the following Wednesday morning by British soldiers who dragged him from his bed and badly beat him. An injury inflicted to his eye at the time would have serious ramifications on his health in later years. After been deported Murphy was interned in Stafford Jail until he was released in early July.

Murphy re-joined in 1917 and participated in all the general activities of his Company. In April 1920 he acted as a scout on the night of the attack on the Clonroche R.I.C. barracks, he was also involved in the raid for petrol the following month at the railway station. Up to The Truce Murphy carried regular dispatches to Ballindaggin, Oylgate, Killanne and Newtownbarry (Bunclody). During the Civil War Murphy took the Anti-Treaty side and throughout the "Battle of Enniscorthy", acted as a medic in the courthouse. He was arrested on the 22nd of February 1923 for throwing a grenade at the Castle which was occupied at the time by Free State troops. He was released a month later due to ill health. For the remainder of the Civil War Murphy carried dispatches to and from the town. Patrick Murphy died aged 69 in 1961.

Philip Murphy (New Street) A Company. Philip Murphy was a member of the I.R.B. before joining the Volunteers as an auxiliary member in 1913. The reason for this auxiliary status was because of his job, he worked in the post office and if it had come to the attention of his superiors that he was a Volunteer, he would have been dismissed immediately. For the two years leading up to the Rising, Murphy copied and deciphered dispatches sent to and from the R.I.C. and handed them over to the leadership. On the first morning of the Rising Murphy reported to the Athenaeum at 8 a.m.. He was placed in charge of the guard and was promoted to Lieutenant. It was his responsibility to send the men to their different locations, make sure they were armed and that the arms were handed back once they were off duty. For the duration he remained at H.Q., save for half a dozen visits to various outposts. Murphy's other roles included taking charge of all weapons commandeered in raids and assessing new recruits on their suitability to serve. After the surrender on Sunday night, he was one of the last Volunteers to leave the Athenaeum.

Murphy was arrested the following Tuesday and deported shortly afterwards. He was interned in Stafford Jail and Frongach Camp. At

Frongach he was appointed as leader of one of the thirteen huts occupied by the prisoners. Murphy was court-martialled for

mutiny and incitement to mutiny

this was for refusing to answer to his name or number and he was sentenced to three months hard labour. He was released on the 23rd of December. Murphy re-joined in 1917 and participated in the routine activities of his Company. At the end of September that year he cycled to Dublin to attend the funeral of Thomas Ashe. There he was recognised by Richard Mulcahy (future General and Minister of Defence) from their time in Frongach, Mulcahy duly placed Murphy in charge of a section of Volunteers for the funeral. After losing his job in the post office Murphy found work as the caretaker of the Showgrounds in Enniscorthy. Using this position he was able to conceal weapons and munitions from 1919 until The Truce. Having got married to Kate Murphy prior to The Truce he withdrew from service and played no part in the Civil War. Philip Murphy died in 1970 at the age of 86.

Thomas Murphy (Irish Street) A Company. Thomas Murphy joined the Volunteers in 1913. On the first morning of the Rising he gathered with the main body of men outside Patrick Keegan's house on Irish Street and marched to the Athenaeum. He remained there until evening and was then detailed to The Duffry for sentry duty. On Friday morning Murphy was instructed to commandeer two horses and their carts. He then went to Davis's Mill for flour and then Lett's Brewery for hops, he delivered this cargo to the town's bakeries. When Murphy returned to H.Q. he was placed on orderly duty in the guard room for the rest of the day. On Saturday, Murphy was assigned guard duty outside the National Bank on Castle Street. He spent Sunday at the Athenaeum and after the surrender helped with the collection of weapons. He evaded arrest by going on the run for several days. In 1917 Murphy re-joined and took part in all the general activities of his Company until he moved to Wexford for a job in 1920. He ceased all service from then. Thomas Murphy died in Brownswood Hospital aged 79 in 1976.

William Murphy (The Shannon) A Company. William Murphy was a member of the I.R.B. before joining the Volunteers in 1913 at their inception. In the months leading up to the Rising Murphy was employed as manager of the munitions department in Donohue's hardware. Through this position he surreptitiously supplied the Volunteers with hundreds of rounds of ammunition for rifles, revolvers and shotguns as well as gunpowder, blasting powder and fuses. On the first morning of the Insurrection Murphy took up a sniping position on the Turret Rocks. According to his statement before the Military Service Pensions Board on the 30th of November 1938, he fired between twenty-five to thirty rounds at the R.I.C. barracks over a two-hour period.. After been relieved he took up sentry duty at Templeshannon. That evening he was once again on the Turret Rocks and fired approximately a dozen more rounds at the barracks. On Friday and Saturday, Murphy was detailed to street patrol around the town. He was present in the Athenaeum on Sunday night for the surrender and helped with the collection of weapons afterwards. Murphy was arrested the following Tuesday at Donohue's and deported not long after. He was interned until July in Stafford Jail and Frongach Camp. On his return to Enniscorthy he was dismissed from his position in Donohue's due to his Volunteer activities. He re-joined in 1917 but was drawn to the political aspect of the movement. He won a seat on the U.D.C. on behalf of Sinn Féin and served for several years. In later years William Murphy moved to Navan. He died in his 66th year in 1959.

Brigid Noctor (Bloomfield) Cumann na mBan. Brigid Noctor (nee Doyle) joined Cumann na mBan in Easter Week 1916. She worked part-time for Seamus Rafter during this period. In the days before the Rising, Rafter showed her some secret compartments in The Bridge House where he lived on Slaney Place. He used these compartments to conceal weapons and boxes of ammunition. Rafter instructed her to hand out these items if requested by Volunteers over the following days. On the first morning of the Rising, Noctor informed Rafter about a quantity of weapons which were in a house where her husband worked as a gardener and where she worked a couple of days a week cleaning. This house belong to a solicitor named Moffatt in Prospect. Rafter sent two Volunteers to relieve the solicitor of his weapons. For the remainder of the Rising Noctor looked after the officers who came to eat and rest in The Bridge House. After the surrender she assisted in removing all weapons and materials from the house. The following week Noctor and her husband were dismissed from their positions with the Moffatts. In August 1918, after the explosion which ultimately killed Seamus Rafter, Noctor cleaned up any traces. She then assisted with his care until he passed away a fortnight later. When the R.I.C. raided the house after his death, Noctor concealed a revolver on her person which belonged to a Volunteer who was present. In early 1920 Noctor had to undergo two serious operations in Dublin. Owing to these health issues she had to cease all activity. Brigid Noctor died in 1962 in her 75th year.

Michael Nolan (Hospital Lane) A Company. A carpenter by trade, Michael Nolan joined the Volunteers in 1913. On the first morning of the Rising he was assigned sentry duty on Lymington Road. After that he claimed in his evidence before the Military Service Pensions board on the 2nd of March 1937 to have fired *nine or ten rounds, maybe more* at the R.I.C. barracks but he did not state from where. On Friday, Nolan spent his entire day at Davis's Mill while on Saturday he was on duty at the bridge. Nolan was sent to Manor Mills House on the Mill Park Road for guard duty on Sunday morning and that evening was back at the bridge until the surrender. He was arrested the following Tuesday and deported shortly afterwards. Nolan was interned in Stafford Jail for a fortnight before he was released. On his return to Enniscorthy he ceased his Volunteer activities. Michael Nolan died at his residence on St. John's Street in 1947 aged 78.

Denis O'Brien (Irish Street) Lieutenant A Company. Denis O'Brien had been a member of the I.R.B. since 1910 when he joined the Volunteers at their inception in 1913. In November 1915 he was chosen by Peter Galligan to join the officer class he was establishing. By the time of the Insurrection O'Brien had been appointed as a section commander in A Company. On the first morning of the Rising, O'Brien was sent to the railway station to take charge of all proceedings there. He remained at the station throughout the day. When he returned to the Athenaeum that evening he was promoted to Lieutenant. On Friday, O'Brien was placed in command of a couple of lorry loads of Volunteers sent to Edermine, their instructions were to intercept any military or police who may have been coming from Wexford. After spending several hours there he returned to the Athenaeum, where upon his arrival he was appointed as Officer in Charge of Transport. From then until the surrender Sunday night O'Brien was stationed at H.Q.. After the surrender, O'Brien helped clear the Athenaeum and then went to "The Dump" and moved material from there to "Antwerp". He went on the run until the following Wednesday. On learning his name was on a wanted list and that the military had already raided his house, O'Brien decided to hand himself in at the R.I.C. barracks to save his family any further hardship. A short time later he was deported. O'Brien was interned in Stafford Jail and Frongach Camp until his release in December.

In 1917 O'Brien re-joined and played an active role in the reorganisation. He held onto his rank and in 1918 was appointed as Adjutant to the 2nd Battalion North Wexford Brigade. That same year O'Brien was arrested after the funeral of Seamus Rafter and jailed for a month. On his release he took up an intelligence role in the Battalion as well as serving as Adjutant. O'Brien knew some individuals working in local hotels who passed him the details of any strangers staying there. He also obtained information from some British soldiers who came to the town. O'Brien was arrested again in December 1920 and was imprisoned until the following December. On his release he stepped back from Volunteer activity and played no role in the Civil War. Denis O'Brien died at the age of 87 in 1972.

Elizabeth O'Brien (Fairview Terrace) Cumann na mBan. Elizabeth O'Brien (nee Cullen) joined Cumann na mBan towards the end of 1915. She reported for duty to the Athenaeum on the first morning of the Rising and remained there until the following Sunday night. Her duties included cooking and cleaning up after the Volunteers. In the days following the surrender O'Brien helped to transfer ammunition between various houses. Her own home was raided, and her stepfather Volunteer Patrick McGrath (my Great Grandfather) was arrested. In the following years her home was used as a safe house for Volunteers on the run. O'Brien cooked for them and kept watch while they slept. The house was also used to store weapons and ammunition for which she had been given the responsibility of looking after. On numerous occasions O'Brien carried weapons and dispatches to and from the town. She also played an intelligence role which entailed her observing the police and military and reporting back on their activities. She served up until The Truce. Elizabeth O'Brien died in 1973, a few weeks shy of her 78th birthday.

James O'Brien (St. John's) Lt. Na Fianna Éireann. James O'Brien joined Na Fianna in 1914. At the time he was working as an apprentice in The Echo Newspaper and helped with the printing of seditious literature including The Irish Volunteer. O'Brien acted as a scout and look out for Patrick Keegan's raiding parties on many occasions. He led a raid himself for shovels, picks and sledgehammers from a railway shed, these implements were used to dig out "The Dump" at the rear of Keegan's house. From Easter Sunday night until the following Wednesday night, O'Brien was on guard duty between "Antwerp and "The Dump". Late Wednesday night he was ordered to go home and sleep. O'Brien reported to the Athenaeum at 10 a.m. Thursday morning and was handed a rifle. That evening he was sent with a dispatch to the Turret Rocks ordering a cease fire. On his arrival, (according to his statement before the Military

Service Pensions Board on the 21st of November 1939) he fired off several rounds at the R.I.C. barracks before passing on the order. But for the exceptions of carrying out sentry duty on Friary Hill and outpost duty at Red Pat's Cross, for the rest of the week O'Brien carried dispatches between the various outposts and H.Q.. After the surrender he evaded arrest.

In the Spring of 1917 O'Brien commenced with the reorganisation of Na Fianna in the town. He was appointed Lieutenant and shortly afterwards Captain. In 1918 he established the first Fianna Battalion and became its Commandant in June. By November a Na Fianna Brigade was up and running and O'Brien was appointed Brigade Commandant. The main roles of Na Fianna were scouting for the Volunteers and carrying dispatches. O'Brien travelled extensively around North Wexford training and organising new branches. In 1919 O'Brien participated in several raids for weapons and documents. He commandeered the lorries which were used for the raid for petrol at the railway station in May 1920 and stood guard as the petrol was loaded. He was arrested in March 1921 and held until that December.

At the outbreak of the Civil War on the 28th of June 1922, O'Brien joined the Republican garrison at the courthouse and fought in the "Battle of Enniscorthy". After evacuating the town he joined up with a flying column but was arrested in August and held until December. Once released he re-joined the column but was again captured in March. O'Brien was one of several prisoners who escaped from Wexford Jail on the 2nd of May 1923. Six weeks later he was involved in the execution of an alleged spy. The following is an excerpt from James O'Brien's sworn statement given before the Military Service Pensions Board on the 21st of November 1939.

Q. *You mention the execution of a spy.*

A. *Yes.*

Q. *Were you in the arrest?*

A. *We were instructed to get him. He was afraid to come with me. We were sent to arrest him. He was one of our own. It had to be kept quiet. We could not get him away from the house he was in.*

Q. *What did you do then?*

A. *He came with another chap. He arranged to meet me later.*

Q. *Was he executed?*

A. *Yes.*

Q. *Had you a part?*

A. *No, I was there immediately after. I was there at the burial; I heard the shot.*

James O'Brien died in Carlow aged 62 in 1962.

James O'Brien (Irish Street) A Company. James O'Brien was a younger brother of Denis O'Brien's. He was a member of the I.R.B. before joining the Volunteers in 1913. Prior to the Rising he helped manufacture munitions at "The Dump" and also carried out guard duty there. The night before the Insurrection O'Brien along with three other Volunteers, William Boyne, James Healy and John Tomkins, were ordered to go to the Boro Bridge and lift rails off the tracks there. On their arrival they were met by an R.I.C. patrol. Shots were exchanged and Tomkins was captured, while Healy was injured making his escape. O'Brien and Boyne helped bring Healy to the hospital beside the County Home and then returned to "Antwerp" to inform the officers what had occurred. O'Brien was then sent to mobilise Volunteers and order them to report to Irish Street. After doing so, he helped cut the lines of communication at the railway and around the town. He was then detailed to commandeer cars in the district.

On Friday O'Brien was a member of a party of Volunteers who raided for weapons outside the town, while on Saturday he spent most of the day on outpost duty. On Sunday O'Brien was placed in charge of D.I. Drake and Father Kehoe after they had arrived with Pádraig Pearse's surrender letter. He escorted them to Mass before accompanying them to Gorey to make sure they got there safely. On their way through Ferns, O'Brien passed on the order from H.Q. to evacuate the village and return to Enniscorthy. After arriving back at the Athenaeum later that night O'Brien helped with the collection and disposal of weapons. He then went to "The Dump" and did the same there. He was arrested the following Tuesday and deported a short time after. O'Brien was interned in Stafford Jail and Frongach Camp until he was released in December. In 1917 O'Brien helped with the reorganisation of his Company and was appointed Lieutenant. He was promoted to Captain a few months later. A month after the Funeral of Seamus Rafter in October 1918, O'Brien was arrested for his role as the officer in charge of a Company of Volunteers at the funeral. He was court-martialled and sentenced to six months hard labour, the last three of which he spent in solitary confinement.

A couple of months after his release O'Brien was appointed as Brigade Adjutant. He used his job as a trade union official as cover for his Volunteer activities. In early 1920 O'Brien was transferred to Gorey for his job and soon realised he couldn't carry out the duties of a Brigade Adjutant fully. He resigned the position and took the rank of Staff Captain. A few months later he moved back to Enniscorthy and although he attended Brigade meetings, his role began to diminish. O'Brien was arrested and jailed in March 1921 and was held until that December. After his release O'Brien had no further involvement. James O'Brien passed away at the age of 70 in 1960.

John Joseph O'Brien (The Duffry) A Company. John Joseph O'Brien joined Na Fianna Éireann in 1914 and the Volunteers and I.R.B. in 1915. From the night of Easter Sunday until the following Wednesday night he was on guard duty at "The Dump". On Thursday morning O'Brien marched from Irish Street with the main body of Volunteers to the Athenaeum where a headquarters was established. O'Brien was placed on outpost duty at St. John's for the day. On Friday he was again on outpost duty as well as commandeering bedding and supplies from several shops. From then until the surrender on Sunday night, O'Brien's duties consisted of scouting and manning outposts. He evaded arrest after the surrender.

O'Brien re-joined in 1917 and while he worked as a tailor during the day, over the next two years he also worked up to four nights a week under the command of Patrick Keegan manufacturing munitions. On one occasion while thawing frozen Gelignite over an open fire, O'Brien was overwhelmed by the fumes. This incident would have a long-lasting effect on his health. Throughout the War of Independence O'Brien played an active part in his Company's operations, he threw grenades at the R.I.C. barracks in Clonroche during the major attack on it in April 1920. The following month he participated in the raid for petrol at the railway station. In May 1921 he was a member of the party who sniped on the R.I.C. barracks in Enniscorthy the night before the Killurin train ambush.. After The Truce, O'Brien joined the Republican police in the town and helped to keep order.

At the outbreak of the Civil War he was a member of the courthouse garrison. On the night the "Battle of Enniscorthy" broke out, O'Brien, while on guard duty at Templeshannon with a colleague, captured a Free State soldier. They attempted to bring him to the courthouse but their route across the bridge was covered by snipers in the Castle, so, under the cover of darkness they brought him across the railway bridge. Once the town had been recaptured by the Free State forces O'Brien left with a flying column, but after travelling four miles had to seek medical attention at a priest's house. His health was poor due to the incident a couple of years previously of inhaling the gelignite fumes. When well enough he returned to Enniscorthy and ceased all activities. John Joseph O'Brien died at the age of 62 in 1958.

Seamus O'Brien (Morriscastle) A Company. Seamus O'Brien was from Morriscastle and served his time as an apprentice in the pub and grocery trade in Cooney's of Oulart before coming to Enniscorthy to work as a shop assistant. On his arrival in the town he joined the Volunteers. There is no record of his activities during Easter Week 1916, however he was arrested on the 2nd of May and interned in Wandsworth Jail and Frongach Camp before he was released in December. In 1917 O'Brien moved to Rathdrum in Wicklow to work in a hotel, at the same time he also joined the Rathdrum Company of the Volunteers. In 1918 he went into business with another Volunteer and opened a grocery shop in the town. O'Brien married a local girl, and they had a daughter in December 1919. On the night of the 12th of February 1920, O'Brien was on the Market Square in Rathdrum with two companions when an R.I.C. patrol consisting of two officers passed by them. One of the men with O'Brien took out a revolver and fired on the policemen wounding one in the shoulder. The other officer turned round and opened fire, fatally wounding O'Brien. The men with him ran away. An internal Volunteer investigation discovered that the Volunteer who opened fire had been under the influence of alcohol and that the shooting had not been premeditated. Seamus O'Brien was 28 years old when he was shot dead and held the rank of Commandant of the Rathdrum Company.

Thomas O'Brien (St. John's) Na Fianna Éireann. Thomas O'Brien was the older brother of Lieutenant James O'Brien. He joined Na Fianna at its inception in 1914. Along with his brother he was under the command of Patrick Keegan. He acted as a scout for raiding parties and carried out guard duty at "The Dump". While working on the trains, O'Brien collected fog lights at various points on route to Dublin, the material in these lights were then used in the manufacture of munitions. On the first morning of the Rising O'Brien marched with the main body of men from Irish Street to the Athenaeum. From there he took up a sniping position on Castle Hill. He was recalled an hour later and sent with a group of Volunteers to commandeer supplies from Donohoe's hardware.

On his return, O'Brien was sent with four others to O'Neill's coal yard to get coal for the heating system in the Athenaeum. The coal yard was approximately fifty yards from the Bank of Ireland on the Mill Park Road. While commandeering the coal they came under fire from two R.I.C. men barricaded inside the Bank. They returned fire (In his testimony before the Military Service Pensions Board on the 9th of February 1940, O'Brien stated he fired once) and the R.I.C. ceased firing. Over the following hours O'Brien raided several shops for supplies. On Friday morning O'Brien carried out sentry duty on the Market Square. After been recalled to the Athenaeum, he was sent to Edermine with a party of Volunteers under the command of Patrick Keegan. There O'Brien was placed on guard duty while the others felled trees to make roadblocks. On Saturday he was on outpost duty at St. Johns and that evening on duty in the guard room at H.Q.. While on outpost duty at Red Pat's Cross on Sunday afternoon, O'Brien arrested the County Surveyor, Stafford Gaffney, who was trying to leave the town without permission. He brought him to the Athenaeum. O'Brien remained there until the surrender, after which he helped with the collection of weapons. Later at "The Dump" Patrick Keegan gave him and his brother some rifles and ammunition to store at their mother's house in St. Johns. O'Brien successfully evaded arrest.

In 1917 O'Brien moved to New Ross on account of his job with the railway and joined the Volunteer Company in the town. For the next couple of years his main activity was the carrying of dispatches and on the rare occasion, munitions. In 1919 he was redeployed to Ferns and joined the Company there. He continued with his dispatch work along with intelligence gathering. On one occasion while working as a guard on a train, O'Brien refused to let British military personnel aboard, for this insubordination he was suspended from work for eight weeks. At the outbreak of the Civil War, O'Brien was based in Wexford town and was a member of the Republican garrison stationed in the old military barracks. He was one of a party of men who attempted to burn Wexford Bridge. O'Brien was arrested shortly after this failed attempt and was imprisoned until December 1923. Thomas O'Brien died in 1980 aged 83.

Seán O'Byrne (Gorey) Gorey Company. Seán O'Byrne was a prominent advocate for Irish freedom in the Gorey area for many years before he joined the Volunteers at their inception in 1913. A close associate of Seán Etchingham, O'Byrne paraded with the Volunteers on Easter Sunday in the expectation of rising up that evening. After receiving the order to stand down he returned to Gorey. Along with four other Volunteers, O'Byrne brought rifles to Enniscorthy on the following Tuesday and stored them in "Antwerp". They remained in the town and on Thursday took part in the Insurrection. On Friday, Etchingham ordered him to go to Gorey and prepare for the suspected advance of the British Military from Arklow. O'Byrne was arrested the following week and deported a short time after. He was interned in Wandsworth Jail and Frongach Camp before he was released in July. In 1917 he re-joined the Volunteers and played an active role in the Gorey Company's activities until his arrest in November 1920. He was released in December 1921. Seán O'Byrne died in 1957 aged 81.

Daniel O'Connor (Ballindaggin) A Company. Daniel O'Connor was employed as a shop assistant in Seamus Rafter's bar and grocery when he joined the Volunteers in 1914. Prior to Easter week he carried and collected dispatches for Rafter. On the first morning of the Rising he marched from Irish Street with the main body of Volunteers to the Athenaeum. He carried out guard duty there while a H.Q. was established. O'Connor's next duty was to take up a sniping position on Castle Hill, from where he fired several times at the R.I.C. barracks. A couple of hours later he was recalled to H.Q. and instructed to go with a party of Volunteers and blow up the Boro Bridge. They ultimately failed in their attempt, only damaging some parapets on the bridge, but they did succeed in lifting rails off the track which would have prevented any train from crossing. On Friday morning Seán Etchingham assigned O'Connor command of two carloads of Volunteers and sent them to Ferns to lift rails off the railway there. Once he returned he was placed on sentry duty on Slaney Street.

On Saturday, again acting on the orders of Etchingham, O'Connor was placed in command of another two carloads, this time they were sent to the country to raid for arms. They raided houses in Ballycarney, Ballinakill, Knockduff, Monalee and Woodbrook before arriving back at the Athenaeum that evening with several shotguns and ammunition. O'Connor spent Sunday on guard duty at the Athenaeum. After the surrender he brought the weapons he had collected to the country to hide. He was arrested the following Thursday and deported shortly afterwards. O'Connor was interned in Stafford Jail and Frongach Camp until December. He re-joined in 1917 and participated in the general activities of his Company as well as continuing his dispatch work. In August 1918, O'Connor was on guard duty outside "Antwerp" when Seamus Rafter was severely injured in an explosion at his premises a short distance away. O'Connor helped carry the stricken Rafter upstairs to his living quarters, where he died a couple of weeks later from his wounds. Over the following years O'Connor was involved in some of his Company's major operations such as the attack on Clonroche R.I.C. barracks, the large raid for petrol at the railway station and the burning of the R.I.C. barracks in Galbally.

One day in the summer of 1920 the daughter of a soldier, who was a customer in Rafters, handed O'Connor a letter which was addressed to the British military. The letter was from a James Doyle of Ballycarney and contained the names and addresses of members of the Ballindaggin Company. O'Connor passed on the letter to the Brigade Staff. That September Doyle was executed by the I.R.A.. In February 1921 O'Connor was arrested and detained at the courthouse. He was regularly beaten and on one occasion used as a hostage by the Black and Tans as they patrolled the town. He was released in May following the intervention of a local priest. Following the split over the Treaty, O'Connor ceased all his activities and took no part in the Civil War. Daniel O'Connor died in 1956 at the age of 62.

Dennis O'Connor (Ballindaggin) A Company. Dennis O'Connor was the younger brother of Daniel O'Connor. He joined the Volunteers in 1914 and a short time after was admitted into the I.R.B.. At the time he was employed as a clerk in a hardware shop belonging to a Laurence Collins. His job gave him access to ammunition and weapons. O'Connor was instructed by his superior officers to make sure these weapons were readily available during Easter Week. The Wednesday evening before the Rising O'Connor received a message to report to Seamus Rafter's house, there, he witnessed Rafter sign his Will. Rafter then told O'Connor to go to the Manse and arrange with the priest to hear the Confessions of the Volunteers. Early the following morning O'Connor took up a sniping position on the Wexford Road opposite the R.I.C. barracks. From there he fired regularly at the barracks until he was relieved at 3 p.m.. He spent the remainder of the day in the Athenaeum. On Friday, O'Connor carried out street patrols around the town centre before marching to Ferns that evening. On Saturday he commandeered supplies amongst other duties in the village. O'Connor was on outpost duty on the Gorey Road when the car containing Pádraig Pearse's surrender letter was let through on Sunday morning. After the surrender he walked back to Enniscorthy arriving at the Athenaeum around 4 a.m.. According to O'Connor in his statement before the Military Service Pensions Board on the 16th of February 1938, as he handed his weapon to Seamus Rafter, Rafter said to him.

"…keep your powder dry."

So, he brought it with him. He went on the run for several days but was arrested on his return to Enniscorthy. O'Connor was one of the youngest Volunteers to be interned, serving his time in Lewes and Woking Jails before he was sent to Frongach Camp from where he was released in

December. In 1917 O'Connor re-joined and took part in all the regular activities of his Company. After Seamus Rafter's funeral in 1918 he was arrested for wearing a uniform and sentenced to one month in Waterford Jail. O'Connor moved to Liverpool in 1919 to find work and ceased all his Volunteer activity, although he did help on the run Volunteers find work. In later years O'Connor returned to Ireland and joined the army, he obtained the rank of Sergeant and settled in Dublin. Dennis O'Connor died in 1981 at the age of 81.

John O'Connor (Ferns) Ferns Company. A member of the Volunteers since 1914, John O'Connor served in Enniscorthy and Ferns during Easter Week. There is not a lot on record to tell us about his actual service. However, he was arrested on the 3rd of May and interned in Wandsworth Jail and Frongach Camp before he was released in December. O'Connor re-joined his Company in 1917 but owing to bad health had very little involvement up to The Truce. At the outbreak of the Civil War he remained loyal to the Pro Treaty side and helped defend Ferns with the Free State Army in July 1922. After the army established control in the village he was stood down, however he remained on call should his assistance have been required. John O'Connor died aged 79 in 1965.

Michael O'Connor (St. John's Street) A Company. Michael O'Connor was a member of the I.R.B. before he joined the Volunteers in 1913. Prior to the Rising he was involved in the manufacture of munitions at "The Dump" on a regular basis. On the first morning of the Insurrection, O'Connor assisted in the raising of the Tricolour above the Athenaeum. He then carried out guard duty outside the building. He remained there until that evening, then he was ordered to the Turret Rocks to keep a watch on the R.I.C. barracks. On Friday morning O'Connor was placed in charge of a small raiding party which was sent to a house in the country rumoured to have weapons, the rumours proved to be false, and they returned to H.Q. empty handed. That afternoon the Athenaeum was thronged with new recruits and O'Connor was given the responsibility to train the most suitable ones on how to use a rifle. He spent Saturday and Sunday on patrol around the town. O'Connor was arrested the following Thursday and deported a short time after. He was interned in Stafford Jail and Frongach Camp before he was released in December.

O'Connor re-joined in 1917 and as well as general Company duties, he once again made munitions. In 1918 he was sent with the party of Volunteers to Waterford to protect the Sinn Féin workers from intimidation at the Bye-Election, while in 1920 he participated in the attack on the R.I.C. barracks in Clonroche. A few months after this O'Connor dropped out of all activities due to ill health. Michael O'Connor died in 1958, he was 75 years old.

Philip O' Connor (Hospital Lane) A Company. Philip (Felix) O'Connor joined the Volunteers at their inception in 1913. On the first morning of the Rising he marched with the main body of men from Irish Street to the Athenaeum. From there he was sent on outpost duty to Red Pat's Cross where he remained until Friday morning. After resting back at H.Q., O'Connor was detailed to the Turret Rocks on Friday evening, from where he claimed to have fired several shots at the R.I.C. barracks. He finished his day by carrying out sentry duty at the bottom of the Ross Road. On Saturday, O'Connor was in Killagoley on outpost duty on the Wexford Road for the day. He remained in the Athenaeum on Sunday until the surrender, after which he made his way to the home of relatives living in Arklow. He stayed there for three months before returning to Enniscorthy when everything had quietened down.

O'Connor re-joined in 1917 and took part in his Company's regular activities. In 1918 he helped guard the General Election ballot boxes which were stored in the courthouse over the Christmas Holidays. In 1920 he was involved in the attack on the Clonroche R.I.C. barracks and the raid for petrol at the railway station. O'Connor was arrested by members of the Devonshire Regiment in March 1921 and imprisoned in the courthouse until July. In April 1922 O'Connor joined the National Army at Beggars Bush and was posted to the barracks in Kilkenny. There he was one of the men who absconded with a large quantity of weapons and ammunition. On his return to Enniscorthy he joined the Republican garrison in the courthouse.

At the outbreak of the "Battle of Enniscorthy", O'Connor took up a sniping position in the steeple of St. Mary's Church and fired numerous times on the Free State positions on the Castle roof. As the Free State forces retook the town O'Connor helped set fire to the courthouse before escaping to the country. He was captured in September and imprisoned until December 1923. At the end of April 1922 O'Connor's brother Henry was shot accidently during a raid for arms by the I.R.A. near Ferns and killed. Another brother, John, on hearing this news returned to Enniscorthy from Liverpool, where he was working, and joined the Anti-Treaty side. He was killed the following March in a fight with Free State troops near Kyle. Philip O Connor died in 1970 in his 74th year.

Arthur O'Keeffe (The Shannon) C Company. A Volunteer since 1913, Arthur O'Keeffe was mobilised on the first morning of the Rising. He was handed a rifle at the Athenaeum and ordered to Salville Cross for outpost duty. O'Keeffe remained there until 2 p.m. and then returned to rest at H.Q.. That evening he was sent on patrol to The Shannon. On Friday he spent the day at Davis's Mill before he was sent once more that evening to patrol The Shannon. O'Keeffe went to Ferns by car on Saturday morning and did guard duty in the village until the evening. Overnight he helped build eight roadblocks on the Camolin Road, finishing this task at 6 a.m.. He then returned to Enniscorthy by car and rested at H.Q.. At 6 p.m. he was detailed for sentry duty on The Shannon, from where he was recalled for the surrender. O'Keeffe avoided arrest and re-joined in 1917. He participated in the general activities of the Volunteers before dropping out in 1919. Arthur O'Keefe died at his residence in St. Senan's Villas in 1957, he was 64 years old.

Michael O'Keeffe (The Shannon) C Company. Michael O'Keeffe was Arthur O'Keeffe's younger brother and joined the Volunteers in 1914. The night before the Rising he was on guard duty at "The Dump". A few hours later he marched with the main body of Volunteers to the Athenaeum. From there he was detailed to take up a sniping position on the Turret Rocks. In his testimony before the Military Service Pensions Board on the 30th of November 1938, O'Keeffe stated he fired up to thirty rounds at the R.I.C. barracks over the course of several hours When he returned to H.Q. he was ordered to raid for arms at the premises of Wm. Armstrong's in Templeshannon. That afternoon O'Keeffe was placed on guard duty at Davis's Mill before he was sent to Salville Cross, where he spent the night on outpost duty. After resting in the Athenaeum O'Keeffe was posted to Clonhaston Cross on Friday afternoon and then to Salville Cross to perform night duty there again. On Saturday he remained at H.Q. all day carrying out guard duty in between rest periods. On Sunday morning he was once again sent to Salville Cross where he remained until he was recalled for the surrender. Once back in the Athenaeum he helped with the collection of weapons. O'Keeffe was arrested the following Tuesday but was released from the R.I.C. barracks after an hour.

O'Keeffe re-joined in 1917 and took part in general Volunteer activities. In 1918 he was involved in election work. During the War of Independence he participated in numerous raids for arms including at Jameson Davis's of Killabeg, Richards's of Solsboro, Kavanaghs of Drumgoold and Hayes's of Greenmount. O'Keeffe also took part in the large raid for petrol at the railway station in May 1920. Throughout the Civil War he worked as a lorry driver for Donohue's, and after taking the Republican side, used his position to deliver dispatches and supplies to the columns around the district as well as transporting the men themselves on several occasions. Michael O'Keeffe died in 1968 aged 73.

Patrick O'Keeffe (Hospital Lane) A Company. Patrick O'Keefe joined the Volunteers in 1913 and became a member of the I.R.B. a short time after. On the Monday and Tuesday nights of Easter Week, O'Keeffe was tasked with keeping watch on the courthouse to make sure none of the rifles stored there belonging to the National Volunteers were removed. On Wednesday night he witnessed Peter Galligan arriving back from Dublin on *a ladies' bicycle*. The same night O'Keeffe stated before the Military Pensions Board on the 9th of February 1940, Seamus Doyle told him to go home and rest,

but not to take off my trousers that I would be getting an early knock.

That knock came at about 2 a.m. and once he had reported to "Antwerp", Seamus Rafter asked him had he the keys to where he worked. O'Keeffe replied he had and was then instructed to get a horse and cart there and go to Donohue's hardware and load up as much munitions as they could and bring them to "The Dump". O'Keeffe made two trips and then returned the horse and cart before marching with the main body of Volunteers to the Athenaeum. From there he was sent on outpost duty to Summerhill. After a number of hours there O'Keeffe was recalled to H.Q. and ordered to commandeer coal with a small number of Volunteers at O'Neill's coal yard. While a couple of the men were scaling the gate, shots were fired from the Bank of Ireland opposite the coal yard, which was occupied by two R.I.C. men. O'Keeffe and the other Volunteers returned fire and the R.I.C. retreated from the windows they had fired from.

On Friday, O'Keeffe was on outpost duty at Red Pat's Cross and on his return to H.Q. that evening, he was placed on guard duty there. O'Keeffe was sent to Salville Cross for outpost duty on Saturday before returning to the town to take part in a recruiting parade that afternoon. On Sunday he was on sentry duty at the top of the Old Barracks Road and that evening on guard duty in the Athenaeum. He was present for the surrender and helped with the collection of weapons before going home. O'Keeffe was arrested a couple of days later and deported shortly afterwards. He was interned in Stafford Jail until he was released in July.

O'Keeffe re-joined in 1917 and along with the general Volunteer activities, he helped with the manufacture of munitions. In 1918 he served at both the Bye-Election in Waterford and the General Election in Wexford. Throughout 1919 O'Keeffe worked as a van driver, he was instructed by his superior officer to compile a list of farmers that he delivered to, whom he believed had access to weapons. These farms were then raided. O'Keeffe himself participated in a raid for rifles and revolvers at Johnston's of Ballinapierce. From then until the Civil War O'Keeffe had little service owing to the fact his wife was an invalid and they had young children. However, on the day hostilities broke out in Enniscorthy he joined the Republican garrison at the courthouse and sniped on the Free State positions on several occasions. O'Keeffe was sent to meet Ernie O'Malley and his Tipperary column outside the town and guide them in. After the Free State Army retook the town O'Keeffe helped set fire to the courthouse and then left with a flying column. He only got as far as the Ringwood before he was ordered to return home because of his family's situation. He avoided arrest and tried to help out as much as he could up until the ceasefire. Patrick O'Keeffe died in Birmingham in 1965 at the age of 69.

Annie O'Leary (Ferns) Cumann na mBan. Annie O'Leary (nee Breslin) was from Ferns but lived and worked in Enniscorthy. She joined Cumann na mBan on the morning of the Rising after reporting to the Athenaeum. She was instructed by Robert Brennan to go with a dispatch to Dunbar's of Ferns for Patrick Ronan, this dispatch was the official order to come to Enniscorthy with the Ferns Company. O'Leary stayed behind in the village and catered for the Volunteers who arrived over the following days. After the surrender she returned to Enniscorthy. In the following months she assisted in raising funds for the prisoner's dependants and sent parcels to the prisoners in Frongach Camp. In early 1917 O'Leary acted as a scout for Patrick Keegan and his small group of Volunteers while they recovered the weapons and munitions hidden after the Rising. Over the next year she participated in plays and concerts which toured the county to raise funds for the Volunteers. After the General Election in 1918 O'Leary cooked for the men who guarded the ballot boxes in the courthouse over the Christmas Holidays.

Throughout the War of Independence she carried dispatches between Enniscorthy and Ferns and on other occasions further afield. O'Leary's lodgings in Enniscorthy was used to store revolvers and ammunition, she would hand them out when required and take them back afterwards. In February 1921 O'Leary acted as a scout for Volunteers John Carroll and James Leacy when they shot and killed the spy Fredrick Newsome in Slaney Place. Later that month she scouted for the attack on the R.I.C. barracks in Ferns. Shortly after, O'Leary was appointed Adjutant of the Ferns branch of Cumann na mBan. In the Civil War she chose the Anti-Treaty side and during the brief occupation of Ferns by the Irregulars in July 1922, she cooked for them in the old R.I.C. barracks. O'Leary continued to carry dispatches and ammunition to various flying columns in her area until the ceasefire. Annie O'Leary died in 1978 aged 81 years.

Liam O'Leary (Main Street) A Company. Liam O'Leary joined the Volunteers in 1914. On the first morning of the Rising he marched from Irish Street to the Athenaeum with the main body of Volunteers. From there he was ordered with a party of men to raid for weapons at some prominent houses in the district. On his return O'Leary joined the party of Volunteers ordered to blow up the Boro Bridge. They only managed to damage parapets on the bridge, but they then lifted rails in order to prevent any train from crossing. Once he was back at the Athenaeum Seamus Doyle gave O'Leary a dispatch to go to Ferns with. On Friday, O'Leary was placed on outpost duty at Red Pat's Cross and later that evening, he was allocated sentry duty at the bottom of Irish Street. For the remaining two days O'Leary carried out sentry and outpost duty at various locations around the town before he was recalled to the Athenaeum for the surrender. O'Leary evaded arrest and re-joined in 1917. Over the following couple of years he was involved in the manufacture of munitions.

At the beginning of February 1920 O'Leary was appointed as Brigade Adjutant. In April he helped to plan the attack on the R.I.C. barracks in Clonroche. He was also involved in the large raid for petrol at the railway station the following month. In June, O'Leary acted as a scout for the men who killed D.I. Lea-Wilson in Gorey. He was arrested in March 1921 in Ferns, and when searched, found to have Brigade documents in his possession. He was sentenced to twelve months imprisonment. That November O'Leary was among the group of inmates who tunnelled out of the jail in Kilkenny. He made good his escape to the Blackstairs Mountains. O'Leary ceased his service in April 1922 and played no role in the Civil War. Liam O'Leary died in 1955 at the age of 58.

Michael O'Leary (Irish Street) A Company. Michael O'Leary mobilised with the other Volunteers early on the first morning of the Rising outside Keegan's on Irish Street. A member of the Volunteers since 1913, he was handed a rifle and marched with the rest of his Company to the Athenaeum. Once there, O'Leary helped remove all the seating from the hall which was then put in the small yard behind the building. After finishing he was assigned to police duty and patrolled the town for the rest of the day. On Friday morning O'Leary was placed on sentry duty at the Gas Yard, while in the afternoon he moved to Hospital Lane. After sleeping in the Athenaeum, he reported for guard duty to Slaney Street on Saturday morning. Later that day he carried out police patrol around the town. On Sunday morning O'Leary was detailed to the top of Irish Street where he remained for most of the day. By the time of the surrender he was back at H.Q. and after handing in his rifle he went home. O'Leary evaded arrest. In 1917 he re-joined and took part in the general activities of his Company over the following years. In March 1921 O'Leary was arrested and held in the courthouse for six weeks. During his captivity he was beaten regularly, and on several occasions used as a hostage by the Black and Tans when they patrolled the town. After The Truce he ceased his involvement and took no part in the Civil War. Michael O'Leary died at his residence in St. John's Villas aged 60 in 1955.

Simon O'Leary (Marshalstown) A Company. Simon O'Leary joined the Volunteers in 1913, at the time he was employed as a shop assistant in Donohue's hardware. After obtaining a better job, he moved to New Ross in late 1915 and transferred to the Volunteer Company there. On Easter Sunday O'Leary played a football match in Wexford Park, after which he spoke to Robert Brennan. Brennan informed him that the Rising was to begin that evening and he was to mobilise with the rest of his Company at Ballywilliam in order to march to Enniscorthy. By the time O'Leary arrived back in New Ross the cancellation order had been issued.

Upon learning that Enniscorthy had risen the following Thursday, O'Leary cycled to the town. He reported to the Athenaeum and was assigned to police duties. For the remainder of the Insurrection he patrolled the streets, checked on people entering the town for provisions and made sure they only received what they needed. He also took keys off some of the publicans so they could not open their premises. On the Monday following the surrender O'Leary cycled back to New Ross in the hope of avoiding capture. However, he was arrested the next day and deported shortly afterwards to Wakefield Prison where he was admitted into the prison hospital. He was released three weeks later suffering from Peritonitis. On his return to Ireland, O'Leary was operated on in St. Vincent's Hospital in Dublin. Afterwards he was transferred to the hospital in New Ross to recuperate. On his discharge he discovered that his job was gone. In February 1917 O'Leary moved to Bagenalstown after getting a job there. He helped establish a Volunteer Company in nearby Paulstown and was appointed Company Captain. From then up until the end of the Civil War all his activities were confined to that general area. In later years O'Leary became a member of the Garda Siochana. Simon O'Leary died in 1964, he was 71 years of age.

Aidan O'Neill (Springvalley) C Company. Aidan "Mogue" O'Neill joined the Volunteers in 1913. On the first morning of the Rising he marched with the main body of Volunteers from Irish Street to the

Athenaeum. From there he was detailed to the Railway Corner on Templeshannon for sentry duty. After a couple of hours there, O'Neill was sent to Killagoley to take up outpost duty. He remained there until night-time and then returned to H.Q. to rest. On Friday morning O'Neill was a member of the advance party that went to Ferns. During his time there he felled trees and erected roadblocks. He remained in Ferns until Sunday evening. After the surrender he hid out in the country for a few days and managed to avoid arrest. O'Neill re-joined in 1917 and participated in general Volunteer activities up until The Truce. Aidan "Mogue" O'Neill died in 1973 at the age of 82.

Annie O'Neill (Ballyhuskard) Cumann na mBan. Annie O'Neill joined Cumann na mBan in 1915. At the time of the Rising she was employed in the laundry at the Enniscorthy Asylum. She had to sneak out on two nights to go to the Athenaeum where she carried out what duties were required of her. Two weeks after the surrender she was brought before the board of the Asylum and threatened with dismissal for *mixing with a bad crowd*. During the War of Independence, O'Neill suggested to the Volunteer leadership that men on the run could use the laundry at the Asylum for refuge. They agreed, so on those occasions, O'Neill would leave a side door open and some food out. The laundry proved such a success that when Volunteers raided for mails they brought the letters to the laundry to go through. O'Neill was suspected of nefarious activity in the laundry by her supervisors, but when accused, she denied it and they could not prove it. Throughout the Civil War O'Neill actively carried dispatches for various Irregular flying columns between Enniscorthy, Wexford and Gorey, she was arrested on several occasions. The last of these arrests occurred in March 1923, after which O'Neill was imprisoned in Kilmainham Jail, while there she went on hunger strike for thirty-four days and had to be released due to her failing health. Annie O'Neill died in her 71st year in 1951.

Jeremiah O'Neill (Market Square) A Company. Jeremiah O'Neill joined the Volunteers in 1916 and served actively in Enniscorthy and Ferns throughout the Rising. Afterwards he evaded arrest. In 1917 O'Neill moved to Maryborough, (Port Laoise) where he was one of the founding members of the Volunteer Company there. O'Neill was involved in the majority of operations carried out by this Company up to The Truce. O'Neill joined the National Army on its formation in 1922, rising to the rank of Captain before his demobilisation in March 1924. He returned to Enniscorthy to live before he settled in Rathevan, Port Laoise in the early 1940's. Jeremiah O'Neill died at the age 79 in 1980.

John O'Neill (Irish Street) A Company. John O' Neill joined the Volunteers three weeks prior to the Rising. After mobilising on the Thursday morning he was sent with a rifle to the Turret Rocks from where according to his statement before the Military Service Pensions Board on the 2nd of March 1937, he fired five rounds at the R.I.C. barracks. That night O'Neill was sent with a party of Volunteers to Scarawalsh in order to fell trees and assemble roadblocks. He returned to the Athenaeum on Friday morning and rested there until the evening. For the next two nights O'Neill dug trenches on the roads leading to Ferns and slept in the Athenaeum by day. He was present for the surrender and after handing in his rifle, went to Ballyorrell to hide out. He returned to Enniscorthy the following night and managed to evade arrest. O'Neill looked after a small dump of weapons which had been hidden after the surrender until Patrick Keegan was released from Frongach Camp. After that he took no further part in Volunteer activities. John O'Neill died at his son's residence in St. Aidan's Villas in 1948, he was 69 years old.

John O'Neill (Hospital Lane) A Company. John O'Neill joined the Volunteers in 1915. During Easter Week his duties included sentry at several locations around the town, commandeering supplies for H.Q. and guard duty at the Banks. Following the surrender O'Neill was arrested and deported shortly afterwards. He was interned in Stafford jail and

Frongach Camp from where he was released in August. In 1917 O'Neill joined a travelling theatrical show and claimed to have offered assistance to various Volunteer Company's around the country. In 1919 he emigrated to Glasgow and joined the I.R.A. in the city. He served with them until his return to Enniscorthy in 1921, after which he ceased all activity. John O'Neill died at the age of 72 at his residence on Pearse Road in 1966.

Laurence O'Neill (Old Church) A Company. Laurence O'Neill joined the Volunteers at their inception in 1913. On the first morning of the Rising he marched with the main body of men from Keegan's to the Athenaeum. From there he took up a sniping position on Castle Hill. Over the following few hours he claimed to have fired multiple times at the R.I.C. barracks. After he was relieved, O'Neill had some refreshments at H.Q. before he was placed on sentry duty at Coffey's Corner, which was the corner of Georges Street (Rafter St.) and the Market Square. Early on Friday morning O'Neill was a member of a party of Volunteers sent to Scarawalsh to fell trees and block roads. On Saturday he spent the day on guard duty at the Gas Yard and that evening he was at the bridge on sentry duty. While there, O'Neill fired a warning shot over the head of a civilian who had ignored his order to halt his pony and trap. O'Neill carried out sentry duty on Sunday at Bellfield and Old Church Road. After the surrender he helped to clear out the Athenaeum before going on the run. He successfully managed to evade capture. O'Neill re-joined in 1917 and participated in the general activities of his Company. In 1918 he assisted at the Bye-Election in Waterford and the General Election later in the year. He served until 1919 when he had to drop out owing to serious issues with his sight. Laurence O'Neill died in Peamount Hospital in Dublin aged 70 in 1966.

Michael O'Neill (Irish Street) A Company. Michael O'Neill was a member of the I.R.B. for several years before he joined the Volunteers at their inception in 1913. He was the father of John O'Neill (Irish Street) who also took part that week. Prior to the Rising, O'Neill assisted in the manufacturing of munitions at "The Dump". Some of these munitions were stored at his own premises on Irish street. On the first morning of the Rising, along with his son, he marched with the main body of Volunteers to the Athenaeum. From there he was ordered to the Turret Rocks to fire on the R.I.C. barracks. After several hours there, O'Neill returned to H.Q. and rested. He was then placed on guard duty at the Gas Yard. On Friday morning O'Neill carried out sentry duty at the top of Irish Street. From Friday afternoon until the surrender on Sunday night, the majority of O'Neill's time was spent on police duty around the town. After the surrender he helped with the collection of weapons at H.Q.. O'Neill personally brought some rifles and a significantly larger number of revolvers to his own home, where he concealed them along with a sizeable quantity of ammunition. He successfully evaded arrest.

Upon Patrick Keegan's release and return to Enniscorthy, O'Neill handed over the rifles to him, however he was told to keep hold of the revolvers and ammunition. He re-joined in 1917 and took part in the general activities of his Company. In 1918 he went to Waterford and assisted at the Bye-Election. After the General Election later that year, O'Neill was a member of the Volunteers who guarded the ballot boxes in the courthouse over the Christmas Holidays. From 1920 up until The Truce, O'Neill supplied and held weapons for the various flying columns in the district which were used in their operations. He had no service during The Civil War. Michael O'Neill died in St. Aidan's Villas in 1948 aged 82.

Patrick O'Neill (Drumgoold) C Company. Patrick O'Neill joined the Volunteers in 1914. On the morning of the Rising he marched with the main body of men to the Athenaeum from Irish Street. After a H.Q. had been established, he was sent with a party of Volunteers to commandeer supplies. At 10.30 a.m. O'Neill was detailed to the Turret Rocks to take up a sniping position, from which he fired sporadically at the R.I.C. barracks below for several hours. On Friday, O'Neill was assigned outpost duty at Salville Cross and that evening, helped to commandeer food for H.Q.. O'Neill carried out sentry duty on Saturday, first at Templeshannon and then on the corner of Lymington Road and New Street. (Wafer St.) On Sunday, O'Neill was back on sentry duty at Templeshannon. He returned to the Athenaeum in time for the surrender, after which he went on the run for three weeks and managed to avoid arrest. O'Neill re-joined in 1917 and served up until The Truce carrying out the routine activities required of him. He did not participate in the Civil War. Patrick O'Neill died at his residence in Drumgoold in 1966, he was 68 years old.

Patrick O'Neill (Old Church) C Company. Patrick O'Neill joined the Volunteers in Dublin in 1913 while he was working in the city, he was attached to the Ringsend Company. On his return to Enniscorthy in 1915 he transferred to C Company. Prior to the Rising, O'Neill was employed as a motor driver in the motor division of The Co-op. Using his work vehicle he transported munitions and materials between "Antwerp" and "The Dump" and vice versa. On the morning of the Insurrection O'Neill marched with the main body of Volunteers from Irish Street to the Athenaeum. From there he was sent to Templeshannon to commandeer a bread van belonging to O'Connor's Bakery of Wexford, which was delivering bread. He brought the van and its contents back to H.Q.. After it was unloaded he was dispatched to Richard King's house in Brownswood to collect ammunition. While driving down the Quay, O'Neill came under fire from the R.I.C. barracks on the opposite side of the Slaney but managed to get through unscathed. On his return to H.Q. O'Neill was sent to Lar Codd's hardware shop on Main Street to commandeer shovels, picks, saws and wrenches. He then transported this consignment to Solsboro where he kept guard as Volunteers felled trees and lifted rails off the track. For the remainder of the day he commandeered motor vehicles from several houses in the district and brought them to the Athenaeum.

On Friday, O'Neill spent the day driving officers to and from outposts. Early on Saturday morning he drove members of the advance party to

Ferns, once there, he stood guard as they cut telegraph lines and lifted rails. O'Neill remained in Ferns until the evening then he returned to Enniscorthy with the car. After having a meal he went to bed. O'Neill was called at 2 a.m. Sunday morning to bring an urgent dispatch to Ferns. He stayed there all day and then brought a group of Volunteers back to town for the surrender. Afterwards O'Neill helped to empty "The Dump" and transport its contents to the country where it was hidden. O'Neill went on the run the next day and remained so until mid-July. He spent the majority of this time camped in Kilpierce Wood. By the time he returned to Enniscorthy his position in The Co-op was gone.

O'Neill re-joined in 1917 and from then until The Truce was used primarily as a driver, transporting arms and men all over the county as well as collecting munitions in such places as Dublin, Kilkenny and Clonmel. In the weeks leading up to the Civil War he was engaged as the principle driver attached to the courthouse garrison. Once the "Battle of Enniscorthy" began on the 2nd of July 1922, O'Neill brought three lorry loads of men from Wexford to the town to fight. He remained active until the ceasefire. When O'Neill initially applied for his Military Service Pension he was turned down and it took a stern rebuttal from his former superior officers to make the Referee reconsider his decision. One of the officers, Michael Kirwan wrote in a letter dated June 27th, 1941.

"…if you still persist in rejecting Patrick O'Neill's appeal after the statements written on his behalf by such responsible and trustworthy officers as T.D. Sinnott former Brigade Commandant and Seamus Doyle former Brigade Adjutant, not to mention other trustworthy people, the working of the 1934 Pension Act is open to grave doubt."

"…he was the first to drive a car at the start of the Insurrection and the last man to drive a load of arms to a dump immediately before the military arrived to take over, everyone else had gone home the previous evening."

Patrick O'Neill died at the age of 56 in 1949.

Thomas O'Neill (Market Square) A Company. Thomas O'Neill was Jeremiah O'Neill's older brother. During the Rising he carried out sentry and outpost duties at various locations. After the surrender he evaded arrest. In 1917 he moved to Port Laoise then known as Maryborough with his brother and helped establish a Volunteer Company in the town. O'Neill played a prominent role in operations in Carlow as well as Laois in the years preceding The Truce. Along with his brother he joined the National Army in early 1922 and by the time he was demobilised in March 1924 he held the rank of Captain. In later years O'Neill served as a Guard and made his home in Carlow. His son Tadhg joined the army and rose through the ranks serving as Chief of Staff from 1986 to 1989. Thomas O'Neill died in Carlow in 1976 at the age of 77.

William O'Neill (Irish Street) A Company. William O'Neill joined the Volunteers in 1913. On Easter Sunday he was assigned guard duty at "The Dump". For the next three days he divided his time between there and "Antwerp". On the first morning of the Rising he marched with the main body of Volunteers from Irish Street to the Athenaeum. After a H.Q. had been established, O'Neill took up a sniping position at the top of Castle Hill and fired several rounds at the R.I.C. barracks according to his testimony before the Military Service Pensions Board on the 30th of November 1938. He remained at this post for over an hour. O'Neill spent the next couple of days on outpost duty at various locations around the town. On Sunday morning he went to Ferns by car and helped collect ammunition to bring back to the town. After the surrender he went on the run for several months, spending time in Kiltealy and Borris before returning to Enniscorthy. O'Neill re-joined in 1917 and carried out routine Company activities until he dropped out in 1919. William O'Neill died at his residence on the Duffry Gate in 1951, he was 70 years old.

John J. O'Reilly (Templeshannon) C Company. John Joseph O'Reilly joined the Volunteers in 1915. On the first morning of the Rising he marched with the main body of men to the Athenaeum from Irish

Street. From there, along with another Volunteer, O'Reilly was sent to a house at The Still to raid for arms. In his statement before the Military Service Pensions Board on the 9th of February 1940 O'Reilly stated that on his return he took up a sniping position on Castle Hill and fired over twenty rounds at the R.I.C. barracks. Later on word was received at H.Q. that coal was being stolen from Donohue's yard, O'Reilly was one of the Volunteers sent to put a stop to it. On Friday morning O'Reilly was placed on guard duty at James Cleary's forge, later in the day he was sent to Davis's Mill.

Early on Saturday morning, O'Reilly went to Ferns and upon his arrival was ordered to commandeer food from the premises of O'Connor-Dunnes and Foleys. On Sunday morning O'Reilly was placed on sentry duty at Station Road, while in the afternoon he carried out police patrol around the village. After the surrender he was a passenger in the car directly behind Peter Galligan's when it crashed on the way back to Enniscorthy. This delay meant it was the early hours of Monday morning before he arrived at the Athenaeum. O'Reilly was arrested the following day and deported shortly afterwards. He was interned in Stafford Jail and Frongach Camp before he was released in July. After returning home O'Reilly had no further involvement. John Joseph O'Reilly died aged 52 in 1943.

John J. O'Reilly (Gorey) A Company. John Joseph O'Reilly was originally from Clonevan near Gorey but lived and worked in Enniscorthy. He joined the Volunteers in 1914. On the Tuesday of Easter Week he was sent to Glenbrien and Oulart to collect munitions and mobilise men for the forthcoming Insurrection. On his return O'Reilly was placed on guard duty at "The Dump". On the first morning of the Rising, O'Reilly marched with the main body of Volunteers from Irish Street to the Athenaeum. He was then assigned a sniping position on the Turret Rocks from where he fired on the R.I.C. barracks below. O'Reilly was recalled to the Athenaeum at around 10.30 a.m. and was appointed as a 2nd Lieutenant. Apart from scouting at Edermine on Friday night, his time was largely spent on visiting outposts to organise relief and at H.Q. He was present for the surrender and after spending the night in his digs, he returned to his home in Clonevan on Monday morning. O'Reilly was arrested there the next day and deported a short time afterwards. He was interned in Stafford Jail and Frongach Camp before he was released in August.

O'Reilly re-joined in Wexford town in 1918 while living there, however, by 1920 he was Adjutant of the Ferns Company after returning to live in the area. He participated in several raids for arms and rate books along with the burning of R.I.C. barracks' in Clonevan and Camolin. In October 1920 O'Reilly was promoted to Adjutant of the 3rd Battalion of the North Wexford Brigade. He was arrested the following month and interned in Kilworth Camp County Cork. O'Reilly escaped in September 1921 during The Truce period. He ceased all activity after his escape and played no role in the Civil War. John Joseph O'Reilly died in 1981 at the age of 91.

Richard O'Rourke (The Leap) A Company. Richard O'Rourke had been a member of the Volunteers since 1914 when he marched with the main body of men from Irish Street to the Athenaeum on the first morning of the Rising. His first role that day was to take up sentry duty on the corner of Castle Street overlooking the Abbey Square. He remained there for three hours before returning to H.Q. for breakfast. O'Rourke was then sent to the Market Square for more sentry duty. That evening he was on duty on Court Street before he finished his day on St. John's Street in the early hours of Friday morning.

While on St. John's Street he had an encounter with a civilian who refused to halt, O'Rourke fired a warning shot over the man's head. The man turned out to be a Dr. Furlong who was making his way to the County Home to do his rounds. On Friday morning O'Rourke assisted in the commandeering of a bread van on the Market Square. While on Saturday he was on sentry duty at the Old Barracks. After attending Mass on Sunday morning, O'Rourke was sent to Arnold's Cross. At the time of the surrender he was recalled to the Athenaeum by the Company Bugler. On his return he helped with the collection and concealment of weapons, personally taking four shotguns to the country and burying them in a field. O'Rourke went on the run for a week before he returned to the town and managed to avoid arrest. He had no further involvement with the Volunteers. Richard O'Rourke died in Brownswood Hospital at the age of 83 in 1975.

William O'Rourke (The Leap) A Company. William O'Rourke was a younger brother of Richard O'Rourke's; he joined the Volunteers in 1914. On the first morning of the Rising he mobilised at "Antwerp" and then went to the Keegan's house on Irish Street, where he was handed a shotgun. From there he marched with the main body of Volunteers to the Athenaeum and helped to establish a H.Q.. After this, O'Rourke took up a sentry position at the Castle gates. A short time later he was placed on guard duty outside the Munster and Leinster Bank at the top of Slaney Street. His final duty of the day was guarding the officer's room in the Athenaeum. On Friday morning O'Rourke was placed on sentry duty at the town side of the Ross Road. In the afternoon he was a member of a party of Volunteers sent to commandeer food for H.Q.. He spent Saturday at the Athenaeum cleaning rifles which had been seized in raids and sorting ammunition. On Sunday evening O'Rourke was on outpost duty at Blackstoops when he was recalled for the surrender. Afterwards he helped to collect and load weapons. He went on the run the following day and did not return to Enniscorthy for approximately six months.

O'Rourke re-joined in 1917 and took part in the general activities of his Company. In 1918 he assisted at both the Bye-Election in Waterford and the General Election later in the year. In between the two elections O'Rourke was wounded accidently while cleaning a revolver, this resulted in a stay of eight weeks in the local hospital. After been discharged he had to go on the run because the R.I.C. were looking for him. In the years up to The Truce he was involved in raids for arms and several attempts to blow up bridges. One of O'Rourke's specific tasks for his Company was to hang Tricolours in inaccessible spots, like telegraph wires and tall trees. This was done purely to annoy the Black and Tans. O'Rourke enlisted in the National Army in March 1922 but returned to Enniscorthy a month later and joined the Republicans in the courthouse. Although he did not participate in the "Battle of Enniscorthy", he acted as a scout for any flying columns in the area throughout the Civil War period. William O'Rourke died in 1986, he was 86 years of age.

William O'Toole (Lower Church Street) A Company. William O'Toole joined the Volunteers in 1913. In 1914 while employed at the Kynoch's munitions factory in Arklow he signed up a dozen or so fellow workers as auxiliary Volunteers. When this was discovered by management a year later he was dismissed. In the weeks leading up to the Rising, O'Toole was involved in raids for materials at Donohue's and the railway stores. He also helped with the manufacture of munitions. On Easter Monday reports were circulating that Seamus Rafter was going to be lifted by the R.I.C.. Along with another Volunteer, O'Toole acted as a bodyguard and stayed by Rafter's side as he went about his business. On Tuesday amidst all the confusion and false narratives, word came through that the Ferns Company were marching to Enniscorthy. Rafter immediately dispatched O'Toole to intercept them and tell them to turn around and return to Ferns to await further orders. He met them at Scarawalsh and after a brief discussion, it was agreed that the Company would camp at Ballinahallin Wood and wait there. O'Toole cycled to Gorey and Courtown on Wednesday morning with dispatches. At 10 p.m. that night he and a fellow Volunteer, Fintan Burke, were ordered to go to Wexford with a message from Robert Brennan for his wife Una. They were both arrested while attempting to do so. After the Rising O'Toole was deported and interned in Wakefield Prison and Frongach Camp until his release that September. O'Toole moved to New Ross for work in 1917 and joined the Company there. In 1918 he helped establish a Company in Ballykelly and was appointed Captain. He returned to

Enniscorthy in 1919 and ceased his Volunteer activities. William O'Toole died on Christmas day in 1953 at the age of 61.

Margaret Peare (Duffry Street) Cumann na mBan. Margaret Peare (nee Cardiff) was the older sister of Joseph John Cardiff and Annie Heneghan. She joined Cumann na mBan in 1915. On the first morning of the Rising she reported for duty to the Athenaeum, where she would remain until after the surrender on Sunday night. Peare's principal duty for the week was cooking for the Volunteers. In the following months she assisted in raising funds for the prisoner's dependants. During the War of Independence Peare carried dispatches and weapons on numerous occasions.

After the attack on the R.I.C. barracks in Clonroche in April 1920, she was sent to Ballindaggin to treat the injured Volunteer Patrick J. Byrne before he was transferred to St. Vincent's Hospital in Dublin. At the time Peare was employed as an insurance agent. In August 1920 while carrying out this work, she called to a house and observed an alleged spy named O'Sullivan in the house. Knowing that he was wanted by the I.R.A., Peare immediately passed on this information and O'Sullivan was taken that very night. Peare's home on Duffry Street was frequently raided during this period by the military under the command of the despised Captain Yeo of the Devonshire Regiment. On one of these raids her brother was arrested and held in the courthouse where he suffered at the hands of Yeo and his men. Peare wrote about the last visit of Yeo to her house in an undated statement.

"…His last visit was the night of my father's wake, June 10th, 1921, when accompanied by another officer, soldiers and the R.I.C., he searched our house holding up and questioning every man who attended the wake, informing us all that it was an illegal assembly."

Margaret Peare died aged 46 in 1941.

Isabella Pender (Bellfield Terrace) Cumann na mBan. Bella Pender (nee Breen) joined Cumann na mBan in 1915. For the first two days of the Rising she was in the Athenaeum cooking and carrying out other duties. On Saturday morning she went to Ferns with a small group to assist with the cooking in the R.I.C. barracks which had been taken over as Volunteer H.Q.. Pender returned to Enniscorthy on Sunday after the surrender arriving in the Athenaeum around midnight. Over the following couple of years she helped to raise funds for the prisoner's dependants and was a member of a travelling company which put on concerts to raise money to buy weapons for the Volunteers. After She married in 1919 she ceased all her activities. Bella Pender died in her 74th year in 1971.

Stephen Pender (Ferns) Ferns Company. Stephen Pender was a member of the Ferns Company and served both in the village and Enniscorthy during the Rising. Afterwards he evaded capture. In 1917 Pender was arrested after taking a rifle and ammunition from a British soldier, for this offence he served a prison term. As an active Volunteer he participated in the attack on the Clonroche R.I.C. barracks in April 1920. He was a member of the Active Service Unit who carried out the ambush at Inch on the R.I.C. cycle patrol and the attack on the barracks in Ferns in 1921. After The Truce Pender joined the National Army and served with them until March 1924. When he was demobilised he emigrated to Canada in search of work but returned the following year. In later years he worked as a Tram driver in Dublin. Stephen Pender died in Dublin at the age of 74 in 1975.

Patrick Pierce (The Shannon) A Company. Patrick Pierce joined the Volunteers in 1914. When Pádraig Pearse visited Enniscorthy in September 1915, Pierce was one of two Volunteers assigned to him as bodyguards, this was owing to the fact he was one of the tallest members of his Company. At the beginning of Easter Week the Volunteers received information that a large consignment of gunpowder and cartridges stored in Donohue's hardware was to be moved elsewhere. The management were under the impression it was going to be stolen. Pierce and a number of his comrades staked out the shop for four nights in order to find out where it would be moved to. The consignment remained in Donohue's and was seized by the Volunteers on the first morning of the Insurrection. Pierce's first duty that morning was to take up a sniping position at the top of Castle Hill. He spent around a half hour there before crossing to the other side of town, where he took up a similar position on the Turret Rocks. He remained there until he was relieved that night.

On Friday morning Pierce was back on the Rocks for a brief spell before he was sent to Ferns on a scouting mission along with Volunteer Michael Maguire. He spent most of Saturday at H.Q. helping to arm the new recruits. On Sunday he was busy blocking roads and felling trees in the Ferns District and on the Wexford Road. After the surrender Pierce evaded arrest and kept a low profile before moving to Dublin a month later.

Pierce remained there until March 1917 before returning to Enniscorthy. He helped to establish a new Shannon Company on his return and was appointed as 1st Lieutenant. Shortly afterwards Pierce went back to work at The Echo Newspaper when it began printing again. Over the following years he was involved in several operations carried out by the Company, including raiding for arms and rate books, the attack on the R.I.C. barracks in Clonroche and the large raid for petrol at the railway station. In January 1921 Pierce was appointed as Captain of his Company and served as such until his arrest in March the same year. While interned on Spike Island, Pierce participated in a hunger strike. He was released from Marlborough (Port Laoise) Jail that December.

At the outbreak of the Civil War, Pierce was attached to the Republican garrison at the courthouse, he held the rank of Battalion Intelligence Officer. When the "Battle of Enniscorthy" began, Pierce was placed in command of a party of men holed up in Bennett's Hotel and Yates's woollen store on the Shannon Quay. These positions were in direct line of fire from the Free State Army in the old R.I.C. barracks on the Abbey Square and the Castle. For three days Pierce and his men exchanged heavy fire with the Free State soldiers. After the town had been retaken he went on the run and joined a flying column. However, he had to return shortly after owing to ill health, the cause of which were the effects of his hunger strike the previous year. Pierce had to undergo an operation and although recuperating, was arrested several times but was never held for long. Patrick Pierce died at the age of 90 in 1988.

Thomas Quigley (Castleboro) A Company. Thomas Quigley joined the Volunteers in March 1916, the month before the Rising. On the first morning he marched with the main body of men from Irish Street to the Athenaeum. While a H.Q. was established, Quigley was placed on sentry duty at the top of Castle Hill. Shortly after he was ordered to help and bring the munitions stored at "The Dump" to the Athenaeum. His next task was to set up beds in the ballroom. After completing this he was sent on outpost duty to the Wexford Road for several hours. When he returned to H.Q. that evening, Quigley was assigned sentry duty on The Duffry. He spent the night on guard duty in the old R.I.C. barracks on Court Street. After resting on Friday morning, Quigley was detailed for outpost duty at Brownswood before completing his days duty at Bellfield Cross. On Saturday morning he was a member of a party of Volunteers who went on a scouting mission along the railway tracks as far as Edermine. After returning, Quigley was placed on sentry duty on Friary Hill and later at the Gas Yard. He spent Sunday on duty in the Athenaeum and was present there for the surrender. Afterwards he evaded capture by going on the run for three weeks.

Quigley re-joined in 1917 and participated in the general activities of his Company until early 1919, then he moved to Arklow for work reasons. Once in Arklow he joined the Company there and played a prominent role in its operations. He served up to The Truce and afterwards took the Republican side in the Civil War. Quigley had to cease activity in early 1923 due to ill health. Despite serving from 1916 until 1923, the Military

Service Pension Board still deemed Quigley not worthy of a pension. In a memo dated the 5th of November 1941, it states.

Service, though good, is of doubtful qualifying standard.

This was despite numerous references from commanding officers in both Wexford and Wicklow. Instead of a pension Quigley was awarded a medal for.

Continuous membership during the period of three months ended the 11th of March 1922.

Thomas Quigley died in 1983, he was 83 years old.

William Quirke (The Shannon) A Company. William Quirke joined the Volunteers in 1913 and the I.R.B. shortly afterwards. At the time of Pádraig Pearse's visit to Enniscorthy in September 1915, Quirke along with his best friend Patrick Pierce were selected as his bodyguards owing to their height. Both also worked for The Echo Newspaper. Prior to Easter Week he was a member of a small party of Volunteers under the command of Patrick Keegan who were involved in raiding for arms and manufacturing munitions. On the night before the Rising, Quirke was dispatched to Riverdale near Crossabeg to collect weapons and bring them to "Antwerp". The next morning Quirke took up a sniping position on the Turret Rocks and remained there for the day. In his testimony before the Military Service Pensions Board on the 8th of October 1937 Quirke stated that he fired on the R.I.C. barracks on numerous occasions. After he was relieved he slept at H.Q. in the Athenaeum. On Friday morning he was back on the Rocks for a short period before he was ordered to take charge of a group of railway workers. Quirke brought these men two miles north along the tracks and had them lift rails. At 6 a.m. Saturday morning he went to Ferns and guarded a group of Volunteers who were lifting rails and felling trees to block roads. He returned to Enniscorthy that evening. Quirke spent Sunday between "Antwerp" and the Athenaeum and was present in the latter for the surrender. He helped to collect and hide weapons before going home in the early hours of Monday morning. He successfully evaded arrest.

In March 1917 Quirke was appointed Captain of the newly formed Shannon Company. In 1919 he led over twenty raids for arms throughout the District. While in 1920 he played a prominent role in some of the major operations in the area, including the attack on the R.I.C. barracks in Clonroche, the raid for petrol at the railway station, collecting shells seized at Pierce's foundry in Wexford and delivering them to the forge in Corrageen. Quirke led the raid on Davis's foundry at St. John's, using boats to cross the Slaney and evade military checkpoints. He also led four separate attacks on R.I.C. and Devonshire Regiment patrols. At the beginning of February 1921, Quirke was arrested and held in the courthouse for three months. Beaten regularly, he was also used as a hostage by the Black and Tans when they patrolled the town.

Shortly after his release in May, Quirke led the biggest military engagement in Enniscorthy since the Rising. Using the cover of darkness, along with eleven others under his command, he took a sniping position on the Turret Rocks. Then at a prearranged time they opened fire on the R.I.C. barracks below. Fire was returned and lasted approximately twenty minutes, with the police using both rifles and machine guns. In that twenty minutes the Active Service Unit was able to pass through the town unbeknownst to the police on their way to Killurin, where they would ambush a military train the following day. Prior to the Civil War Quirke was appointed as an auxiliary officer in the Free State Army.

When the "Battle of Enniscorthy" broke out in July, Quirke was in the Castle. From there he fired on and was fired upon by former comrades over a three-day period before the Free State Army surrendered. He was given safe passage afterwards. After the Free State Army retook the town, Quirke assisted in the release of a number of Republicans familiar to him who had been arrested. A few weeks later Quirke saved his best friend, work colleague and former brother in arms, Patrick Pierce from a severe beating by Free State officers. That September he resigned his post and resumed working at The Echo full time. William Quirke died in 1973 at the age of 75.

Seamus Rafter (Slaney Place) O/C Enniscorthy Battalion. Seamus Rafter was a founding member of the Gaelic League in Enniscorthy, and a longstanding member of the I.R.B. before the Volunteers were established in 1913. In late 1915, on the resignation of William Brennan Whitmore, (Over an argument about Volunteers attending Dances) Rafter was appointed as Officer in Charge of the Enniscorthy Battalion, having already served as Captain of A Company. Throughout the Rising Rafter spent the vast majority of his time in the Athenaeum planning and organising. After the surrender he and his fellow officers handed themselves over to the British military on the Monday afternoon. He was court-martialled and sentenced to death, which was commuted to five years penal servitude. Rafter was released in June 1917 and on his return to Enniscorthy, threw himself back into Volunteer activities.

On the 26th of August 1918 Rafter was at his pub and grocery at 3 Slaney Place when an explosion rocked the building leaving him severely injured. Not wanting the police involved, he was carried upstairs and nursed for over a fortnight before he succumbed to his injuries on the 12th of September. Rafter was 45 years of age. He was buried with full military honours in his native Ballindaggin. Over the following weeks many of those who paraded in uniform were harassed and arrested by the police. In later years Rafter was honoured in Enniscorthy with a statue in the Abbey Square, which was unveiled in 1958 opposite the old R.I.C. barracks. Georges Street was also renamed after him.

Thomas Rafter (Ballindaggin) A Company. Thomas Rafter was an older brother of Seamus Rafter's. He joined the I.R.B. in 1911 and the Volunteers in 1913. Rafter was a member of the Ballindaggin Company which was attached to A Company. On the first day of the Rising he went to Enniscorthy with members of his Company. There they were ordered by his brother to return to Ballindaggin and block the road leading to The Curragh in order to prevent the British military from passing through. Over the weekend along with Volunteer George Stafford, Rafter visited the Parishes of Kiltealy, Rathnure, Coutnacuddy, Killane and Caim to encourage the young men there to join them. However their endeavours proved fruitless. In Ballindaggin they closed the two pubs and took over the post office. They also cut the telegraph lines but were still in daily contact with Enniscorthy through dispatches. After the surrender in the town Rafter evaded arrest.

He re-joined in 1917 and in April the following year led an ambush on the vehicle belonging to the County Surveyor and his assistant, which reaped a large quantity of Gelignite and other explosives. After the death of his brother Seamus, he removed munitions and weapons from a lock-up belonging to him on Main Street and brought them to Corrageen. From then up until The Truce Rafter was involved in carrying dispatches, manufacturing munitions and scouting for various flying columns that passed through his area. He played no part in the Civil War. Thomas Rafter died at the age of 93 in 1961.

Charles Redmond (Killagoley) A Company. While working and living in Liverpool, Charles Redmond joined the I.R.B. in 1908. He returned home to Enniscorthy in 1912 and joined the Volunteers the following year. On the first morning of the Rising he left "Antwerp" and went to Keegan's at 2 a.m.. From there he was sent to Blackstoops to keep watch. Redmond returned a few hours later and marched with the main body of Volunteers to the Athenaeum. His next assignment was outpost duty at Drumgoold Cross and then after a rest and something to eat, he was placed on guard duty at the bridge overnight. On Friday night Redmond was sent to the Castle where he remained until Saturday morning. That afternoon he took a sniping position on the Turret Rocks and according to his statement before the Military Service Pensions Board on the 11th of February 1941, he fired three times at the R.I.C. barracks. On Saturday night he was at Blackstoops before he was sent to Drumgoold early on Sunday morning. Redmond returned to H.Q. at noon and rested there until 6 p.m.. He was then assigned sentry duty on Irish Street until he was recalled at the surrender. Redmond evaded capture and in 1917 joined the Boolavogue Company with whom he served until The Truce. Charles Redmond died in Brownswood Hospital in 1967 aged 79.

Laurence Redmond (Morriscastle) A Company. Laurence Redmond joined the Volunteers in 1914, three years after becoming a member of the I.R.B.. A native of Morriscastle, he came to Enniscorthy on the Tuesday of Easter Week and stayed with friends. He was called out on the Thursday morning and sent to block roads on The Shannon, after which he was placed on sentry duty there. Redmond spent the majority of his time Friday on sentry duty on the Market Square, while on Saturday he was once again posted to The Shannon. That evening Redmond was sent to the residence of T.D. Sinnott in Davidstown with dispatches. He remained there until the following Tuesday, when he returned to Enniscorthy to obtain intelligence before reporting back to Sinnott's. Redmond went home to Morriscastle on Thursday and evaded arrest.

In 1917 Redmond joined the Kilmuckridge Company. Over the following years he was involved in setting fire to the R.I.C. barracks in Kilmuckridge and the destruction of the Coastguard Station in Morriscastle, during which he had to fire a number of warning shots. In March 1920 Redmond was arrested and sentenced to three months in Waterford Jail. He was accompanied on the journey to Waterford by District Inspector Percival Lea Wilson, who threatened to shoot Redmond if the journey was interrupted in any manner. Wilson himself was shot dead less than three months later by the I.R.A. in Gorey. Redmond chose the Republican side in the Civil War. He was badly burned while handling explosives in July 1922, the results of his injuries confined him to bed for a couple of months. After recovering he resumed his activities until the ceasefire in 1923. Laurence Redmond died aged 83 in 1969.

Owen Redmond (The Harrow) Ferns Company. Owen Redmond joined the Volunteers in 1914 and during the Easter Rising served in both Enniscorthy and Ferns. He was arrested afterwards and interned in Wandsworth Jail and Frongach Camp from where he was released that July. Redmond re-joined his Company in 1917 and played a prominent role in all their activities up until The Truce. During the Civil War he served with the rank of Captain in the Free State Army until he was demobilised in 1923. Owen Redmond died of Tuberculosis in 1924, he was 31 years old.

Myles Roban (The Leap) A Company. Myles Roban joined the Volunteers in 1914. On the first morning of the Rising he marched with the main body of men from Irish Street to the Athenaeum. There he was ordered to take up a sniping position behind the Castle wall, from where (according to his testimony before the Military Service Pensions Board on the 8th of February 1940) he fired approximately thirty shots at the R.I.C. barracks on the Abbey Square. After Roban was relieved, he joined a party of Volunteers who commandeered provisions from Matt Ryan's shop on the Market Square and then bedding from Bolger's on Georges Street (Rafter St.). After resting and getting something to eat, he was assigned outpost duty to Davis's Mill until the early hours of Friday. On Friday morning Roban did police duty around the town. Later he was placed on guard duty outside The National Bank, which was situated opposite the Athenaeum on Castle Street. That night he spent on outpost duty at Blackstoops. Roban returned to H.Q. on Saturday morning and slept there until evening. Once back on duty, he was sent to Bellfield to investigate the theft of a sheep. He then did outpost duty at Summerhill until Sunday morning after which he rested until the evening. Roban was present in the Athenaeum for the surrender and helped to load vehicles with weapons and materials that were taken away and hidden. He evaded arrest.

On the reorganisation of the Volunteers in March 1917, Roban joined the Shannon Company. Over the Christmas Holidays in 1918 he guarded the General Election ballot boxes in the courthouse. In May 1921, Roban was a member of the party of Volunteers under the command of William Quirke, who sniped on the R.I.C. barracks in Enniscorthy the night before the Killurin Train Ambush. Roban also used his position as a rate collector to gather intelligence on the movements of the R.I.C.. When the Civil War broke out, Roban aligned himself with the Republican side and fought in the "Battle of Enniscorthy". He was one of the men sent to meet Ernie O'Malley and his Tipperary column, to guide them into the town. As the Free State Army retook the town, Roban helped to set fire to the courthouse. Following a short period of time with various flying columns he returned to Enniscorthy and took charge of a small group of men who carried out attacks on Free State soldiers. They also burned the signal box at the railway and an empty passenger train at Solsboro. Roban was arrested shortly after the ceasefire in May 1923 and was interned until July 1924. Myles Roban died in 1957 at the age of 67.

Thomas Roche (Ferns) Ferns Company. Thomas Roche founded a branch of the Gaelic League in Ferns in 1902, he also served as a member on the G.A.A.'s County Board. In 1909 he joined the I.R.B. and was the driving force behind the setting up a Volunteer Company in the village in 1914. Prior to the Rising Roche's home was used as a weapons store and a place to manufacture munitions. During the Rising itself, he served in Enniscorthy and Ferns. Roche was arrested the day after the surrender and deported not long afterwards. He was interned in Wandsworth Prison and Frongach Camp until the following December. After his release Roche wasted no time in helping to reform his Company. In 1918 he was appointed as Director of Elections and *the success of some was down to him*. Roche was selected as a Parish Judge and served until courts were set up. Despite all this work he still found time for all the general Volunteer activities as well as participating in several operations. Thomas Roche died at the age of 81 in 1952.

Patrick Ronan (Ferns) O/C Ferns Company. Patrick Ronan joined the I.R.B. in 1912 and the Volunteers in 1914. Prior to Easter Week he held the rank of 2nd Lieutenant of the Ferns Company. With Captain Brennan Whitmore in Dublin for the Rising and 1st Lieutenant Patrick Doyle in jail for possession of rifles, Ronan was in charge of the Ferns Company on Easter Sunday afternoon when they paraded in the village. They had gathered under the impression they would march to Enniscorthy that evening for the imminent uprising. Instead Ronan received a message ordering the Company to stand down and await further orders. On Monday evening Ronan and his Company learnt of the events in Dublin and were left in a state of confusion, having not yet received any instructions from Enniscorthy. Early Tuesday morning he received an order to proceed to Enniscorthy, only to meet a Volunteer, William O'Toole, at Scarawalsh with a countermanding order and the instruction to return to Ferns. Ronan decided against that and instead set up a camp in nearby Ballinahallin Wood. They remained there until early Wednesday morning and then returned to Ferns demoralised. Later on Wednesday morning Ronan received an order to mobilise and march to Enniscorthy, this order was cancelled and renewed several times that day.

On Thursday morning he received a further order to proceed but decided to wait for certainty. Later in the day word came through from Cumann na mBan member Annie O'Leary that Enniscorthy had risen. Ronan gathered what remained of his Company, around twenty men, and marched to Enniscorthy. They arrived at nightfall and reported to H.Q. in the Athenaeum. On Friday morning Ronan was placed in charge of collecting all the available bicycles in the town. Early on Saturday morning he returned to Ferns under the command of Seán Moran (who was killed by the Black and Tans in Drogheda in 1921) to take control of the village. Ronan was present at the R.I.C. barracks on Sunday morning when Canon Kehoe and D.I. Drake were brought under guard with Pádraig Pearse's surrender letter. After the surrender in Enniscorthy, he was ordered to evacuate the village and return to the town. He was in the last car to leave and was behind Peter Galligan's when it crashed on-route. Ronan and others helped the injured and by the time a doctor had arrived, Galligan told him it was too late to go to Enniscorthy and to go home instead and hide as many weapons as he could. Ronan was arrested the following Tuesday and deported soon afterwards. He was interned in Wandsworth Prison and Frongach Camp until December.

After his release he re-joined his Company and over the next couple of years helped to establish a separate Company in Kilrush. He drilled and trained Volunteers there two nights a week until he was observed and informed on, this led to his arrest in November 1920. Ronan was held in the courthouse in Enniscorthy for four months, there he suffered beatings on an almost daily basis. He was then sent to Kilworth Prison Camp in Cork. While at Kilworth, Ronan participated in the digging of an escape tunnel, unfortunately for him the day before the planned escape he was moved to Spike Island. However, twenty-one men left behind managed to escape. Ronan was freed in December 1921 from Maryborough (Port Laoise) Jail, but due to the ill treatment he had received during his captivity he was unable to play any further active part. Patrick Ronan died in 1981, he was 85 years of age

Patrick Sheehan (Irish Street) A Company. A member of the Volunteers since 1914, Patrick Sheehan's primary role throughout the Rising was that of a driver. He transported Volunteers between outposts, brought them to raid for arms and made several journeys to Ferns. He was arrested afterwards and interned in Stafford Jail for a month. Sheehan re-joined in 1917 and continued to be used as a driver. The night of the attack on the R.I.C. barracks in Clonroche in April 1920, Sheehan transported over three hundred grenades and a quantity rifles to the village for use in the attack. During the Civil War Sheehan joined the Free State Army and was assigned to the Transport Corps. Patrick Sheehan died at the age of 62 in St. John's Hospital in1960.

Martin J. Shiel (Slaney Street) A Company. Martin J. Shiel was an auxiliary member of the Volunteers in 1916. During the Insurrection he carried out policing duties in the town. After the surrender his licensed premises on Slaney Street was used to hide weapons and munitions. Shiel was one of the few business owners in the town who refused to do business with members of the crown forces. His establishment was raided and looted on several occasions by said forces up until The Truce. In 1918 Shiel was the local Director of Elections and his premises were visited by Michael Collins and Ernest Blythe amongst others. His home was used for meetings throughout the War of Independence.

In 1922 Shiel chose the Pro-Treaty side. At the outbreak of "Battle of Enniscorthy" Shiel scaled a fourteen-foot wall at the back of his premises to deliver supplies to the besieged soldiers in the Castle, he did this on several occasions. He also went to the former R.I.C. barracks on the Abbey Square, then occupied by the Free State Army, under the cover of darkness to obtain ammunition for the soldiers in the Castle. He did all this while the fighting was at its heaviest. After the Free State Army recaptured the town, Shiel was used as an intelligence asset and passed on important information. He obtained valuable contracts for food and supplies from the Free State Army, however, these were cancelled shortly afterwards leaving him severely out of pocket. After the Civil War ended, his business collapsed altogether due jointly to a boycott by members of the Anti-Treaty side and the unpaid bills of the Free State Army. Martin J. Shiel died in Dublin at the age of 77 in 1957.

Alicia Shortall (Templeshannon) Cumann na mBan. Alicia Shortall (nee French) was one of the youngest members of Cumann na mBan when she joined in 1916. On the first morning of the Rising she reported for duty at the Athenaeum. From there she was sent to commandeer bedding from Burke-Roches on Castle Street, medical supplies from Taylors Chemist on the Market Square and finally, groceries from Buttles shop in Templeshannon. Once back at H.Q. Shortall was tasked with filling basins of hot water for Volunteers to bathe their feet in when they returned off duty. In the early hours of Friday morning she helped to tend a Volunteer who was brought back to H.Q. after he had been accidently shot by a comrade. A few hours later Shortall fainted at Mass from a combination of exhaustion and the shock of treating the wounded man. She was brought to her home and after a rest reported back for duty to the Athenaeum that evening. She remained there until after the surrender. In the months following the Rising, Shortall assisted in the collection of funds for the prisoner's dependants. She also participated in a series of concerts and plays that travelled the county to raise funds to buy weapons for the Volunteers. After moving to Carlow in the middle of 1920, Shortall ceased her activities and got married shortly afterwards. Alicia Shortall died at the age of 72 in 1971.

Patrick Sinnott Jr. (Bellfield) A Company. Patrick Sinnott Jr. was an apprentice machinist at The Echo Newspaper at the time of the Rising. On the first morning of the Insurrection he was assigned sentry duty on Georges Street. (Rafter St) While there he was involved in an exchange of gunfire with members of an R.I.C. patrol which lasted for several minutes before the patrol retreated down Friary Hill. There is no other details in his file of his activities for the rest of the week. Sinnott was arrested on the day after the surrender and deported shortly afterwards. He was interned in Lewes Jail and Frongach Camp from where he was released in December. Sinnott re-joined in 1917 and was involved in the manufacture of munitions for the next two years. He took part in the attack on the R.I.C. barracks in Clonroche and the large raid for petrol at the railway station in 1920. Sinnott moved to Wexford later that year and joined a Company there. He was involved in several operations carried out in that area up until The Truce. During the Civil War Sinnott served with the Free State Army and held the rank of Sergeant Major at its conclusion. Sinnott moved to the United States shortly after in order to find work. By 1940 he was back in Ireland and had re-joined the army, he served until 1945 and held the rank of Corporal. Patrick Sinnott Jr. died in 1947 five days shy of his 52nd birthday.

Patrick Sinnott Snr. (Bellfield) A Company. The father of Patrick Sinnott Jr., Patrick Sinnott Snr. was a member of the I.R.B. for several years before joining the Volunteers in 1913. He worked as a printer for The Echo Newspaper which at the time held strong Republican beliefs and had the likes of Robert Brennan, Seán Etchingham and Larry de Lacy on its staff. Sinnott worked at night and weekends printing various seditious pamphlets for de Lacy and Liam Mellows which were then distributed countrywide. On the morning of the Rising Sinnott was posted to the Castle roof from where he fired several rounds at the R.I.C. barracks. For the remainder of the week he was placed on sentry duty around the town and on a couple of occasions helped to commandeer supplies. On the Monday after the surrender he was arrested and brought to the R.I.C. barracks where he was questioned for three hours before he was released. Sinnott then went to Wexford and stayed there for several months.

In early 1917 he returned to Enniscorthy and re-joined his Company; he also went back to work at The Echo once it re-opened. Over the following years Sinnott's home was raided several times by the authorities. In 1920, during one such raid, he was so badly beaten by the Black and Tans that it led to sight loss and eventually, total blindness. After this beating Sinnott moved to Wexford to live, as he was incapable of carrying on in both his work life and Volunteer duty. Patrick Sinnott Snr. died at the age of 73 in 1943.

Patrick Sinnott (Ballyhuskard) A Company. Patrick Sinnott joined the Volunteers in 1914. A carpenter by trade, he used his skills to make pike handles for several months prior to the Rising working out of Cleary's Forge. On the first morning of hostilities he reported to the Athenaeum at 8 a.m., he was then sent with a party of Volunteers in a commandeered lorry to scout Ferns. On arrival in the village he saw the

R.I.C. barracks had sandbags around it. In his testimony before the Military Service Pensions Board on the 4th of June 1940, Sinnott claimed to have fired a shot at the barracks before the lorry turned around. On their way back they helped to fell trees and block roads at Scarawalsh and Solsboro. On his return to H.Q. Sinnott was instructed by Patrick Keegan to go to the Wexford Road. At 9 p.m. he was sent on outpost duty to Drumgoold Cross, from where he was relieved at 4 a.m. on Friday morning. Later that morning Sinnott was on outpost duty at the gates of the Enniscorthy Asylum. In the afternoon he was placed on guard duty outside the Munster and Leinster Bank at the top of Slaney Street. After resting and having something to eat in the Athenaeum, he was sent back to the gates of the Asylum. For the majority of his time on Saturday and Sunday, Sinnott was on duty in the vicinity of the Athenaeum. After the surrender he evaded arrest.

Sinnott re-joined in 1917 and was primarily occupied in the manufacture of munitions at "Antwerp". In 1920, O'Brien's licensed premises on Irish Street was owned and run by two elderly spinster sisters. Both were staunch Republicans and refused entry or service to the British military. For this reason the Volunteers often kept an eye out for the sisters. On one particular night, Sinnott, in the company of Volunteers Cleary and Holbrook intercepted three British officers trying to gain entrance through the backyard. After a brief skirmish the officers were relieved of their weapons and sent gingerly on their way. A couple of nights later a large party of drunken Black and Tans forced their way into O'Brien's and smashed the place to pieces. The Volunteers received strict orders from G.H.Q. in Dublin not to retaliate as the situation was too precarious at that moment. Shortly afterwards Sinnott moved to Wexford and played no further role. Patrick Sinnott died in Bridgetown at the age of 65 in 1956.

Thomas D. Sinnott (Davidstown) A Company. Thomas D. Sinnott joined the Volunteers in Dundalk at their inception in 1913. On his return to Enniscorthy he took up a position as a Science Teacher in the local

Christian Brothers School and joined A Company. The first morning of the Rising, Sinnott reported for duty to Irish Street at 4 a.m. and marched to the Athenaeum with the main body of men. At 6.30 a.m. he was sent to make contact with Phil Lennon, the Battalion Commandant of New Ross who was to have brought his men to Clonroche. On arriving in Clonroche Sinnott soon realised that the New Ross men were not coming, he returned to Enniscorthy arriving by 9 a.m.. Sinnott then joined two Volunteers and accompanied them on a horse and cart to Donohoe's, there they commandeered any practical supplies they could and returned to the Athenaeum. After unloading their cargo they were sent to James Cleary's Forge to bring any weaponry that was ready back to H.Q.. On each occasion they crossed the bridge, they came under heavy fire from the R.I.C. barracks. Sinnott was then ordered to go to an outpost and escort three prisoners into town, two farmers and a shopkeeper from Dublin who had each tried to force their way into the town.

On his return to H.Q. Sinnott was appointed Captain of *"Ingress and Egress"*, this meant no one could leave or enter the town without a permit signed by Sinnott. He had a car and a driver plus ten messengers at his disposal and from that point on this was his role until the surrender. Sinnott was arrested on the Tuesday following the surrender and deported shortly afterwards. He was interned in Stafford Jail and Frongach Camp until December. On the re-establishment of the Volunteers in 1917, Sinnott was appointed Captain of B Company. That June he was made Deputy Brigade Adjutant and by the end of the year had been promoted to Brigade Adjutant. In January 1918 he was appointed Brigade Vice Commandant and in February led a party of fifty Volunteers to Waterford to protect Sinn Féin workers at the Bye-Election there. In September 1919 Sinnott was promoted to Brigade Commandant.

Following the fatal shooting of Ellen Morris in The Ballagh during a botched raid for arms by a flying column belonging to his Brigade, Sinnott was court-martialled and demoted to the rank of Private in March 1920. Despite this, he continued to play an active role, he was one of the riflemen at the attack on the Clonroche R.I.C. barracks in April and was also involved in the large raid for petrol at the railway station the following month. In June Sinnott organised the transport for the men who killed D.I. Lea Wilson in Gorey. He was re-appointed as Commandant in October 1920. Sinnott was arrested in November 1921 and released the following month. He did not participate in the Civil War.

As a Chemistry teacher, in the years following the Rising, Sinnott was one of the driving forces behind the setting up of a munition's factory on the top floor of "Antwerp". His recollections on the death of Seamus Rafter differ from some of his comrades who stated it was in "Antwerp" that Seamus Rafter suffered fatal injuries from an explosion in August 1918. When he was before the Military Service Pensions Board on the 1st of July 1936 Sinnott gave this detailed account of the incident.

"It was in his own house, about 50 yards from the munition factory. Antwerp was well known. There was always an armed man in the house. We made powder and explosives in the house and made it up into parcels which were left on the shelves (of Rafter's shop) *labelled "Mrs. Murphy, Morrissey and Malone." The different Companies came and took what they wanted. The parcels were supposed to contain tea and sugar and even though the place was raided, no one suspected what was in the parcels. This occurred on the 24th or 25th of August 1918. I had made up the cartridge powder and the explosive powder-a certain quantity of each and at about nine o'clock the parcels were left on the shelves. I went out and was just about 60 yards from the door when Rafter's place went up. We broke in, we had to put a guard of our men on the place. For seventeen nights and seventeen days five men remained there under arms, they never slept. The police were not allowed in all this time, not till the man was waked. He died eventually. He would not let us go away all the time, but he never told us, even in his delirium, what happened. He was always trying something or other different – the thing had a fascination for him; and he was a man of 44 or 45. His death disorganised the whole thing. Everything fell through after that – we were all caught after that. Up to that it was one of the most active Brigades in the country."*

In later years Sinnott worked in local government and in 1942 he was appointed as the first County Manager of Wexford, serving in the position until his retirement in 1953. Thomas D. Sinnott died in 1965 at the age of 72.

Loftus H. Smith (Tomnalosset) A Company. During the Easter Rising Loftus H. Smith was a member of a party of Volunteers who raided numerous houses in the Enniscorthy District. He also carried out street patrol. After the surrender Smith evaded arrest and when the organisation was reformed in 1917 he re-joined. From then until The Truce he was involved in the manufacture of munitions, raids for arms and materials and later was appointed as Brigade Police Officer. In 1922 Smith joined the National Army and was one of the soldiers who took over the former R.I.C. barracks on the Abbey Square when the R.I.C. left. During the "Battle of Enniscorthy" in July, he spent four days in the Castle attempting to repel the Anti-Treaty forces attack until finally surrendering. That September, Smith was in command of the Free State soldiers who captured a flying column of Irregulars at Ballindaggin. He joined the Garda Siochana on its formation and retired as a Superintendent in 1941. Loftus H. Smith died at the age of 75 in 1967.

Patrick F. Stokes (The Duffry) A Company. Patrick F. Stokes joined the Volunteers in 1915 and served as the Company Bugler. On the first morning of the Rising he sounded the fall in at Irish Street and marched with the main body of men to the Athenaeum. For the remainder of the week Stokes acted as Seamus Rafter's *Aide de Camp* and for the exceptions of a short spell on sentry duty on the Market Square and one raid for arms outside the town, he remained at the Athenaeum. With the news of the surrender, Stokes was sent with his bugle to recall the Volunteers from their posts. He was arrested the following day and interned in Dublin for a month.

Stokes's mother died within days of his return to Enniscorthy. With his father also in bad health, Stokes tried to take over his business as a painter and decorator, however this proved too difficult. He moved to Swords in Dublin where he found work as a painter and joined the local Volunteer Company. After a couple of years in Swords, Stokes moved again, this time to Bagenalstown where he joined the Company there. He played an active role up until The Truce, after which he ceased his activities.

Stokes's older brother Thomas also participated in the Easter Rising. Afterwards he was interned in Stafford Jail and Frongach Camp where he became very ill. After his release his health deteriorated to such an extent he was dead by the end of 1917, he was only 24 years of age. His sister Marion, a member of Cumann na mBan, also took part in Easter Week. Along with Una Brennan and Greta Commerford, she is credited with raising the Tricolour above the Athenaeum on the first morning of the Rising. Patrick F. Stokes died in Dublin where he resided at the age of 85 in 1984.

John Sunderland (Ferns) Ferns Company. John Sunderland joined the Volunteers in 1914 and served in Enniscorthy and Ferns during Easter Week. Afterwards he was arrested and interned in Wakefield Prison and Frongach Camp, from where he was released in July. Sunderland re-joined in 1917 and carried out the general activities of his Company as well as manufacturing munitions. He took part in the burning of the Clonevan R.I.C. barracks in 1920. At the outbreak of the Civil War, Sunderland chose the Pro-Treaty side and although not a member of the Free State Army, took up arms to defend Ferns against the Anti-Treaty forces. John Sunderland died in 1938 at the age of 50.

Michael Sutton (St. John's Street) A Company. Michael Sutton joined the Volunteers in 1913. He reported for duty to the Athenaeum on the first morning of the Rising. From there he was placed on sentry duty on Lymington Road. After a couple of hours there he was moved to Castle Hill. According to Sutton's testimony before the Military Service Pensions Board on the 8th of February 1940, that afternoon he followed two R.I.C. men along the Mill Park Road, he stated one of them entered his residence while the other continued towards the barracks in the Abbey Square. Sutton said he fired three shots at this man and that fire was returned. He spent Friday on sentry duty on Irish Street and that evening at Maudlin's Folly. On Saturday he was on duty at Davis's Mill before he was sent to Macmine that night. Sutton was on duty on The Duffry all day Sunday until he was recalled to H.Q. for the surrender. He was arrested in Newtownbarry (Bunclody) the following Tuesday and was held for six days before he was released.

Sutton re-joined in 1917 and along with the regular activities of his Company he carried dispatches on a number of occasions. In 1920, while in the company of two Volunteers, they observed a small number of Black and Tans hiding in O'Neill's coal yard on the Mill Park Road. One of the Volunteers fired a shot in their direction before the three of them made their escape. Following The Truce, Sutton ceased his activities and played no part in the Civil War. Michael Sutton died in his 84th year in 1977.

William Thorpe (The Shannon) C Company. William Thorpe joined the Volunteers in 1913. On the first morning of the Rising he reported to Keegan's on Irish Street and marched from there to the Athenaeum with the main body of Volunteers. After a H.Q. had been established, Thorpe was sent on outpost duty to Salville Cross and remained there all day. On Friday morning he was detailed to Drumgoold Cross for more outpost duty. That night Thorpe marched to Ferns with a column of Volunteers, arriving early Saturday morning. Thorpe spent Saturday and Sunday in Ferns before returning to Enniscorthy after the surrender. He was arrested the following Thursday on the bridge and was deported a short time afterwards. Thorpe was interned in Stafford Jail and Frongach Camp until he was released at the end of July. Once he returned home he ceased his Volunteer activities. William Thorpe died at his residence in Vinegar Hill Villas in 1953 at the age of 58.

Margaret Tobin (Killagoley) Cumann na mBan. Margaret Tobin (nee Howlin) joined Cumann Na mBan in 1915. She had three brothers in the Volunteers, James, Patrick and Thomas. Tobin arrived at the Athenaeum at 10 a.m. on the first morning of the Rising. She immediately started catering for the men, fixing up beds and generally making the place suitable as a H.Q.. Tobin remained there until Sunday night. Over the next couple of years she was involved in raising funds for the movement. She acted as a pianist for the concert party that put on shows around the county. In late 1918 she obtained a job in Dublin and resigned from her Cumann. Tobin had no further service. Margaret Tobin died in 1963 at the age of 74.

Patrick Tobin (Irish Street) A Company. Patrick Tobin joined the I.R.B. in 1884, the same year as "Antwerp" was established as a meeting place for the organisation. They used the G.A.A., which had been founded that year, as cover to operate. Tobin joined the Volunteers at their inception in 1913. Prior to the Rising, while working for the railway as a carter, he was able to pass on information to Patrick Keegan regarding shipments of suitable materials for his munition factory. In 1915 Tobin was arrested and jailed for a month after he was caught tearing down British army recruiting posters. On the first morning of the Rising, Tobin called on several houses to rouse Volunteers and then marched with the main body of men from Irish Street to the Athenaeum. Once a H.Q. had been established, he took up a sniping position overlooking the R.I.C. barracks. He remained in this position for three hours and would later claim to never have fired a shot. After he was relieved, Tobin was placed on sentry duty at the top of New Street (Wafer St.) and then later was assigned outpost duty at Blackstoops.

On Friday morning Tobin was sent to intercept the post and bring the letters back to H.Q.. After doing so, he was told to question a man who lived on Slaney Street regarding the contents of one of the letters. Tobin was then ordered with a fellow Volunteer to seize any weapons in houses belonging to ex-British soldiers. They returned that evening with one rifle. He spent Saturday on outpost duty at Clonhaston Cross and in H.Q.. Except for going to mass on Sunday morning, Tobin remained in the

Athenaeum until the surrender. He was arrested the following Friday and deported shortly afterwards. Tobin was interned in Lewes and Woking Jails before he was released from Frongach Camp in December.

He re-joined in 1917 and was placed in charge of a small group of Volunteers who made Buckshot. Tobin also continued his work as a carter and helped to seize munitions from the railway. He was arrested in May 1919 and held for two months in the courthouse. Tobin was again arrested on the 2nd of February 1921 - this was the night the Black and Tans broke up "Antwerp"- and was held until the end of April. He took an active part in enforcing the Belfast Boycott, destroying goods at the railway on a thrice weekly basis up until The Truce. Although Tobin participated in the Civil War he did not claim for it on his pension application. When he was before the Military Service Pensions Board on the 2nd of March 1937 he said.

"…I am not claiming for the Civil War. I prefer it did not happen."

Patrick Tobin was 73 years old when he died in 1940.

Pádraic Tóibín (Irish Street) Na Fianna Éireann. The son of Patrick Tobin, Pádraic Toibin joined Na Fianna in 1915. He was only 12 years old when he participated in the Easter Rising. He was used to deliver dispatches throughout the week and on one occasion came under fire while on his way to Killagoley. After the surrender Tóibín helped carry arms to a farm in The Moyne. In 1917 Tóibín re-joined Na Fianna and was appointed as a Section Commander. Along with the routine activities of his section, he acted as a look out for the members of the Volunteers engaged in the manufacture of munitions. With Na Fianna expanding throughout the county, a brigade was formed and Tóibín was appointed Brigade Quartermaster and afterwards, Brigade Vice Commandant. Throughout 1919 and 1920 he participated in numerous raids for weapons and materials. Tóibín was a member of a party who raided the Wexford to Dublin train for mails in October 1920 and was subsequently arrested and imprisoned for this deed. He was released in early 1921.

That summer Tóibín carried dispatches to and from Dublin on several occasions.

When the Civil War broke out Tóibín chose the Republican side and fought in the "Battle of Enniscorthy". On the morning of the 5th of July, the fourth and final day of the battle, Tóibín along with a small party of men made their way up Friary Place to the rear of the post office, which they mistakenly believed was occupied by Free State soldiers. Once in position they broke a back window and threw in some grenades. The loud explosions were heard by a Free State sniper hiding across the road in an upstairs room of number seven Castle Hill. He opened fire and fatally wounded two of Tóibín's comrades. Maurice Spillane from Hospital Lane was killed instantly, while Patrick O'Brien, who had arrived from Dublin to fight, died a short time later. After the Free State retook the town Tóibín fled to the country where he remained until November.

On his return he got a job on The Echo Newspaper. Part of his job was as The Echo correspondent in Gorey. Here Tóibín made contact with a member of the Free State Army, who on several occasions, passed on information about the planned movements of the army. Tóibín gave this intelligence to local leaders who were able to warn various flying columns of impending raids. He was arrested in April 1923 when his nefarious activities came to light. Tóibín was interned until December 1923 when he was released from Hare Park Camp in The Curragh. Pádraic Tóibín died in 1995 in his 90th year.

Patrick Tomkins (Ballycarney) A Company. On the first morning of the Rising Patrick Tomkins sniped on the R.I.C. barracks. Later in the week he was sent to Ferns with a party of Volunteers to try and derail a military train supposably coming from Arklow. This information would prove to be false. Tomkins was arrested on the Tuesday following the surrender and was deported shortly afterwards. He was interned in Wakefield Prison and Frongach Camp until the end of July. In 1917

Tomkins joined the Ballcarney Company and served with them up to The Truce. Afterwards he served with the Free State Army in the Civil War. Tomkins's brother John was arrested the night before the Rising, he was one of four Volunteers who were sent to lift rails off the tracks at the Boro Bridge. Patrick Tomkins died in the County Home in 1929 aged 32.

Thomas Treanor (Monaghan) Lt. Wexford Company. Thomas Treanor was originally from County Monaghan. He moved to Wexford town in 1912 after obtaining the position of Assistant County Surveyor. He joined the Volunteers in 1913. By 1916 he was living in Enniscorthy. During Easter Week he was at several meetings along with Robert Brennan that were held to decide whether they should fight. On the first morning of the Rising Treanor heard volleys of rifle fire at around 7 a.m. and reported to the Athenaeum. He spent the day there handling dispatches. That night he slept at home. On Friday Volunteer Patrick Kehoe suggested the two of them should go to Wicklow and try to get the Companies there to destroy railway bridges, for there was a rumour the British military would come from Dublin by train. The two men were given permission and set off that night by bicycle. They first visited Shillelagh then Avoca before arriving in Wicklow town on Saturday night. In each location they were greeted with indifference. After been chased out of Wicklow by the R.I.C. they spent the night in a hotel in Ashford. The following morning after attending Mass, Treanor spotted the car containing Seamus Doyle and Seán Etchingham on their way to see Pádraig Pearse in Arbour Hill. Etchingham saw the two men and took out a white handkerchief, waved it and then dropped it out of the car. The two men immediately recognised what that meant, Enniscorthy had surrendered. They got on their bicycles and made their way back. Treanor was arrested the following Tuesday and was deported shortly afterwards. He was interned in Stafford Jail before he was released in June after the intervention of his father-in-law, who was an influential man.

In 1917 Treanor moved back to Wexford. Not long after the Volunteers were reorganised Treanor notified Brigade H.Q. in Enniscorthy that he would be transporting a large amount of Gelignite and Detonators on a specific day. He arranged for the Volunteers to hold him up along with the County Surveyor and their police escort. This plan was followed to the last detail and the Volunteers got away with the consignment. Treanor came under scrutiny over the hold-up but was eventually exonerated.

In October 1920 Treanor was appointed Adjutant of the South Wexford Brigade and that December he drew up a plan to blow-up the R.I.C. barracks in Carraig on Bannow. The barracks was attached to a small shop and the Volunteers planned to leave fifty pounds of Gelignite at the wall inside the shop. On the evening of the attack, Treanor and another Volunteer entered the shop and were surprised to find the shopkeeper there, thinking he was normally gone on a break at that hour. The shopkeeper was immediately suspicious of the two strangers and tackled Treanor's companion to the ground. Treanor attempted to intervene, but the shopkeeper was too strong. Treanor took out his revolver and shot the man twice, killing him. He then helped the injured Volunteer up and with the rest of the attack party who were hidden outside, made their escape with the sounds of shots ringing in their ears. Treanor was arrested in February 1921, not for the killing, but for various other activities and was interned until Christmas. After his release he played no further part. Thomas Treanor died at the age of 72 in 1963.

Patrick Tumbleton (Mary Street) A Company. Patrick Tumbleton joined the I.R.B. in 1911 and the Volunteers at their inception in 1913. At midnight on the Wednesday before the Rising, he was ordered by Denis O'Brien to mobilise other Volunteers. After doing this he was then sent with a party of men to commandeer supplies from Donohoe's hardware. He then reported to Keegan's on Irish Street and marched with the main body of Volunteers to the Athenaeum. Once the H.Q. was up and running, Tumbleton was detailed to the railway station with a party of

Volunteers to stop the Kynoch worker's train. He returned to H.Q. with the train driver and fireman and was then sent to Summerhill on outpost duty. After he was relieved from there, he took up a sniping position on Castle Hill and fired several times over the period of an hour at the R.I.C. barracks. Tumbleton spent Friday on sentry duty, first on the Market Square, then on the corner of Irish Street and finally on Court Street. On Saturday morning he went to Ferns in a lorry. He returned shortly after and for the rest of the day was placed on sentry duty on The Duffry. Tumbleton spent Sunday in the vicinity of the Athenaeum and was present for the surrender, after which he helped with the collection and disposal of weapons.

At approximately 4 a.m. on Monday morning Tumbleton lowered the Tricolour from the Athenaeum and handed it to Fr. Patrick Murphy of the Mission House. He was arrested the following Thursday and was interned in Stafford Jail and Frongach Camp. While in Frongach, Tumbleton became known as the camp barber, (he was one in civilian life) he cut the hair and shaved the likes of Michael Collins, W.T. Cosgrave, Dick McKee and Richard Mulcahy. After Tumbleton was released in December he ceased his Volunteer activities, although he did store munitions on his premises at various times. His barber shop was raided and broken up on three occasions by the Black and Tans. On the 26th of September 1938, T.D. Sinnott wrote to the Military Service Pensions Board about their failure to call Tumbleton before it, he wrote.

"…Please arrange to get him heard. He has my heart broken. He thinks because he cut the hair and shaved most of the faces of most of the leaders of this country's struggle he should have been amongst the first heard and, naturally he blames us down here."

Patrick Tumbleton died in 1945, he was 69 years old.

Eileen Twomey (Cork) Cumann na mBan. Eileen Twomey (nee O'Hegarty) was a close associate of Robert and Una Brennan. She worked as a secondary teacher in the Loreto Convent in Wexford and joined

Cumann na mBan in 1916. Twomey returned to Wexford from a holiday at her home in Cork on Holy Saturday with the understanding the Rising was beginning the next day. Over the following days she carried dispatches for Brennan as the confusion mounted about what was going to happen. Twomey arrived in Enniscorthy on the Tuesday evening and went to the Keegan house on Irish Street, where she remained until the Rising began on Thursday. Throughout the Insurrection she assisted the Brennans in the Athenaeum.

Following the surrender Twomey hid out in Oylgate for a couple of months. She then went back to Wexford with the intention of resuming her teaching post. However, upon her arrival she was dismissed due to her activities. She then went home to Cork before leaving for London that December. Twomey returned to Wexford in December 1917 and took up a position as a Gaelic League teacher. This consisted of mostly teaching classes in the evening time which left her days free for Cumann activity. Her main roles involved dealing with correspondence, the preparation and distribution of propaganda literature and assisting in fund raising. Twomey carried out these duties for two years before she got married in late 1919 and moved to Athlone. From Athlone she moved back to Cork the following year. Twomey was actively involved in her home county all the way up to the Civil War ceasefire. Eileen Twomey died at the age of 85 in 1979.

Patrick Tyrell (The Duffry) Captain A Company. Patrick Tyrell was a former British soldier who joined the I.R.B. in 1906 and the Volunteers in 1913. He acted as his Company's drill instructor and was also a member of Patrick Keegan's small group of Volunteers who raided for materials and manufactured munitions at "The Dump" prior to the Rising. On Easter Sunday Tyrell was on guard duty at Blackstoops for most of the day before returning to "Antwerp" to sleep. Over the following three days he raided for weapons and commandeered some cars. He spent the majority of his time on the railway keeping watch and every night he slept at "Antwerp".

On the first morning of the Rising, Tyrell led approximately fifteen men to the Turret Rocks where they spent the day firing on the R.I.C. barracks. On Friday and Saturday he was on outpost duty on the railway while on Sunday he was on duty around the town and at H.Q.. He was arrested a week after the surrender and deported shortly afterwards. Tyrell was interned in Stafford Jail and Frongach Camp before he was released from Wandsworth Prison at the end of October.

When the Company was reorganised in 1917, Tyrell was appointed Lieutenant and placed in charge of musketry training. Over the following years he used his job as a carter for Donohoe's to steal boxes of ammunition and cartridges as well as other materials used for the manufacture of munitions. Tyrell participated in several raids for arms around the district and also took part in the large raid for petrol at the railway station in April 1920.. After The Truce he ceased his activities. Patrick Tyrell died in St. John's Hospital in 1962 at the age of 87.

John Wafer (The Shannon) A Company. John Wafer joined the Volunteers in 1913 and the I.R.B. in 1914. Prior to the Rising he was a member of the group of Volunteers under the command of Patrick Keegan who raided for weapons and manufactured munitions. On Easter Sunday, Wafer was sent with a dispatch to Edward de Lacey in Oulart. From that time until the following Thursday morning he remained on standby for any developments. On the morning of the Rising Wafer was mobilised at 5.30 a.m. and ordered to cut telegraph lines on the roads and railway lines around the town. He also helped to dismantle the signal box at the railway station. In the afternoon he was tasked with commandeering cars and petrol. On Friday morning Wafer was sent to the Turret Rocks, from where he sniped sporadically on the R.I.C. barracks over a three-hour period. After he was relieved, he was ordered to scout the Wexford Road. He got as far as Oylgate before returning. Wafer was on outpost duty at the graveyard on Saturday before marching to Ferns that evening with the column of Volunteers under the command of Peter Galligan. He spent Sunday on duty in Ferns until the surrender order was received, he then returned to Enniscorthy. At the Athenaeum, Wafer helped collect weapons before going to "The Dump" to assist with the removal of weapons and munitions there. In the early hours of Monday morning he brought a quantity of rifles to Ballindaggin to be hidden. He was arrested on the following Wednesday and deported shortly afterwards. Wafer was interned in Stafford Jail and Frongach Camp before he was released at the end of August.

In 1917 Wafer re-joined and carried out the general activities of his Company. He moved to Dublin in 1918 and joined D Company of the 2nd Battalion, with whom he served prominently until returning home in the middle of 1920. From his return up until The Truce, Wafer manufactured munitions and blocked roads. He joined the Republican garrison at the courthouse several weeks before the Civil War broke out. When the "Battle of Enniscorthy" began, Wafer took up a sniping position in the steeple of St. Mary's Church, which overlooked the Free State Army positions in the Castle. He then moved to Askins's Shop on Georges Street (Rafter St.) which had a clear line of fire down Church Street to the Castle. Wafer was in command of eight men here and they remained there for two days. After the Free State soldiers surrendered, he helped to disarm them as they left the Castle. As the Free State reinforcements arrived Wafer assisted in setting fire to the courthouse before evacuating the town for the country. Wafer spent two months with a flying column before he was captured in September, he was interned for three weeks before he had to be released after catching Pneumonia. Wafer was laid up until the following January and after this, his only actions were to carry dispatches to flying columns on a couple of occasions.

Wafer's brother was Captain Thomas Wafer, who fought and died in the Rising in Dublin. He was killed while in charge of the Volunteer position in the Hibernian Bank which was located on the corner of O'Connell Street and Lower Abbey Street. His body was never recovered due to the fire which engulfed much of that area. Thomas Wafer was killed on Wednesday the 26th of April, the day before his Enniscorthy comrades rose. A witness to his killing was Leslie Price, the future wife of Tom Barry, the famous Rebel from Cork. She was a member of Cumann Na mBan and her account of Wafer's death is featured in Barry's biography written years later. Another of Wafer's brothers Patrick, also fought in Dublin that week. John Wafer died in St. Vincent's Hospital Dublin in 1960 aged 62.

Patrick Wafer (The Shannon) A Company. Patrick Wafer was the father of Thomas, Patrick and John Wafer., and was a long-time member of the I.R.B. before joining the Volunteers at their inception in 1913. In 1915 acting under the orders of Thomas Clarke, Wafer collected as much gold as he could from around the Enniscorthy area and brought it to Dublin. He had managed to collect several hundred pounds worth, which was then used to buy weapons for the Volunteers. On other occasions he brought packets of Amberite Gunpowder and returned with several revolvers. On Holy Saturday Wafer travelled to Dublin with his daughter Mary who was a member of Cumann na mBan. On his arrival he went to his eldest sons Thomas's home and helped him distribute weapons to the members of his Company. Wafer returned to Enniscorthy on Easter Sunday unaware that he would never see his son again.

On the following Thursday Wafer reported for duty to the Athenaeum. For the remainder of the Rising he spent his time between H.Q. and "The Dump" where he helped to organise and distribute weapons and munitions. After the surrender he brought twelve rifles home and hid them until the Company's reorganisation in 1917. He successfully evaded arrest. During the War of Independence Wafer's home was used on numerous occasions as a refuge for Volunteers on the run and also for the storage of arms. Taking the Republican side in The Civil War, Wafer fed the Republican forces holed up in Bennetts Hotel and Yates Wool Store throughout the "Battle of Enniscorthy". In honour of his fallen son Thomas, New Street was renamed Wafer Street, although it would take until November 2016 for the proper spelling of his name to be officially recognised. A hall in Springvalley was also named after him. Patrick Wafer died in 1944 at the age of 77.

James J. Walsh (Dublin) A Company. James Joseph Walsh joined the Volunteers in 1913. In the days leading up to the Rising he was a member of the small party of Volunteers assigned to guard Seamus Rafter's premises, which were under observation by the R.I.C.. Walsh later stated before the Military Service Pensions Board on the 20th of December 1937, that their orders were

to shoot the first policeman who entered the hall.

On the first morning of the Rising he mobilised at Keegan's, from there he was sent to guard the Volunteers tasked with climbing poles to cut telegraph wires. After reporting back to the new H.Q. in the Athenaeum, Walsh was then detailed to the Market Square where he was placed on guard duty over the licensed premises. On Friday morning while on sentry duty at Templeshannon, Walsh claimed to have come under fire from the R.I.C. barracks. He stated he ran into Bennett's Hotel's yard and up into the hay loft from where he returned fire on the barracks. That night he was sent to Lett's Brewery for sentry duty, he remained there until Saturday morning. On Saturday afternoon Walsh took part in the parade around the town before the column of Volunteers left for Ferns. He was placed on sentry duty that night in the town centre. After spending Sunday morning on guard duty on the Market Square, Walsh was sent with Thomas O'Brien to Red Pat's Cross for outpost duty. That evening they arrested the County Surveyor Stafford Gaffney, who was attempting to leave the town without permission, and brought him back to the Athenaeum. Walsh was present for the surrender and successfully evaded capture afterwards.

During 1917 Walsh was arrested on a couple of occasions but was never detained. However, on the third occasion he was, and over a period of days was severely beaten. After a doctor was called to examine him, he ordered that Walsh should be brought to the Enniscorthy Asylum. He was detained for two weeks before his release was ordered by the head Psychiatrist who refused to certify him as insane. After he was discharged Walsh left Enniscorthy due to the shame and stigma he felt after been locked up in the Asylum. James Joseph Walsh died in 1954 aged 76.

Joseph Walsh (Court Street) A Company. Joseph Walsh joined the Volunteers in 1913. On the first morning of the Rising he marched with the main body of men from Irish Street to the Athenaeum. He was sent from there to a nearby hardware shop to commandeer some axes and timber. Once he returned he helped to assemble tables and a kitchen. Later Walsh was a member of the party of Volunteers who came under fire while getting coal from O'Neill's coal yard on the Mill Park Road. In the afternoon he carried out sentry duty on New Street (Wafer St.) before ending his day on police patrol around the town centre. On Friday Walsh spent his day at H.Q., serving in the armoury, kitchen and guard room. That night along with Michael Jordan, he was on outpost duty at Blackstoops, where he remained until he was recalled on Saturday morning. When Walsh reported back on duty Saturday night, he was sent with a dispatch to Ferns by car. He remained in Ferns overnight and returned to Enniscorthy at 8.30 a.m. the next morning.

After the surrender was announced, Walsh was sent back to Ferns with Laurence Leacy to collect Peter Galligan and bring him back for a conference with the leaders. On their way back Leacy took a wrong turn and crashed. Walsh was badly injured. He was transferred to his home and placed in bed. The following Thursday he was arrested while in his sick bed and brought at first, to the R.I.C. barracks and then the Athenaeum, where the captured Volunteers were held. There he was examined by three doctors who insisted upon his release. After Walsh was released he spent the next four months recuperating. Walsh re-joined in 1917 and carried out the general activities of his Company up until The Truce. As a member of the Republican garrison during the "Battle of Enniscorthy", he claimed to have fired on a Free State Army position in Lett's Brewery from the roof of their headquarters in the courthouse.

Over the following months Walsh carried ammunition to various flying columns on a number of occasions. Joseph Walsh died in 1951 aged 60.

Patrick Walsh (Irish Street) A Company. Patrick Walsh joined the Volunteers in 1913 and the I.R.B. shortly afterwards. On the morning of the Rising he marched with the main body of men from Irish Street to the Athenaeum. From there he was placed on sentry duty on Cathedral Street. After returning to H.Q., Seamus Doyle instructed Walsh to report to Michael De Lacey in the old R.I.C. barracks on Court Street. De Lacey was in charge of the Republican police which had been established there. He sent Walsh to police the Market Square and Main Street.

Some accounts of the Rising in Enniscorthy state that throughout that week there were only two gunshot victims, R.I.C. Constable Grace and a young local girl named Foley. However, there was at least one other. At 1 a.m. on Friday morning Walsh was sent with another Volunteer to relieve the outpost at Arnold's Cross. As they approached, Volunteer Philip Murphy opened fire believing they were enemy combatants. Walsh was wounded in the chest, stomach and arm. He was brought back to the Athenaeum where Doctor William Kelly examined him. He was then transferred to the local hospital where he remained for three months. Walsh evaded arrest due to his condition. He re-joined in 1917 but had to drop out after a couple of months as a result of his injuries. Patrick Walsh died in 1961, he was 69 years of age.

Patrick Walsh (Court Street) A Company. Patrick Walsh was the older brother of Joseph Walsh, he joined the I.R.B. in 1911 and the Volunteers at their inception in 1913. After reporting for duty on the first morning of the Rising, he was sent with a party of Volunteers to the railway station to search for a consignment of sporting ammunition, which was supposably stored in one of the goods sheds. When he returned to H.Q., Walsh was ordered to go to Clonroche with a dispatch. That night he was placed on outpost duty at Salville Cross until 5.30 a.m. Friday morning. After resting in the Athenaeum, he spent Friday evening on sentry duty on the Market Square. Walsh was detailed for outpost duty at Summerhill on Saturday morning and then to Lucas Park later in the day. On Sunday Walsh was on duty at H.Q. until the surrender, after which he was sent with a nurse and *a supply of bandages* to the scene of the car crash involving Peter Galligan outside Ferns. Walsh did not return until 6.45 a.m. and after discovering the Athenaeum was empty, he went home. He evaded capture and re-joined in 1917. Walsh participated in the general activities of his Company up until March 1921, when he was arrested. He was held prisoner at the courthouse and was beaten on several occasions. He was also used as a hostage by the Black and Tans who marched him around the town with a revolver shoved in his back. Walsh was released in the middle of May and although available for duty, played no further part. Patrick Walsh died at the age of 66 in 1956.

Christina Ward (Friary Hill) Cumann na mBan. Christina Ward joined Cumann Na mBan in 1916. Throughout the Rising she reported daily to the Athenaeum for duty. She slept at home; her house was only a short distance from H.Q.. Her roles included cooking and clerical work for the officers. In the months following Ward collected funds for the prisoner's dependants and sent parcels to the prisoners. She was involved in election work during the 1918 General Election. In 1920, Ward converted stolen insurance stamps into cash for the movement at her place of work. She also typed warning letters which were used to intimidate witnesses in cases against Volunteers. Christina Ward died at the age of 78 in1973.

John Webster (The Shannon) C Company. John Webster joined the Volunteers in 1913. On the first morning of the Rising he mobilised on Irish Street and marched with the main body of men to the Athenaeum. After a H.Q. had been established there he was sent to the Turret Rocks under the command of Michael Cahill. Webster took up a sniping position and fired several times on the R.I.C. barracks over a period of a few hours. At around noon, Webster was ordered along with two other

Volunteers to go to Salville Cross for outpost duty. After he was relieved that evening, he returned to the Athenaeum for something to eat. Webster finished his days service on police duty, he patrolled the town to prevent any looting. On Friday Webster was detailed to Clonhaston Cross for outpost duty and that evening was on sentry duty on the Market Square. Webster was sent to Edermine on Saturday morning to help block roads and rested on his return to H.Q.. Later he took up sentry duty on the Market Square again. On Sunday Webster spent his day between the Athenaeum and the Market Square. After the surrender he evaded capture. In 1917 Webster re-joined and carried out the general activities of his Company up until The Truce. He had no involvement in the Civil War. John Webster died in 1949 aged 68.

James Whelan (Irish street) A Company. James Whelan joined the Volunteers in 1913 and the I.R.B. shortly after. Prior to the Rising, he was a member of the party of Volunteers under the command of Patrick Keegan tasked with the manufacture of munitions and raiding for arms. On the Wednesday of Easter Week, Whelan was sent to Wexford with a dispatch. On his return he went to "The Dump" and it was from there he mobilised early the following morning. After the H.Q. had been established in the Athenaeum, he took up a sniping position on Castle Hill (according to his statement to the Military Service Pensions Board on the 8th of February 1940) from where he fired several times at the R.I.C. barracks. On Friday morning Whelan again sniped on the barracks, this time from Yates's woollen store on the Shannon Quay. That evening he was on the Turret Rocks. Early on Saturday morning Whelan was placed on sentry duty on Irish Street, while that evening, he marched to Ferns with the column of Volunteers under the command of Peter Galligan. In Ferns, he was placed on sentry duty outside the R.I.C. barracks, which now served as Volunteer headquarters in the village. After news of the surrender on Sunday night, Whelan returned to the Athenaeum and collected a couple of rifles and brought them to Ballycarney to be hidden. He then made his way to Carlow and evaded arrest.

After moving to Wexford in 1917, Whelan joined a Volunteer Company there. He kept in close contact with his Enniscorthy comrades and in September 1920, while wearing the disguise of a British officer, he called to the home in Ballcarney of a spy named James Doyle along with a couple of Volunteers dressed as soldiers. Doyle had been discovered passing information about the Ballindaggin Company to the R.I.C.. Whelan had him lead them to the home of the Doyle brothers in Ballindaggin before revealing his true identity. He then participated in Doyle's trial and execution.

As a member of the North Wexford Brigade Active Service Unit, Whelan was involved in three further executions of spies in 1921. Firstly in March the killing of two brothers named Skelton from Booladurragh and then in May an auxiliary postman named James Morrisey from St. John's Street. Morrisey had served in the British Army for two years and was a leading figure in the ex-servicemen's association in Enniscorthy. A frequent visitor to the military headquarters in the courthouse, he had paraded around the town in uniform with the Black and Tans on occasions. When his body was found near Marshalstown, rosary beads were wrapped around his hands and a note on the body which stated. *Spy and traitor, others beware. I.R.A..*

In March 1922 Whelan joined the National Army but deserted after the split and joined the Republican garrison in the courthouse. At this time he was appointed Brigade Adjutant and Police Officer. Whelan fought in the "Battle of Enniscorthy" and after the town was retaken by the Free State Army, joined up with a flying column. Whelan was captured in September and imprisoned until December 1923. James Whelan died at the age of 85 in 1983.

John "Seán" Whelan (Irish Street) A Company. Seán Whelan was the older brother of James Whelan. He joined the Volunteers in 1913 and the I.R.B. not long after that. Prior to the Rising, like his brother he was a member of the small party of Volunteers under the command of Patrick

Keegan. On the first morning of the Insurrection, Whelan marched with the main body of men from Irish Street to the Athenaeum. He was present outside when the Tricolour was raised and followed by a volley of three shots and three cheers. Whelan then took up sentry duty at the top of Castle Hill for a brief period before returning to "The Dump", where he spent the majority of his time until the surrender.

Early on the Monday morning following the surrender, he accompanied his brother James to their maternal grandfather's house in Ballycarney and gave him rifles to hide. Their grandfather's two sons, their uncles, Patrick and John Tomkins were also involved that week. Whelan evaded capture, but on his return to Enniscorthy he was dismissed from his job and had to move to Kildare to find work. He returned in mid-1919 and by the beginning of 1920, had been appointed O/C of A Company. Whelan played a leading role in the attack on the R.I.C. barracks in Clonroche in April that year and the large raid for petrol at the railway station the following month.

In June 1920, Whelan was selected by G.H.Q. in Dublin to participate in the killing of District Inspector Lea Wilson in Gorey. When Whelan appeared before the Military Service Pensions Board on the 11th of May 1937 he was asked was he involved in the actual shooting.

Yes in the actual shooting. I was supposed to be the best shot and I was selected, and it turned out I was not.

Board member.

You missed him?

Whelan.

No, the gun I had was too accurate. I fired to get him but got the top of the shoulder. I allowed for the gun to kick but it didn't.

Board member.

He was shot.

Whelan.

Yes he was shot then, we emptied four 45s and then we gave him six.

In September Whelan was involved in the trial and conviction of the spy James Doyle, whose execution was carried out by his brother James among others. In November he was arrested, and while he was held in the courthouse for three weeks, was the victim of severe beatings. He was interned in Cork and Kilkenny. During his imprisonment in Kilkenny, Whelan stood on a nail and caught Tetanus. His condition deteriorated to such an extent he was given the Last Rites. After he had recovered he was released in August 1921.

Whelan joined the National Army in March 1922, but after the split over The Treaty he chose the Republican side. He was one of the ringleaders in the Kilkenny barracks who orchestrated the theft of a large quantity of rifles and ammunition. Back in Enniscorthy, Whelan was appointed Brigade Q/M in May and shortly after Divisional Q/M.. Throughout the "Battle of Enniscorthy" in July, Whelan was involved in the fighting. He was captured by Free State soldiers at the end of that month and interned until March 1924. John "Seán" Whelan died on his 73rd birthday in 1968.

John Whelan (St. John's Street) A Company. John Whelan joined the Volunteers in 1914. On the morning of the Rising he marched from Irish Street to the Athenaeum with the main body of men. From there he was sent with a few other Volunteers to the courthouse to confiscate rifles belonging to the National Volunteers that were stored there. Once back at H.Q. with the rifles, they oiled and cleaned them. Whelan was then placed on guard duty outside The National Bank on Castle Street. In the afternoon he went with a group of railway workers a couple of miles north along the railway line to remove rails. That evening Whelan was assigned sentry duty at the Gas Yard. On Friday morning Whelan was ordered to go by bicycle to New Ross and deliver a dispatch to Phil

Lennon, who was in charge of the Volunteers there. Whelan returned that evening with Lennon's reply. After a meal he was placed on sentry duty on Lymington Road.

The following morning Whelan was ordered to commandeer a lorry from Buttle's Bacon Company, where he was employed. After carrying out this assignment he was detailed to the corner of New Street (Wafer St.) and the Pig Market Hill for the remainder of the day. On Sunday, Whelan was on duty in the Athenaeum and after the surrender helped to load vehicles with munitions. He was arrested the following Tuesday and deported shortly afterwards. Whelan was interned in Stafford Jail until he was released in June. Whelan believed his release was down to the intervention of his employer Mr. Buttle. However after resuming his job as a shop assistant, he was dismissed in the first week of 1917. Whelan then left Enniscorthy and moved to Blackwater. He joined the Company there and served up until The Truce, rising to the rank of Company Adjutant. Whelan did not participate in the Civil War. John Whelan died at his residence in Askasilla, Blackwater in 1966 at the age of 78.

Kathleen Whelan (Church Street) Cumann na mBan. Kathleen Whelan (nee Moran) joined Cumann na mBan in 1914. She came from a staunch Republican family who all participated in the Rising. Whelan reported for duty to the Athenaeum at 7.30 a.m. on the Thursday morning and remained there until Sunday night. She served as a typist and was under the command of Seamus Doyle, for whom she typed out dispatches and commandeering orders. After the surrender, Whelan helped to load munitions into cars. In the months and years following, Whelan worked actively raising funds for the prisoner's dependents and for weapons for the Volunteers. Throughout the War of Independence she carried dispatches and ammunition to flying columns as far afield as New Ross, Gorey and Wicklow.

She chose the Republican side in the Civil War and during the "Battle of Enniscorthy", Whelan and her sister, Brigid Christina Moran, came under fire from Free State soldiers in the Castle while removing munitions from their home on Church Street. She also tended to wounded I.R.A. men in St. Mary's Church and helped prepare the body of Volunteer Maurice Spillane for his wake. In the following months Whelan was a member of the Cumann na mBan Active Service Unit established by another of her sisters, Marie Fitzpatrick, which travelled the county delivering dispatches, food and ammunition to various flying columns whenever they were called upon. She served with this unit until April 1923, when she got married and ceased her activity. Kathleen Whelan died in 1941 in her 52nd year.

Patrick Whelan (Ferns) Ferns Company. Patrick Whelan joined the Volunteers in 1914. He arrived in Enniscorthy with members of his Company on the first evening of the Rising and was assigned a sentry post. The following day Whelan returned to Ferns and helped to erect roadblocks and dismantle the railway. Over the remaining days of the Rising he carried out sentry and outpost duty in the village. Whelan was arrested three days after the surrender and deported shortly afterwards. He was interned in Wandsworth Prison before he was released at the end of May. Whelan re-joined his Company in 1917 and served with it until The Truce. He joined the National Army in April 1922 and was assigned to the garrison in Ferns. He participated in a fight with Anti-Treaty forces in the village that July. When the army left Ferns in September 1922, Whelan resigned his position. Patrick Whelan died in 1933 aged 61.

Thomas Whelan (Ferns) Ferns Company. Thomas Whelan was a member of the I.R.B. prior to joining the Volunteers in 1913. He marched with about twenty men from his Company to Enniscorthy on the first day of the Rising, arriving in the early evening. After reporting to the Athenaeum he was detailed for outpost duty on the Wexford Road. On Friday morning Whelan was one of the Volunteers who cycled to Ferns in advance of the main column. He remained in the village until the surrender on Sunday. Whelan was arrested on the following Tuesday and deported not long afterwards. He was interned until December in Wandsworth Prison and then Frongach Camp. In 1917, Whelan re-joined and took part in the general activities of his Company. On two separate occasions he was involved in attacks on the R.I.C. barracks in Ferns. Whelan was appointed Sergeant in the Republican police in August 1921 and served in that position until the Free State Army took over the village in July 1922. Thomas Whelan died in Wexford town aged 72 in 1963..

Mary White (Castle Street) Cumann na mBan. Mary White was one of the founding members of Cumann na mBan in Enniscorthy. After the split in the organisation in 1915 she became President of the Enniscorthy Branch. Throughout Easter Week she was in command of the women in the Athenaeum and assigned them to their specific duties. On the Saturday she went to her family's shop which was next door to the Athenaeum (Peter White's) and handed out groceries and supplies to the Volunteers. After the surrender White helped to clear out the Athenaeum, remaining there until 2 a.m. Monday morning. In the following months she organised the prisoner's dependant's fund. White served as Branch President until the Autumn of 1918 when she resigned her position. Mary White died at the age of 85 in 1966.

James Willis (Templeshannon) C Company. James Willis joined the Volunteers in 1913. On the first morning of the Rising he marched with the main body of men from Irish Street to the Athenaeum. There he was placed on sentry duty outside the building. His next assignment was to carry out guard duty at the Gas Yard, he remained there until early Friday morning. After resting at H.Q., Willis was on street patrol around the town centre. That evening he was sent back to the Gas Yard to relieve the Volunteers there. On Saturday, Willis was on sentry duty outside the Athenaeum and later, took part in the recruiting parade around the town. He spent Sunday afternoon in H.Q., sorting through the various types of ammunition. Willis was present for the surrender, after which he helped to collect and load weapons into vehicles. He evaded capture. Willis re-joined in 1917 and over the following years, used his position as a signalman at the railway station to carry dispatches. The dispatches were brought from Dublin by guards on the train. They would pass them to Willis who then brought them to Seamus Rafter, and after Rafter's death, to Philip Murphy in the post office. In May 1920, Willis was on night duty at the railway station when the large raid for petrol occurred, he kept watch throughout the operation. After The Truce he ceased his activities. James Willis died in1972 at the age of 75.

Edward Wilson (Hospital Lane) A Company. Edward Wilson joined the Volunteers in 1913 and was one of four brothers who participated in the Easter Rising. He marched to the Athenaeum from Irish Street with the main body of Volunteers early on the Thursday morning. From there he was sent to the grounds of the Mercy Convent School to take up a sniping position, he had a clear view of the R.I.C. barracks across the Slaney. In his testimony before the Military Services Pensions Board on the 4th of June 1940, Wilson stated he fired *a couple of shots*. After a few hours there he returned to H.Q.. Later that evening Wilson was placed on sentry duty on Friary Hill and remained there until the early hours of Friday morning. After resting in the Athenaeum, Wilson was placed on sentry duty at St. John's Street and later on in the day at The Mill. He slept in H.Q. that night. On Saturday morning Wilson was detailed to sentry duty, firstly on The Duffry and then on the Market Square in the afternoon before finishing his days duty at the bottom of the Bohreen Hill. On Sunday he was assigned outpost duty at Red Pat's Cross for part of the day. The rest of his time was spent in the Athenaeum. He was present for the surrender and afterwards helped with the collection and disposal of munitions. Wilson was arrested on the following Tuesday and deported a short time later. He was interned in Stafford Jail and Frongach Camp before he was released at the end of August. Wilson re-joined in 1917 but dropped out the following year. Edward Wilson died in 1953 at the age of 69.

Joseph Wilson (Hospital Lane) A Company. The oldest of the Wilson brothers, Joseph Wilson was a member of the I.R.B. for several years before joining the Volunteers at their inception in 1913. He was mobilised on the first morning of the Insurrection. For the following four days his activities included raiding for food and supplies, street patrols, sentry and outpost duties. Wilson was present for the surrender, after which he handed in his rifle and went home. He was arrested on the 4th of May and deported a short time afterwards. Wilson was interned in Stafford jail and Frongach Camp before he was released from Wandsworth Prison in August. On his return home he ceased his Volunteer activities. Joseph Wilson died at his home on Hospital Lane in 1938 aged 62.

Owen Wilson (Hospital Lane) A Company. Owen Wilson joined the I.R.B. in 1908 and the Volunteers in 1913. From Easter Sunday until the morning of the Rising he spent every night at "The Dump". He marched with the main body of Volunteers from there to the Athenaeum early on Thursday morning. After a H.Q. had been established there, Wilson took up a sniping position on Castle Hill, from where (according to his statement before the Military Service Pensions Board on the 8th of December 1937) he fired about a dozen rounds at the R.I.C. barracks over the period of an hour. He then returned to H.Q.. Later in the day Wilson was placed on guard duty on the Market Square. After spending the night in the Athenaeum he was assigned sentry duty on St. John's Street. On Saturday he carried out a similar role on the Island Road. Wilson spent Sunday in the vicinity of the Athenaeum and after the surrender, helped to remove munitions to safety. He was the only Wilson brother to evade arrest and afterwards ceased all Volunteer activity. Owen Wilson died in 1957 at the age of 76.

Robert Wilson (Hospital Lane) A Company. Robert Wilson was the youngest of the Wilson brothers and like his brothers was a member of the I.R.B. before joining the Volunteers in 1913. After marching from Irish street to the Athenaeum with the main body of Volunteers, Wilson was placed on sentry duty at Mitchell's Corner. (Corner of Rafter St. and Church St). While there he encountered two R.I.C. constables attempting to make their way to their D.I.'s house, they exchanged fire from a distance of a hundred yards. Later in the day he was sent to Davis's Mill for outpost duty. For the next two days Wilson carried out sentry duty at various locations around the town. On Saturday night he marched to Ferns with the column of Volunteers under the command of Peter Galligan. Wilson remained in Ferns until the surrender, then he returned to Enniscorthy and helped with the disposal of weapons. He was arrested the following Tuesday and deported shortly afterwards. Wilson was interned in Stafford Jail for a month before he was released. On his return home he ceased all Volunteer activities. Robert Wilson died in St. John's Hospital at the age of 68 in 1953.

Myles Wildes (Springvalley) A Company. At the time of The Rising Myles Wildes was a member of the British Army who was home on leave. Once he heard of the Insurrection, he reported to the Athenaeum and joined up. Wildes carried out sentry and outpost duty throughout the week. After the surrender he re-joined his Regiment. When he left the army in 1919 he joined the Volunteers and served up to The Truce. Wildes joined the National Army in March 1922 and by the time he was demobilised in October 1924 held the rank of Sergeant.

Myles Wildes died at his residence in St. Aidan' Villas in 1960 at the age of 76.

Involved, Arrested or Interned

Patrick Adams, The Shannon.
Aidan Allen, Castle Street.
James Armstrong, Galbally.
Michael Balfe, The Shannon.
Sylvester Balfe, The Shannon.
Patrick Bolger, Irish Street.
Richard Bourke, Springvalley.
Patrick "Red" Boyne. The Shannon
Matthew Brennan, Camolin.
Patrick Brennan, Island Road.
James Breslin, Ferns.
James Browne, Ferns.
Kathleen Browne, Rathronan Castle.
Dudley Butler, Courtown.
Daniel Byrne, Ferns.
John Byrne, Gorey.
Michael Byrne, Camolin.
James Carroll, Ferns.
Daniel Carton, Ferns.
James Casey, Ross Road.
William Coady, Court Street.
Gretta Comerford, Templeshannon.
Edward Connolly, Glenbrien.
John Connolly, Springvalley.
Valentine Connolly, Court Street.
Frank Conway, Killagoley.
William Cooney, Ross Road.
Thomas Cordon, St. John's Street.
John Coughlan, Wexford.
William Cowman, Ferns.
James Curran, Bunclody.

Joseph Cummins, Edermine.
Edward Dagg, The Shannon.
James Daly, Templescoby.
William Darcy, Courtown.
Edward de Lacey, Oulart.
Laurence de Lacey, Oulart.
Michael de Lacey, Oulart.
James Dempsey, Oulart.
John Devereux, Mill Park Road.
John Dillon, The Shannon.
Michael Dillon, St. John's Street.
Patrick Dillon, The Shannon.
Edward Donegan, Cathedral Street.
Nicholas Donnelly, Springvalley.
John Doran, The Shannon.
Katie Smyth-Doyle, Milehouse.
Lawrence Doyle, Lower Church Street.
John Doyle, Ferns.
John Doyle, Gorey.
James Dunbar, Ferns.
Patrick Dunbar, Ferns.
Arthur Dunne, Gorey.
Thomas Dunne, Island Road.
Denis Dwyer, The Shannon.
Matthew Ennis, Tomnalosset.
Michael Fenlon, Hospital Lane.
William Fenlon, Hospital Lane.
James Fitzharris, Clonhaston.
Margaret "Ita" Forrestal, The Shannon.
Daniel Fortune, Gorey.
William Fortune, Slaney Street.
Michael Franklin, St. John's Street.
Thomas Franklin, Inch.

Joseph Funge, Courtown.
Thomas Furlong, The Shannon.
William Gahan, The Duffry.
Michael Gethings, Ferns.
Frank Gibbons, Dublin.
Annie Godfrey, Enniscorthy.
James Goff, The Shannon.
Harry Goff, The Shannon.
John Gowan, Hollyfort.
Patrick Hall, Old Church.
Walter Hall, Old Church.
T.J. Haye, Court Street.
Thomas Hayes, Court Street.
John Hawkins, Killagoley.
Edward Hearne, Killagoley.
James Hearne, Killagoley.
John Hearne, Friary Hill.
James Hedley, Irish Street.
Matthew Heffernan, Edermine.
John Hennessy, Monfin.
Patrick Hennessy, Tomnalosset.
Patrick Hinch, Askamore.
John J. Hogan, Borris.
Patrick Hogan, Gorey.
Thomas Hollywood, Offaly.
James Howlin, Killagoley.
Thomas Howlin, Killagoley.
Joseph Hunt, Courtown.
C.J. Irwin, Kilcannon.
Thomas Jordan, Drumgoold.
John Kavanagh, Ferns.
Michael Kavanagh, Castle Hill.
Thomas Kearney, Island Road.

Thomas Keegan, Irish Street.
John Kehoe, Ballinapierce.
Martin Kehoe, The Shannon.
Mary Eileen Kehoe, Enniscorthy.
Patrick Kehoe, The Duffry.
Patrick Kehoe, The Shannon.
Nicholas "Clem" Kelly, The Shannon.
Patrick Kelly, Slaney Place.
William Kelly, St. John's Street.
Moses Kenny, Gorey.
Patrick Kenny, Ballycarney.
Matthew Kent, Ballycarney.
J. Keyes, Ardmine.
Joseph Killen, Ferns.
John Kinch, Ferns.
Daniel Kirwan, Bree.
Matthew Lafferty, Tomnalosset.
James Larkin, Templeshannon.
John Larkin, Ballindaggin.
T.J. Larkin, The Duffry
Fred Lawton, New Street.
Anastatia Leacy, Georges Street.
Charles Lynch, Court Street.
James Lynch, Court Street.
John Lynch, Ferns.
Laurence Lynch, Court Street.
James Lyndon, Slaney Street.
William Lyons, Ferns.
Barney Maguire, Ferns.
Jeremiah Maguire, Camolin.
John Maguire, Ferns.
John Maguire, The Moyne.
Michael Maher, Irish Street

Thomas Maher, Island Road.
Ambrose Martin, Oulart.
Andrew McCann, Gorey.
Thomas McCarthy, Georges Street.
Edward McDonagh, Gorey.
J. McDonagh, Gorey.
Edward McDonald, Camolin
Patrick McDonald, The Shannon.
Mark McGrath, Ballywilliam.
.Andrew McKeever, Court Street.
Joseph Meagher, Castle Hill.
James Moran, Friary Place.
Liam Moran, Church Street.
Michael Moran, Church Street.
Seán Moran, Church Street.
William Moran, Friary Place.
J. Morgan, Friary Place.
John Moynihan, Ferns.
Annie Murphy, Blackwater.
Arthur Murphy, St. John's Street.
Francis Murphy, Springvalley.
James Murphy, Bunclody.
Jeremiah Murphy, Castleboro.
Jeremiah Murphy, The Harrow.
John Murphy, Ferns.
Kitty Murphy, The Shannon.
Nicholas Murphy, The Duffry.
Robert Murphy, St. John's Street.
Simon Murphy, Drumgoold.
Sylvester Murphy, Ferns.
Thomas Murphy, Kilcotty.
William Murphy, Irish Street.
Winifred Murphy, The Shannon.

James Murray, Ross Road.
James Mythen, Oulart.
John Mythen, Blackwater.
Nicholas Newport, Wexford.
Edward Nolan, Court Street.
Hugh O'Brien, The Shannon.
John O'Brien, Old Church.
Michael O'Brien, Ferns.
Matthew O'Brien, Hospital Lane.
Michael O'Brien, Hospital Lane.
Sarah O'Brien, Irish Street
William O'Gorman, Dublin.
Michael O'Leary Snr, Irish Street.
Michael J. O'Leary, Clonhaston.
Seán O'Leary, New Street.
John O'Neill, Friary Hill
M.J. O'Neill, Ferns.
Peter O'Neill, Gorey.
Christopher O'Toole, The Shannon.
John Pender, St. Patrick's Place.
James Pembroke, Irish Street.
Michael Pierce, The Shannon.
James Quinn, Camolin.
Thomas Rafferty, Ballindaggin.
William Reddy, The Shannon.
Edward Redmond, Court Street.
Patrick Rigley, Court Street.
Thomas Rigley, The Shannon.
James Roban, The Leap.
James Roche, Ferns.
John Roche, Ferns.
Edward Ronan, Ferns.
Edward Rossiter, Templeshannon.

James Rossiter, St. John's Street.
Mary F. Rossiter, Court Street.
William Royce, Slaney Street.
William Ruth, St. John's Street.
James Ryan, Templeshannon.
John Ryan, Old Church.
William Sears, The Shannon.
Thomas Scallan, Gorey.
John Shannon, St. Patrick's Place.
Matthew Sheridan, New Street.
Robert J. Shortall, St. Mary's Hill.
John Sinnott, Ferns.
Michael Sinnott, Ferns.
Michael Sinnott, Georges Street.
Pierce Sinnott, Gorey.
Albert F. Smith, Tomnalosset.
Christopher Smith, Friary Hill.
Peter Smyth, Castle Street.
Moses Somers, St. John's Street.
George Stafford, Ballindaggin.
Marion Stokes, Duffry Street.
Patrick Stokes, Duffry Street.
Thomas Stokes, Duffry Street.
Peter Sutton, St. John's Street.
Walter Sutton, Clonhaston.
John Tallon, The Moyne.
John Tomkins, Ballycarney.
Michael Tobin, Bohreen Hill.
Thomas Tobin, Market Square.
John Travers, Ballymurtagh.
James Walsh, Court street.
Patrick Walsh, Old Church.
Thomas Walsh, Old Church.

Kate Ward, Friary Hill.
Mary Ward, Friary Hill.
Thomas Watkins, Templeshannon.
Robert Webster, The Shannon.
John Whelan, Blackwater.
Martin Whelan, Marshalstown.
Michael Whelan, Wexford.
Michael White, Castle Street.

Arrested and Interned after Rising

Patrick Chapman, Ballymitty.
Thomas Chapman, Ballymitty.
James Clegg, New Ross.
T. Colgan, Ballymitty.
Richard Corish, Wexford.
Michael Crowley, New Ross.
T. Cullen, Duncormick.
Martin Deegan, New Ross.
Thomas Devereux, Danescastle.
Dr. Edward Dundon, Borris.
Arthur Dunne, New Ross.
John Doyle, New Ross.
William Doyle, New Ross.
John Fanning, New Ross.
Thomas Fielding, Barntown.
Ed Foley, Wexford.
Michael Foley, New Ross.
John Furlong, Bargy Commons
J. Furlong, Cleariestown.
Maggie Furlong, Skeeterpark.
James Hadley, New Ross.
D.J. Hanley, New Ross.
John Hartley, New Ross.
Patrick Hanley, New Ross.
J. Hayes, Bridgetown.
J. Kavanagh, Duncormick.
Maggie Kavanagh, Skeeterpark.
Tim Kehoe, New Ross.
P. Kehoe, Bridgetown.
P. Kehoe, Cleariestown.
Joseph S. Kelly, New Ross.
Thomas Kelly, New Ross.

G. Kennedy, New Ross.
John Kennedy, New Ross.
Michael J. Kennedy, New Ross.
Philip Kennedy, New Ross.
Sean Kennedy, New Ross.
T. Kennedy, New Ross.
T.J. Kennedy, New Ross.
Philip Lennon, New Ross.
P. Lynch, New Ross.
James Lyng, Ballinabanogue.
William Lennon, New Ross.
William Maddock, Duncormick.
Daniel McEvoy, New Ross.
William Maddock, Duncormick.
Joseph McCarthy, New Ross.
T. McGrath, New Ross.
John McGuire, Wexford.
Fred McLoughlin, Glenmore.
T Moran, Duncormick.
Ed. Murphy,. New Ross.
J. Murphy, Bridgetown.
John Murphy, New Ross.
John Murphy, New Ross.
N.J. Murphy, Wexford.
William Murphy, Bridgetown.
William Murphy, New Ross.
Matthew O'Connor, Wexford.
Michael O'Keeffe, New Ross.
Simon O'Leary, New Ross.
John O'Neill, New Ross.
James Prendergast, New Ross.
Myles Redmond, Wexford.
William Rice, Wexford.

Nell Ryan, Tomcoole.
J. Scarmill, Duncormick.
Michael Sheehan, New Ross.
Joseph Shelby, New Ross.
J. Sinnott, Wexford.
T. Stafford, Barntown.
William Stafford, Barntown.
James Walshe, New Ross.
Peter Warner, New Ross.

Wexford Men and Women who Fought elsewhere in 1916

John Bolger, Blackwater. The G.P.O..
Maria Clince, Ballymoney. Jameson Distillery.
James Corcoran, Craanford. Killed at St. Stephen's Green 25/4/16.
Daniel Forde, Wexford. Athenry, Galway.
Joseph Furlong, Wexford. Boland's Mill.
Nicholas Jackman, Kilgorman. The Four Courts.
James Lawless, Gorey. Jacob's Biscuit Factory.
Liam Mellows, Inch. Athenry, Galway.
Edward Murphy, Newtownbarry. Father Matthew Hall.
Henry O'Hanrahan. New Ross. The G.P.O..
Michael O'Hanrahan, New Ross. The G.P.O.. Executed 4/5/16.
Michael Roche, Ballycullane. Jameson Distillery.
James Ryan, Tomcoole. The G.P.O..
Frederick Stephens, Gorey. St. Stephen's Green.
Thomas Wafer, The Shannon. Killed in the Hibernian Bank, O'Connell Street 26/4/16
Richard Whelan, Lower Church Street. South Dublin Union.
William Brennan Whitmore, Clonee. The G.P.O..

Sources

Bureau of Military History

Witness Statement of Edward Balfe. Document No. 1,373.
Witness Statement of John Carroll. Document No. 1,258.
Witness Statement of James Cullen. Document No. 1,343.
Witness Statement of James Daly. Document No. 1,257.
Witness Statement of Michael de Lacey. Document No. 319.
Witness Statement of Patrick Doyle. Document No. 1,298.
Witness Statement of Seamus Doyle. Document No's 315 and 1,342.
Witness Statement of Thomas Doyle. Document No. 1,041
Witness Statement of John Dwyer. Document No. 1,293.
Witness Statement of Thomas Dwyer. Document No. 1,198.
Witness Statement of Maria Fitzpatrick. Document No's. 1,344 and 1,345.
Witness Statement of Patrick Fitzpatrick. Document No. 1,274.
Witness Statement of Peter Paul Galligan. Document No. 170.
Witness Statement of Joseph Killen. Document No. 1,215.
Witness Statement of Michael Kirwan. Document No. 1,175.
Witness Statement of Thomas Francis Meagher. Document No. 1,156.
Witness Statement of Rev. Michael Murphy. Document No. 1,277.
Witness Statement of Rev. Patrick Murphy. Document No. 1,216.
Witness Statement of Laurence Redmond. Document No. 1,010.
Witness Statement of Patrick Ronan. Document No's. 299, 1,157 and 1,256.
Witness Statement of Seán Whelan. Document No's. 1,294 and 1,085.

Military Service Pension Collection.

National Archives: Census of Ireland 1901/1911.

Archives.Oireactas.ie

The Irish Times Rebellion Handbook 1917

Ancestry.com

Findmypast.co.uk

Enniscorthy 2000 Book of the Millennium.
Enniscorthy A History. ISBN 978-0-9560574-7-1

Printed in Great Britain
by Amazon